HEROES' TWILIGHT

A Study of the Literature of the Great War

Bernard Bergonzi

CARCANET

First published in 1965 by Constable
Second edition published in 1980 by Macmillan
Third edition published in 1996 by
Carcanet Press Limited

A CIP catalogue record for this book
is available from the British Library
ISBN 1 85754 135 9

The publisher acknowledges financial assistance
from the Arts Council of England

Set in 10pt Sabon by Bryan Williamson, Frome

Printed digitally since 2001.
Carcanet Press Limited, *now at* Conavon Court, Blackfriar Street
Manchester M3 5BQ UK   www.carcanet.co.uk

HEROES' TWILIGHT

Contents

In Memory of Gabriel

Preface

The first edition of this book was published by Constable in 1965, and a second edition with minor changes appeared from Macmillan in 1980. That has been out of print for some years, and as readers have been kind enough to express a wish for a third edition I have taken this opportunity to make some fairly extensive revisions and additions, though the plan of the book and most of the material in it remain as they were in 1965. I have removed obviously dated or dating references, and I have tried to improve the style where it seemed to need it, often by excising words, phrases or sentences, and occasionally whole paragraphs. I have added an appendix, 'The Problem of War Poetry', an earlier version of which was delivered as the Byron Foundation Lecture at the University of Nottingham in 1990 and subsequently published in *PN Review*. This develops ideas that emerged from the book, and modifies some of my original assumptions, particularly about the extent to which the poetry of the war expresses a clear disjunction between early idealism and later disillusionment. The treatment of Edward Thomas and Ivor Gurney in the first edition was very inadequate; the achievement of these two poets is now much more evident, helped by recent scholarship, and I have inserted a new chapter about them. There are significant works of fiction or autobiography by survivors, such as Vera Brittain's *Testament of Youth*, which I passed over or did not know about when I first wrote, and I now say about something them in the appropriate chapters.

Thirty years on, *Heroes' Twilight* has unavoidably become a different book from the one I orginally wrote even where the text remains unchanged. The context in which it is read has altered with time. When it first appeared the First World War was well within living memory, many of the writers I discussed were alive, and some were still actively working. Now they have all gone, and so has direct memory, and discussion of the war and the writing it generated is divided between scholarship and mythology (modes which can interact in unexpected ways). The final chapter of the original edition discussed poems and novels invoking the war by writers born after it ended, who were conscious of its mythic aspects. I have enlarged this chapter under a new title to take in more material. For the most part I have kept comments on later criticism and scholarship to the notes, though in a few places where editorial or biographical work has added to understanding of a writer I have inserted references in the text.

Heroes' Twilight was not written as an academic study, even though I was a university teacher when I wrote it. I conceived it as a work of critical literary history which would be of interest to a general educated readership that wanted to know something about the way English writers had responded to the cataclysm of the Great War, whether or not they had survived it. The annotation is correspondingly less extensive and rigorous than is the norm in present-day scholarly works. Academic literary study has expanded rapidly since 1965, and 'war writing' and particularly the 'war poets' are now established subjects for teaching and research, generating an extensive secondary literature. John H. Johnston's *English Poetry of the First World War*, a work by an American scholar, appeared in 1964 while I was writing *Heroes' Twilight*; as far as I know it was the first critical study of the poetry of the war, and it has had a string of successors.[1] In 1975 another American, Paul Fussell, made a major and seminal contribution in *The Great War and Modern Memory*, a work of cultural history as well as literary criticism, which has transformed our view of the subject. He takes the canonical poets and prose writers whom I discussed, plus a number of others,

---

[1] They include Jon Silkin, *Out of Battle: The Poetry of the Great War* (London, 1972); Hilda D.Spear, *Remembering We Forget: A Background Study to the Poetry of the First World War* (London, 1979); John Lehmann, *The English Poets of the First World War* (London, 1981); Desmond Graham, *The Truth of War: Owen, Blunden, Rosenberg* (Manchester, 1984); Fred D. Crawford, *British Poets of the Great War* (London and Toronto, 1988); George Parfitt, *English Poetry of the First World War: Contexts and Themes* (Hemel Hempstead, 1990); Adrian Caesar, *Taking It Like a Man: Suffering, Sexuality and the War Poets* (Manchester, 1993). Anne Powell has edited *A Deep Cry: A Literary Pilgrimage to the Battlefields and Cemeteries of British Soldier-Poets Killed in Northern France and Flanders* (Aberporth, 1993). This includes poetry and prose by the writers, biographical essays and other documentary material, with maps of battlefields and lists of regiments, cemeteries and memorials. Sixty-six poets are represented, most of whose names are no longer familiar. Nosheen Khan, *Women's Poetry of the First World War* (Hemel Hempstead, 1989) discusses poets who were necessarily remote from the battlefield – though a few came close to it as nurses or ambulance drivers – and whose attitudes range from fervent patriotism to pacifism.

and places them in a variety of contexts, drawn from historical records, from the letters and diaries of serving soldiers, from contemporary journalism, from popular culture, from rumour and legends. Fussell is concerned with the interpenetration of literature and history in the British experience of the Western Front, and in the way in which soldiers' immediate response was often apprehended in literary terms, and in the literary means in which it was later recalled, modified and ultimately mythologized. As Fussell puts it: 'I have tried to understand something of the simultaneous and reciprocal process by which life feeds materials to literature while literature returns the favour by conferring forms upon life.' His book provides many illuminations. He points out, for instance, that for the front-line soldiers the most crucial parts of the day were dawn, when attacks might be launched, and dusk, when raiding parties would set out. The sky was always visible from the trenches, and sunrise and sunset were much more apparent to the soldier than to the civilian town-dweller. The peculiar significance of dawn underlies one of the greatest of war-poems, Isaac Rosenberg's 'Break of Day in the Trenches'. Ruskin had started a tradition of describing skies and sunrises and sunsets, and during the war it directed both the observation of such things, and the mode of writing about them, whether in poems, memoirs or letters.

It was, as Fussell says, a very literary war. In 1914 the English people were at a high pitch of literacy. The young officers had received a classical education and were very well read in English poetry, so that Shakespeare and Milton, Wordsworth and Keats, would be constantly quoted or alluded to when they wrote about the war. English poetry provided a sense of identity and continuity, a means of accommodating to life in a bizarre world as well as a source of consolation. The private soldiers, though formally less educated, were still part of a traditional literary culture, and many of them naturally expressed themselves in the idiom of the English Bible and *Pilgrim's Progress*. Englishmen of all classes, enduring a seemingly endless war, could readily see the waterlogged battlefields of Passchendaele as a literal Slough of Despond. Again, the poems by Wilfred Owen and others, lamenting the premature deaths of fine young men were in an ancient tradition reaching back to classical pastoral. But they had a more immediate source in the *fin de siècle* cult of Uranian love, which produced poems of sublimated devotion to young men, usually called 'boys' or 'lads'. Such knowledge does not detract from the originality of Owen's poems; but it indicates the complex fusion of tradition and unprecedented reality that formed them.

The cultural-historical vein that Fussell opened up has proved fruitful to later writers. Stuart Sillars' *Art and Survival in First World War Britain* (1987) is an account of how key events of the war, like the battle of Jutland, the protracted campaigns on the Somme, and the war in the air, were presented to the population via fine art, posters and illustrations, films, the press, and other writings with a wide circulation. Peter Buitenhuis's *The Great War of Words: Literature as Propaganda in 1914-18 and After* (1989) shows how prominent English writers willingly engaged in a secret propaganda effort to influence neutral and especially American opinion against the Germans and in favour of the Allied cause. Books that were seemingly independent and brought out by established publishers were in fact commissioned by the Government's propaganda department, and writers who in peacetime had cherished their intellectual integrity showed themselves very ready to surrender it in wartime. Samuel Hynes's *A War Imagined: The First World War and English Culture* (1990) is a long and thorough study in the cultural history of the war years and their aftermath in the 1920s and 1930s, exploring the war as an imaginative event. Hynes writes: 'the Myth that took shape at the end of the Twenties was more than simply a story of what the war *was*...It expanded as it evolved, from a myth of war to a myth of ruination that included life among the ruins, a myth of the world that the war had made.'

In the preface to the first edition of *Heroes' Twilight* I remarked that though I was concerned largely with the British literary response to the Western Front, this was only one aspect of a large subject, and I expressed the hope that one day the literature of the Great War would be discussed with a comprehensiveness which would take in its many international strands. Several such studies have since appeared, looking at the treatment of the war in other languages and literatures; these are of great interest in their own right, and are valuable in providing a relativizing context for the work of English writers, checking any tendency to treat as universal attitudes which may be national and cultural. A book edited by Holger Klein, *The First World War in Fiction* (1976), contains critical essays on work by French, German, Austrian and Italian writers as well as English and American ones. Elizabeth A. Marsland's *The Nation's Cause: French, English and German Poetry of the First World War* (1991) is a learned and valuable comparative study of poetry in three languages, based not on a limited number of canonical authors but on an extensive trawl of poems published in wartime anthologies, newspapers and magazines. Her approach is social-historical rather than literary-critical, but she provides provocative insights for the reader of war poetry, as when she argues that protest poetry is as much open to the charge of being propagandist as the patriotic writing it tended to replace.

In 1988 a remarkable anthology, *The Lost Voices of World War I*, edited by Tim Cross, appeared to mark the seventieth anniversary of the Armistice and to commemorate the writers from all countries who had died in the war, whether in action or in other ways as a result of it. The book contains poems – in the original languages as well as in translation – or prose extracts from many such writers, together with essays on their work. The English include Rupert Brooke, Charles Sorley, T.E. Hulme, Edward Thomas, Isaac Rosenberg and Wilfred Owen. The other writer-victims represented are French (notably Charles Péguy and Guillaume Apollinaire), German, Italian, Polish, Czech, Serb, Slovene, Bulgarian, Hungarian, and Armenian (Russians, though, are conspicuous by their absence). *The Lost Voices of World War I* contains an introduction and a concluding essay by Robert Wohl, who is the author of a distinguished discussion of the international intellectual contexts of the war, *The Generation of 1914* (1980). In that work Wohl traces the development of 'generational consciousness' in major European countries from the early 1900s; he argues that many intellectuals born in the 1880s or a little later felt they were part of a new generation, at odds with everything that had gone before. This consciousness, as it developed in the early years of the twentieth century, had affinities with the emerging modernism in art, music and literature; it was strongly reinforced in the war and its aftermath, and in some cases led to Fascism and in others to Communism. Wohl focuses his discussion on key writers and intellectuals from several countries. His chapter on English developments, where he considers Rupert Brooke, Siegfried Sassoon, and T.E. Lawrence, is slighter than the others, perhaps because intellectuals are reluctant to identify themselves as such in England. Wohl shows that in Continental countries not all writing about the war, even when acknowledging its horrors, was anti-war. He also modifies Fussell's rather exaggerated insistence on 1914 as a total break in history by indicating to what extent attitudes usually associated with the war were apparent before it.

There is a similar approach in Modris Eksteins' ambitious and impressive book, *Rites of Spring: The Great War and the Birth of the Modern Age* (1989). This is a study in European cultural history that is organized like a literary text, and specifically a three-act drama. It moves from the first performance of Stravinsky's *Rite of Spring*, which provoked a riot in a Paris theatre in May 1913, through the war and its aftermath, to the last days of the Third Reich in the spring of 1945. Although the author gives imaginative and dramatic form to history, his study is copiously documented, drawing on a wide range of published and unpublished sources in English, French and German. Eksteins states he wants to extend the notions of modernism and the avant-garde to the realm of the social and the political: 'Culture is regarded as a social phenomenon and modernism as the principal urge of our time. The book argues in the process that Germany has been the modernist nation *par excellence* in this century.' Germany is seen as the prime mover of a cataclysmic phase of history, the restless, dynamic, forward-looking power at the heart of Europe; German values were based on subjectivity and inner feeling, not on an objective sense of the order of things. Eksteins argues that Germany was primarily responsible for the First World War, an opinion generally taken for granted in Britain during the war, and then virtuously rejected by liberal opinion after it. He advances it less on diplomatic and political grounds than from his sense of Germany's expansionist energy. Germany, he says, was fighting to change *the* world, while conservative Britain was fighting to save *a* world. His book is strongly influenced by Nietzsche's belief that the world can only be understood as an aesthetic phenomenon. Out of the ruin of First World War Germany rose Nazism, which was an aesthetic, subjective and voluntaristic mode of confronting experience, led by the failed artist, Hitler. Eksteins is fascinated by the German experience, whilst believing that the philistine and backward-looking British had the better values. His book is intellectually exciting, even if it is not always convincing.

Returning to the narrower literary and English concerns of *Heroes' Twilight*, I have been struck by the realization that I wrote it during the approach to the fiftieth anniversary of the outbreak of the First World War in 1914, and that I have been revising it during the weeks leading up to the fiftieth anniversary of the end of the Second World War in Europe in 1945. Western Europe has been at peace and increasingly united for half a century, but in the rest of the world men have gone to war with much the same energy and enthusiasm that they showed in 1914. Since the second edition of my book appeared in 1980, British servicemen have died in small wars in the Falklands and the Gulf, in a bloody guerilla campaign in Ulster and in peacekeeping in Bosnia. New wars keep breaking out.

Wilfred Owen called for unqualified pacifism (though he went back to war and fought bravely, winning the Military Cross a month before he was killed). I increasingly feel he may have been right, but am restrained by memories of the war in which I grew up; the First World War and the follies of the victors led to Hitler, and Hitler had to be defeated. I have had, too, a sense that there is something artificial and unreal in writing about writing about war: violent death and wounds and destruction can seem both unbearably close and comfortably remote. Yet the works I discuss were written as an act of anamnesis, to make experience clear to their authors and to preserve the memory of what they had seen and undergone. Literature preserves memory, and at the same time transforms it, however terrible, into something strange and beautiful. I hope this book will give readers a better access to those memorials.

I should like to repeat the acknowledgements in the first edition to Tony England, Christian Hardie, Sylvia Mulvey, Brocard Sewell, Dennis Welland, and the late Marcus Cunliffe; and to add the name of Michael Schmidt, for his active encouragement of this edition. I am indebted, too, to the Computer Services Centre and – as so often in the past – the Library of the University of Warwick.

1: Between Hotspur and Falstaff:
Reflections on the Literature of War

We can begin with Shakespeare, who may or may not have been a soldier, but who wrote about war with uncommon completeness: showing us the glory and the trumpets in *Henry V* and the sickness and the taste of death in *Troilus and Cressida*. In *Henry IV*, Part I, he invents two characters who stand for opposing attitudes to war, and who illustrate these attitudes with great lucidity and an almost clinical exaggeration. Hotspur exemplifies the moral virtues of heroism and the single-minded pursuit of honour, but carries them to a ludicrous pitch:

> By heaven methinks it were an easy leap,
> To pluck bright honour from the pale-fac'd moon,
> Or dive into the bottom of the deep,
> Where fadomline could never touch the ground,
> And pluck up drowned honour by the locks,
> So he that doth redeem her thence might wear
> Without corrival all her dignities.
> But out upon this half-fac'd fellowship.

To which Worcester sourly replies that Hotspur does not know what he is talking about: 'He apprehends a world of figures here,/But not the form of what he should attend.'

At the end of the play Hotspur has died in battle and his body is discovered by Sir John Falstaff, who habitually puts life before honour. Falstaff embodies the biological virtue of cowardice: he combines the blind impulse to survive of a low writhing organism with the human burden of consciousness and a far more vivid imagination than Hotspur's:

> Well, 'tis no matter, honour pricks me on; yea, but how if honour
> prick me off when I come on? how then? how then? can honour set to a leg?
> no, or an arm? no, or take away the grief of a wound? no, honour

hath no skill in surgery then? no, what is honour? a word, what is
in that word honour? what is that honour? air, a trim reckoning.
Who hath it? he that died a'Wednesday, doth he feel it? no, doth
he hear it? no 'tis insensible then? yea, to the dead, but will it not
live with the living? no, why? detraction will not suffer it, there-
fore I'll none of it, honour is a mere scutcheon, and so ends my
Catechism.

By constant reiteration Falstaff evacuates the word 'honour' of all
the densities of meaning that it held for Hotspur, and reduces it to 'a
word...air'. Shakespeare does not endorse either of these attitudes:
each of them is an unacceptable extreme, though stemming from a
genuine value: Falstaff's will arouse a more immediate response,
since it flatly embodies, in its most basic form, the desire for self-
preservation.

One or other of these attitudes, though usually expressed in a
more moderate form, will certainly be present when war is talked
about. A film of the 1960s depicted an attempted escape by a number
of British officers in a prisoner-of-war camp during the last war; the
attempt failed and many of them were shot. A female critic com-
plained of the futile heroics that led these men to make the attempt.
They were well out of the war, she implied; wouldn't they have been
better off taking correspondence courses in some useful pursuit, and
so preparing themselves for peacetime, instead of throwing their
lives away in a futile gesture? A male correspondent replied, in some-
what Hotspurian tones, that they were by no means out of the war;
they were still serving soldiers, obliged to harass the enemy wherever
possible, and this their attempted escape succeeded in doing.

In Renaissance images of war, Hotspur was likely to be in the
dominance, whether seen as the helmeted, gesturing superman of
Verrocchio's statue of Bartolommeo Colleoni, or the loudmouthed
colossi who strode across the dramatic stages of the Elizabethan age:
Tamburlaine, Coriolanus, Bussy D'Ambois. (Shakespeare, however,
would sometimes permit his heroes to be undercut by the scoffing,
sceptical intellect of a Falstaff or a Thersites.) In the Romantic era,
Scott exploited a nostalgia for the clear-cut heroics of a past age of
chivalry. Byron, on the other hand, savagely castigated the inglorious
pursuit of glory in those cantos of *Don Juan* that deal with the siege
of Ismail:

> 'Let there be light! said God, and there was light!'
> 'Let there be blood!' says man, and there's a sea!
> The fiat of this spoiled child of the Night

> (For Day ne'er saw his merits) could decree
> More evil in an hour, than thirty bright
>   Summers could renovate, though they should be
> Lovely as those which ripened Eden's fruit,
>   For war cuts up not only branch, but root.

General Suvorov, who might have been seen as a figure of traditional heroic splendour, is calmly stripped of his pretensions:

> Suwarrow, who was standing in his shirt
>   Before a company of Calmucks, drilling,
> Exclaiming, fooling, swearing at the inert,
>   And lecturing on the noble art of killing, –
> For, deeming human clay but common dirt,
>   This great philosopher was thus instilling
> His maxims, which, to martial comprehension,
> Proved death in battle equal to a pension.

In stressing the physical horror of death in battle Byron is close to what we think of as a characteristic note of twentieth-century war poetry:

> The groan, the roll in dust, the all-white eye
>   Turned back within its socket – these reward
> Your rank and file by thousands, while the rest
> May win perhaps a riband at the breast!

Mocking Wordsworth, for unguardedly referring in his 'Thanksgiving Ode' to Carnage as the daughter of God, Byron seems to anticipate the angry gibes that Siegfried Sassoon and other poets of 1914-18 directed at the crass utterances of civilian propagandists. (Wordsworth wisely removed the reference when he came to revise the poem.) Byron eloquently condemns war, but not without reservations: he runs up against the hard paradox that to be a complete pacifist is to acquiesce in tyranny. *Some* wars – wars in defence of freedom, as opposed to wars fought for mere empty glory – are just. And here the paradox closes its jaws, for *all* wars are claimed as being in defence of freedom by those who initiate them.

> History can only take things in the gross;
>   But could we know them in detail, perchance
> In balancing the profit and the loss,
>   War's merit it by no means might enhance,
> To waste so much gold for a little dross,
>   As hath been done, mere conquest to advance.

The drying up a single tear has more
Of honest fame, than shedding seas of gore.

And why? because it brings self-approbation;
    Whereas the other, after all its glare,
Shouts, bridges, arches, pensions from a nation,
    Which (it may be) has not much left to spare,
A higher title, or a loftier station,
    Though they may make Corruption gape or stare,
Yet, in the end, except in Freedom's battles,
Are nothing but a child of Murder's rattles.

And such they are – and such they will be found.
    Not so Leonidas and Washington,
Whose every battle-field is holy ground,
    Which breathes of nations saved, not worlds undone.
How sweetly on the ear such echoes sound!
    While the mere victor's may appal or stun
The servile and the vain, such names will be
A watchword till the future shall be free.

It is in the novel, the dominant literary form of the nineteenth century, which in its very nature is realistic, bourgeois-centred, anti-heroic, and frequently ironic, that the Hotspurian or heroic attitude to war is most radically undermined. Stendhal, Byron's contemporary, provides in *La Chartreuse de Parme* a superb account of Fabrice del Dongo's misadventures on the field of Waterloo. Overflowing with martial aspirations and eager for a place in the fight, Fabrice plunges into the battle and meets a scene of inextricable confusion. Neither he nor anyone else can grasp the pattern of what is going on, and there is little opportunity to play the part of a hero: Fabrice day-dreams of glory and is thrilled to catch sight of the red-faced Marshal Ney, one of his idols; but Stendhal ironically contrasts his state of mind with the reality that surrounds him, the carnage and the spreading disorder of an army in retreat. He provides the sharply observed and bloody detail that one more readily associates with Barbusse or Remarque:

Fabrizio sat on, horror-struck. What most impressed him was the mud on the feet of the corpse, which had been stripped of its shoes and of everything else, indeed, except a wretched pair of blood-stained trousers... The corpse was hideously disfigured. A bullet had entered near the nose and passed out at the opposite temple. One eye was open and staring.

A little later Fabrice comes upon a wounded horse, its hooves entangled in its own entrails, and reflects, 'Well, I am under fire at last. I have seen the firing. Now I am a real soldier.'

Thackeray, too, dealt with Waterloo, though not with the actual fighting; his irony, though a good deal less subtle than Stendhal's, is sharply anti-heroic. He expresses that typically British attitude which, whilst prepared to be actively patriotic at times of crisis, is generally contemptuous of the military virtues as such, an attitude of which Kipling complained in 'Tommy': 'Yes, makin' mock o' uniforms that guard you while you sleep/Is cheaper than them uniforms, an' they're starvation cheap.' But the fullest treatment of the war in nineteenth century fiction occurs in the great battle scenes of *War and Peace*, in which Tolsoy combines Stendhal's cruel detail and awareness of confusion with a huge panoramic sweep that dwarfs all the participants, whether generals or ordinary soldiers, reducing them to agents of the historical process. Also in the Tolstoyan manner, though on a far smaller scale, is Stephen Crane's astonishing recreation of a war that he had never experienced, *The Red Badge of Courage*. Crane said of this masterpiece: 'of course, I have never been in a battle, but I believe that I got my sense of the rage of conflict on the football field, or else fighting is a hereditary instinct, and I wrote intuitively.'

English writers were less adventurous, but at intervals, when the occasional far-away wars of the period demanded it, feelings rose to an unusual pitch of patriotic fervour and were given appropriate literary expression. One of the most notorious and wretchedly unforgettable instances, in a thoroughly atavistic mode, is Tennyson's 'Charge of the Light Brigade'. Tennyson writes with a large and confident innocence about the state of mind of the unhappy cavalrymen forced to charge the Russian guns:

> 'Forward, the Light Brigade!'
> Was there a man dismay'd?
> Not tho' the soldier knew
> Some one had blunder'd...

He displays a curious and presumably inadvertent tact in *not* giving the phrase 'someone had blundered' any kind of sardonic weight: the blunder merely makes the glory of the fallen heroes all the more spectacular. One can imagine what Sassoon would have made of the incident.

In the final years of the nineteenth century, the period of self-assertive Imperialism, British writers were increasingly aware of the martial and heroic virtues; and there was at the same time an increasing preoccupation with violence: I shall say more about this in the next chapter. But the anti-heroic mode also had its energetic protagonists, of whom Bernard Shaw was one of the most illustrious and skilful. *Arms and the Man* provided a thoroughly Falstaffian view of war, and was recognized by some patriots as being a subversive work. Writing in 1916, T.E. Hulme, an intellectual militarist, complained of the humanistic (or Falstaffian) ethic: 'As *life* is its fundamental value, it leads naturally to pacifism, and tends to regard conceptions like Honour, etc., as empty words, which cannot deceive the *emancipated*.' Defending the case for heroic values, Hulme continued:

> The rationalists (though they could not have said why) seem to have known *instinctively* that this conception of heroism was the central *nerve* of the ethic they opposed; and have consequently always tried to disintegrate it by ridicule. The author of 'Arms and the Man' thus reminds one of the wasps described by Fabre, who sting their prey in the central ganglia in order to paralyse it, in this way acting as if they were expert entomologists, though in reality they can have no conscious knowledge of what they are doing.[1]

Hulme remains a singular and exotic figure (at least in an English context), who was prepared to argue about and advance intellectually positions which most people only upheld in a blind and purely instinctive way. In the essays he published during the Great War, containing a dispute about the war with Bertrand Russell, he provided fresh manifestations of the perennial debate between Hotspur and Falstaff (though Hulme, as a serving soldier, disliked the trenches as much as anyone else). Amongst those who fought, the Hotspurian mode in time gave place to the Falstaffian, or something rather like it. Hulme may have vigorously defended the traditional heroic virtues, which had been so nobly upheld at Thermopylae and even, in Tennyson's vision, in the Crimea; but after the mechanized, large-scale slaughter on the Somme in July 1916, a certain necessary balance and proportion had been lost, and these virtues were increasingly devalued. One may contrast Julian Grenfell's hymn to battle:

> And Life is Colour and Warmth and Light,
> And a striving evermore for these;

[1] *Further Speculations*, ed. S. Hynes (Minneapolis, 1955), pp.200-202.

And he is dead who will not fight;
And who dies fighting has increase...

with the depressed utterance of Arthur Graeme West (in a diary entry of 19 August 1916): 'What right has anyone to demand of me that I should give up my chance of obtaining happiness – the only chance I have, and the only thing worth obtaining here.' West was a keen admirer of Bertrand Russell, Hulme's opponent in controversy.

The war of 1914-18 can still very properly be referred to by its original name of the Great War; for despite the greater magnitude of its more truly global successor, it represented a far more radical crisis in British civilization. In particular, it meant that the traditional mythology of heroism and the hero, the Hotspurian mode of self-assertion, had ceased to be viable; even though heroic *deeds* could be, and were, performed in abundance. For later evidence of the way in which anti-heroic attitudes to war have become dominant we can turn to one of the most famous novels of the Second World War, Joseph Heller's *Catch 22*.[2] The anti-hero of it is Captain Yossarian, a bomber-pilot who has flown gallantly on a large number of missions but has now frankly had enough of the war: his principal opponent is not the Germans, but his commanding officer, Colonel Cathcart, who for reasons of personal glory is constantly increasing the number of missions his men must undertake before being sent home. In this situation Yossarian proclaims a belief in the absolute value of survival; in the face of Julian Grenfell's passionate assurance that 'who dies fighting has increase' he would probably have replied with equal passion that 'who dies fighting is *dead*!' In the face of Yossarian's energy and conviction, the old absolute distinction between 'heroism' and 'cowardice' ceases to have much meaning: Yossarian asserts the primacy of the biological, for which 'cowardice' is a virtue. In this discussion with a fellow-officer, Yossarian gives the Falstaffian arguments a fresh emphasis:

> 'You are talking about winning the war, and I am talking about winning the war and keeping alive.'
> 'Exactly,' Clevinger snapped smugly. 'And which do you think is more important?'
> 'To whom?' Yossarian shot back. 'Open your eyes, Clevinger. It doesn't make a damned bit of difference who wins the war to someone who's dead.'

---

[2] Philip Larkin described Heller's novel as 'the American hymn to cowardice, *Catch 22*'; *Selected Letters*, ed. A. Thwaite (London, 1992), p.531.

Clevinger sat for a moment as though he'd been slapped. 'Con-
gratulations!' he exclaimed bitterly, the thinnest milk-white line
enclosing his lips tightly in a bloodless, squeezing ring. 'I can't
think of another attitude that could be depended upon to give
greater comfort to the enemy.'

'The enemy,' retorted Yossarian with weighted precision, 'is
anybody who's going to get you killed, no matter *which* side he's
on, and that includes Colonel Cathcart. And don't you forget
that, because the longer you remember it, the longer you might
live.'

But Clevinger did forget it, and now he was dead.

Joseph Heller takes the Falstaffian approach further by making
one of his characters argue that, on the whole, it is better to lose wars
than to win them. In a Roman brothel an airman called Nately, who
is a normally patriotic young American, meets an old man who
claims to be a hundred and seven years old and who talks like this:

'You put so much stock in *winning* wars,' the grubby iniquitous
old man scoffed. 'The real trick lies in *losing* wars, in knowing
which wars can be *lost*. Italy has been losing wars for centuries,
and just see how splendidly we've done nonetheless. France wins
wars and is in a continual state of crisis. Germany loses and pros-
pers. Look at our own recent history. Italy won a war in Ethiopia
and promptly stumbled into serious trouble. Victory gave us such
insane delusions of grandeur that we helped start a world war we
hadn't a chance of winning. But now that we are losing again,
everything has taken a turn for the better, and we will certainly
come out on top again if we succeed in being defeated.'

Under the stress of Hotspurian emotions, much blood has been
spilt in the pursuit of wars whose outcome made no difference at all
to most of the inhabitants of the countries involved. But not all wars
might as well be lost as won: in our own age, where totalitarianism
and the technology of genocide go hand in hand, the price of losing
a war might be the surrendering of one's fellow countrymen to
torture, deportation or mass extermination.

2: Preludes

It is always tempting to mythologize the past, and no period of recent history lends itself so readily to such a habit of mind as the years immediately before 1914. We imagine long, brilliant afternoons, with the costumes and décor out of *My Fair Lady*, the champagne and strawberries inexhaustible, premières of the Russian Ballet, yachting at Cowes, veteran motor-cars with their brass and paint-work gleaming. And for the poor, beer was cheap and the pubs were open all day. The sun always shone and the sky was triumphantly, everlastingly blue. This whole, magnificent, fragile order was shattered in pieces by a pistol shot at Sarajevo, and then trodden deep in the mud and darkness of Flanders and the Somme. It is a compelling myth, and, of course, some of it is true. When we read that David Lloyd George observed in a speech on 17 July – three weeks before Britain declared war on Germany – 'In the matter of external affairs the sky has never been more perfectly blue', we are struck by the poignancy of such child-like unawareness, enhanced by that familiar and characteristic image of a sky of perfect blue.

One cannot say that myths are untrue: it is not in their nature to be contradicted, but one can point out their insufficiencies. And the picture of the England of the years before the outbreak of the Great War as a peaceable Eden, happily unconscious of the fate about to sweep it away, contains very much less than the whole truth. Many people were aware of the clouds already forming in that apparently flawless sky. George Dangerfield's *The Strange Death of Liberal England 1910-1914* (1935) showed how the civilized and placid surface of life in those years barely covered alarming areas of violence and disorder: huge cracks were already appearing in the structure that toppled with such apparent suddenness in 1914. Indeed, Dangerfield argues that the Great War did no more than accentuate a process that was already under way: the stability of English life was threatened by a triple outbreak of violence: from industrial troubles, from the suffragette movement, and from the Tory revolt over Ulster. If the country had not gone to war in August 1914, England would have been faced with a possible civil war in Ireland, and something like a general strike in industry, provoked by union leaders of extremely militant temper.

As one might expect, some of the imaginative writers of the time were conscious of the spreading cracks in the social façade and the hints of impending disaster. In 1910, the year of George V's accession, two books, both to become famous, were published. One of them, Norman Angell's *The Great Illusion*, an impressive work of liberal optimism, argued that a general European war was impossible for economic reasons. The other was *Howards End*, the fourth novel by E.M. Forster, then aged thirty-one: it advanced no propositions, save perhaps the mild argument in favour of togetherness contained in its epigraph, 'only connect'; but it contained a more penetrating insight into the attitudes and preoccupations of its time than many overtly discursive works. Though an imperfect and often contrived novel, *Howards End* remains highly relevant for anyone concerned with the intellectual, moral and social quality of life in the England of 1910-14. C.K. Stead has suggested[1] that its decent, worried liberalism, deeply in love with the English countryside and past, and conscious of impending dissolution, was to form the staple attitude of the Georgian poets of two or three years later, an attitude which was to find both fulfilment and catastrophe during the Great War. In many passages of *Howards End* Forster shows himself strangely prophetic, already concerned with problems that were to be dominant many years later: the volume of traffic in London streets, the demolition of well-loved buildings, the sprawl of suburbia into open countryside. There is a key passage in the final pages of the novel: Margaret, Helen and Helen's baby are arranged in a precarious tableau in the garden of Howards End, the house that has symbolized the continuity of English tradition.

> 'I hope it will be permanent,' said Helen, drifting away to other thoughts.
> 'I think so. There are moments when I feel Howards End peculiarly our own.'
> 'All the same, London's creeping.'
> She pointed over the meadow – over eight or nine meadows, but at the end of them was a red rust.

---

[1] *The New Poetic*, (London, 1964) p.83.

'You see that in Surrey and even Hampshire now,' she continued. 'I can see it from the Purbeck Downs. And London is only part of something else, I'm afraid. Life's going to be melted down, all over the world.'

Margaret knew that her sister spoke truly. Howards End, Oniton, the Purbeck Downs, the Oderberge, were all survivals, and the melting pot was being prepared for them. Logically, they had no right to be alive.

Forster could not have viewed open violence, and still less the prospect of war, with anything other than utter repugnance. Nevertheless, there is a surprising amount of violence in his earlier novels, usually of a flatly melodramatic kind, and the topic is clearly one which the author found interesting if distasteful. As an example, one can refer to the scene in Chapter XLI of *Howards End* in which Leonard Bast, the wretched, upstart young autodidact from the lower orders, is beaten by Charles Wilcox with the flat of a sword, and falls dead; as he falls, he brings down a bookcase on top of him and so is buried, with heavy symbolism, under a pile of books.

A similar interest in violence is noticeable in many other works of the early years of the century, and in much late-Victorian literature. In authors who do not share Forster's liberal convictions it is a good deal more pronounced: Kipling comes immediately to mind, but there were other exemplars. In 1892 the crippled Imperialist, W.E. Henley, published a strange poem called 'The Song of the Sword', which he dedicated to Kipling. This is a passionate paean to violence, perhaps inspired by early heroic poetry, in which Henley seems to hint at something as radically un-English as the Spanish cult of death:

Clear singing, clean slicing;
Sweet spoken, soft finishing;
Making death beautiful,
Life but a coin
To be staked in the pastime
Whose playing is more
Than the transfer of being;
Arch-anarch, chief builder,
Prince and evangelist,
I am the Will of God:
I am the Sword.

A very different writer, G.K. Chesterton, was a Liberal of sorts, a Little Englander, and a Christian apologist. His fantastic novel, *The*

Napoleon of Notting Hill (1904), contain accounts of street fighting
in the West London suburbs in which a good deal of blood is spilt
but no one is really hurt: 'down the steep streets which lead from the
Waterworks Tower to the Notting Hill High Road, blood has been
running, and is running, in great red serpents, that curl out into the
main thoroughfare and shine in the moon.' There is something
deeply innocent about such a vision, the product of a period when
England had been at peace for a very long time (save for the Boer
War and various colonial adventures) and peace had come to seem
insupportably dull.[2] How much more modern, by contrast, are
Byron and Stendhal.

Another example of purely literary violence can be seen in an early
poem by Ezra Pound, 'Altaforte', which commemorates with con-
siderable gusto the bellicose inclinations of a Provençal nobleman:

> And let the music of the swords make them crimson!
> Hell grant soon we hear again the swords clash!
> Hell blot black for always the thought 'Peace'!

One does not need to look far to find literary evidence of a concern
with violence that was to erupt in the large-scale political and social
turbulence of the years immediately before 1914.

A particular preoccupation of many writers in the early years of
this century was the fear of a future war and a possible invasion of
England. This was not, in itself, a new theme. From the Franco-
Prussian war of 1870 onwards many books and pamphlets had been
published which dealt with such an invasion; some of them were
written by professional soldiers and aimed at arousing the nation
and strengthening its defences, while others, of a more sensational
kind, merely wanted to make their readers' flesh creep. One of the
earliest and most famous was *The Battle of Dorking* (1871) by
General Sir George Chesney, about a successful Prussian invasion of
southern England, which inspired many imitations. Representative
later examples included *The Invasion of England* (1882) by General
Sir William Butler, and *The Great War in England in 1897* (1894) by
William Le Queux. In the same genre, but of incomparably greater
literary and imaginative power, was H.G. Wells's *The War of the
Worlds* (1898), which described an invasion of England, not by
human enemies, but by Martians. Many of these works were of a
frankly ephemeral nature, but there seems to have been a fairly

---

[2] For more about *The Napoleon of Notting Hill* see my introduction to the World's
Classic's edition (Oxford, 1994).

steady demand for them, and no doubt their output varied according
to the international situation: the hypothetical enemies involved
were usually France, Germany or Russia, or a combination of two or
three of these powers; but in one or two instances America was seen
as a possible opponent.

After the turn of the century, however, Germany came to be
regarded more and more as Britain's most likely enemy, reflecting
the increasing German attempt to rival Britain as a world power;
and the warning note became more urgent. As, for instance, in
Kipling's impassioned rebuke in 'The Islanders' (1902) to his fellow-
countrymen – 'the flannelled fools at the wicket or the muddied oafs
at the goals' – for their slackness in the matter of national defence:

> Do ye wait for the spattered shrapnel ere ye learn how a gun
>   is laid?
> For the low, red glare to southward when the raided coast-
>   towns burn?
> (Light ye shall have on that lesson, but little time to learn.)

A celebrated popular novel of about the same time was Erskine
Childers's *The Riddle of the Sands* (1903), a splendid adventure
story in which an English yachtsman sailing in the East Frisian
islands stumbles upon plans for a German invasion of England.
Childers wrote the book with an overtly didactic aim, though in later
years, after fighting throughout the Great War, he abandoned his
English patriotism and became an Irish nationalist; he was finally
shot by the Free State Government as an adherent of the Republican
side in the Civil War.

Wells was another writer somewhat preoccupied with the threat
of war and the menace of Imperial Germany. In 1908 he published
The War in the Air, in which a German attempt to obtain world
domination begins with an airship attack on the United States.
Global war ensues and leads to the virtual collapse of civilization
throughout large parts of the world. This novel embodies an apoca-
lyptic vision of a kind which had obsessed many writers of the *fin de
siècle* era and to which Wells had previously given a more profoundly
imaginative embodiment in *The War of the Worlds*. But *The War in
the Air*, though a shapeless book, has some powerful passages, and
contains a fairly good anticipation of the horrors of aerial bombard-
ment. Wells returned to the topic of war in *The World Set Free*, an
inferior fantasy which appeared in 1914, not long before the out-
break of the Great War. It describes a war fought in the 1950s (it is
mankind's last war, and the prelude to Utopia), but the line-up is

appropriate to 1914: Britain and France, allied with the 'Slav Con-
federation', against Germany and the other Central European
powers. Wells displays his characteristic flair for prophecy in
imagining the use of atomic bombs, but gets the detail wrong by
making them two feet in diameter and dropped from aeroplanes by
hand. He displays a more accurate anticipation of the conflict that
was to follow hard on the publication of his book when one of his
characters reflects:

> ' "From Holland to the Alps this day," I thought, "there must be
> crouching and lying between half and a million of men, trying to
> inflict irreparable damage upon one another. The thing is idiotic
> to the pitch of impossibility. It is a dream. Presently I shall wake
> up."...'

More directly concerned with the German menace as it was under-
stood by many people in the immediate pre-war period, is a novel by
Saki (H.H. Munro), *When William Came*. Published in 1913, ten
years after Childers's novel, it reflects the same preoccupation.
Britain has already been occupied by Germany, after a brief war, not
described in detail, in which the British forces were decisively defeated:
the King has fled to India, and the British Isles have been annexed as
a province of the German Empire, with bilingual notices and news-
papers and German troops much in evidence. The story is told
through the eyes of Murrey Yeovil, a Tory patriot who had been
travelling in Siberia whilst the war was being fought and returns to
discover, in horror, a defeated nation. Most of the novel is set in
fashionable London, among Saki's familiar circle of epigrammatic,
world-weary socialites, Murrey's wife, Cicely, prominent amongst
them; they are prepared to accept the new situation and collaborate,
with varying degrees of enthusiasm, with the occupying power.
Murrey's disgust with the prevailing decadence is heightened when
an Imperial Rescript is published stating that subjects of British birth
will not, as had been anticipated, be conscripted for military service,
since they are not of sufficient martial calibre; instead they will be
prohibited from handling arms at all, even in rifle clubs, though they
will be very heavily taxed to help support the occupying German
troops. Thus the will and capacity to resist of the British will be
finally eradicated: it was part of Saki's didactic message in this novel,
as it had previously been Kipling's, to denounce the British for their
unwillingness to accept conscription in peacetime. The point is
rather heavily underlined when Murrey sees a company of Bavarian
infantry marching down a London street:

A group of lads from the tea-shop clustered on the pavement and watched the troops go by, staring at a phase of life in which they had no share. The martial trappings, the swaggering joy of life, the comradeship of camp and barracks, the hard discipline of drill yard and fatigue duty, the long sentry watches, the trench digging, forced marches, wounds, cold, hunger, makeshift hospitals, and the blood-wet laurels – these were not for them. Such things they might only guess at, or see on a cinema film, darkly; they belonged to the civilian nation.

This is, perhaps, a somewhat civilian concept of the martial virtues, though a traditional one: within a year or so the 'blood-wet laurels' were to seem a distinctly inadequate symbol for the realities of twentieth-century warfare. (Saki himself died in action in 1916.) At the end of his book, Saki permits a faint note of hope: the youth of Britain, it seems, have not been won over by the conquerors, and a parade of boy-scouts in front of the Kaiser in Hyde Park is boycotted and a complete failure.

German rule in the England of 1913, as Saki describes it, though irksome, is remarkably mild when compared with what we now know of Nazi or Communist occupation; but it would have been a shocking enough picture for contemporary readers. One may doubt if such works were very successful in their directly propagandist aims: but they point to a deep-seated fear of German domination. They may suggest, too, that the outbreak of war in August 1914, though in one way such an unexpected event, had been imaginatively anticipated for some time. And a subconscious fear of invasion and occupation is perhaps why so many Englishmen reacted as if it were England herself that was being invaded, rather than Belgium. To this extent, a war propaganda poster showing German soldiers mounting guard in a British factory and maltreating the workers fulfilled expectations and fears aroused by books like *When William Came*.

There is another sphere, much more remote from politics and everyday affairs, in which one also finds a certain preoccupation with violence, and an impatience with the pacific virtues. In the world of avant-garde art and literature there was a cult of the virile and dynamic virtues: Futurism as an international artistic movement, under the leadership of the ebullient Italian, Marinetti, briefly flourished from about 1911; and the Futurists idolized the machine – notably the aeroplane and the motor-car – and were very excited by the dynamism manifested in modern war. Before long Futurist aspirations were to be surpassed in the artillery bombardments of the Western front: shortly before his death in 1915 the young French sculptor of genius, Henri Gaudier-Brzeska, remarked in a letter:

> we have the finest futuristic music Marinetti can dream of, big guns, small guns, bomb-throwers' reports, with a great difference between the German and the French, the different kinds of whistling from the shells, their explosion, the echo in the woods of the rifle fires, some short, discreet, others long, rolling, etc.; but it is all stupid vulgarity, and I prefer the fresh wind in the leaves with a few songs from the birds.[3]

Futurism never made any great impact in England, though the painter C.R.W. Nevinson considered himself an adherent of the movement. But there were comparable currents of thought in advanced London intellectual and artistic circles during the years before 1914. One can again consider the enigmatic figure of T.E. Hulme, for instance, who was killed in 1917: had he survived he might have become the principal theoretician of English fascism, if such a movement had developed on a large scale. Hulme, as a begetter of Imagist poetry and the defender of Epstein's sculpture, was actively engaged in the artistic manifestations of the early modern movement; and whilst not a systematic thinker, he professed a number of highly influential attitudes. Hulme's aesthetic was, above all, anti-vital; just as he admired heroic values, as against an ethic based on *life*, so he desired in art – particularly in sculpture – a kind of creation that was geometrical, non-organic and more or less abstract. In his excursions into political thought Hulme strongly admired the writings of the French syndicalist, Georges Sorel, whose mystical cult of 'proletarian violence' appealed to the extreme Right as much as to the Left (Sorel himself was an admirer of Lenin, but was also a dominant influence on Mussolini). Hulme helped to translate Sorel's *Reflections on Violence* (1916), where we find such sentiments as these:

> Proletarian violence, carried on as a pure and simple manifestation of the class war, appears thus as a very fine and very heroic thing; it is at the service of the immemorial interests of civilisation; it is not perhaps the most appropriate method of obtaining immediate material advantages, but it may save the world from barbarism.

Hulme was associated for a time with Ezra Pound and Wyndham

---

[3] Ezra Pound, *Gaudier-Brzeska: A Memoir*, (Hessle, 1960), p.69.

Lewis, who founded early in 1914 the Vorticist movement, as some-
thing of an English counterblast to Futurism. There are similarities
between the two movements, though the Vorticists condemned the
Futurists; the principal difference between them is that the Vorticists
were less concerned with dynamism and movement. Their aesthetic
principle was the 'Vortex', defined variously as a point of stasis
amidst the flow of 'vital' activity, or as a unit of creative energy (it
also had affinities, never very clearly defined, with the Image in
poetry). Hulme was suspicious of the Vorticists, and not on good
personal terms with them, but they seemed to reflect his ideas: above
all a stress on the abstract, geometrical, anti-human element in art.
Like the Futurists, they admired machinery. This, at least, was true
of the painters and sculptors in their midst: Lewis, Edward Wads-
worth, and Henri Gaudier-Brzeska. Pound was in the group princi-
pally as an enthusiastic publicist, and Lewis said that the artists
secretly despised his literary interests as hopelessly old-fashioned
and backward-looking, compared with their own revolutionary
zeal. (Though once the war had started, Gaudier-Brzeska, a belligerent
patriot who joined the French army at the outbreak, could find
inspiration in Pound's purely literary bellicosity; in a letter to
Wadsworth in November 1914 he remarked: 'you may imagine how
difficult it is to concentrate your mind upon any subject when you
are obsessed by fighting. Now would be the time to read over and
over again Ezra's "Altaforte".'[4])

The first number of *Blast*, the Vorticist magazine, was dated
20 June 1914: its huge magenta cover and stark, angry typography
were in themselves aggressive acts. Still more so were the manifestoes
that it contained, those lists of 'blasts', more trenchant than coherent,
directed at the survivals of the Victorian era and the various idols
and comfortable assumptions of the philistine British middle-class.
Much of the contents of *Blast* have their permanent place in the
literary and artistic history of the twentieth century: the reproductions
of paintings by Lewis and Wadsworth, of sculpture by Gaudier-
Brzeska, the early chapters of Ford Madox Ford's *The Good Soldier*,
and, in the second number, some of Eliot's first poems. But in the
present context, the most poignant thing about *Blast* is the contrast
between its small-scale belligerency, so emphatic at the time and so
frail in retrospect, and the wave of mechanized violence, thoroughly
geometrical and anti-vital, that was to sweep over Europe a few

---

4 Ibid., p.72.

weeks later. Knowing what we do, is it sinister or pathetic to find reproduced in *Blast* an angular abstract design by Lewis with the caption 'Plan of War'?

The War provided a far greater Vortex; and this was recognized by Gaudier-Brzeska, in the manifesto that he wrote from the trenches and which appeared posthumously in 1915 in the second number of *Blast*.

I HAVE BEEN FIGHTING FOR TWO MONTHS and I can now gauge the intensity of life.

HUMAN MASSES teem and move, are destroyed and crop up again.

HORSES are worn out in three weeks, die by the roadside.

DOGS wander, are destroyed, and others come along.

WITH ALL THE DESTRUCTION that works around us NOTHING IS CHANGED, EVEN SUPERFICIALLY. LIFE IS THE SAME STRENGTH, THE MOVING AGENT THAT PERMITS THE SMALL INDIVIDUAL TO ASSERT HIMSELF.

THE BURSTING SHELLS, the volleys, wire entanglements, projectors, motors, the chaos of battle DO NOT ALTER IN THE LEAST the outlines of the hill we are besieging. A company of PARTRIDGES scuttle along before our very trench.

IT WOULD BE FOLLY TO SEEK ARTISTIC EMOTIONS AMID THESE LITTLE WORKS OF OURS.

THIS PALTRY MECHANISM, WHICH SERVES AS A PURGE TO OVER-NUMEROUS HUMANITY.

THIS WAR IS A GREAT REMEDY.

IN THE INDIVIDUAL IT KILLS ARROGANCE, SELF-ESTEEM, PRIDE.

IT TAKES AWAY FROM THE MASSES NUMBERS UPON NUMBERS OF UNIMPORTANT UNITS, WHOSE ECONOMIC ACTIVITIES BECOME NOXIOUS AS THE RECENT TRADE CRISES HAVE SHOWN US.

MY VIEWS ON SCULPTURE REMAIN ABSOLUTELY THE SAME. IT IS THE VORTEX OF WILL, OF DECISION, THAT BEGINS .[5]

And so on.

Traditional England, prosperous, pacific, humane, optimistic, the England seen in an exalted light in *Howards End*, in Margaret Schlegel's vision of a countryside that 'would vote Liberal if it could', was sadly undermined in the years that led up to the Great War: attacked by strikers and suffragettes, threatened by military revolt

[5] Ibid., pp.27-8.

over Ireland, and on the intellectual plane riddled with self-doubt and preoccupied with violence; berated by Tories like Kipling and Saki for being pacific, and by the artistic avant-garde for being philistine and bourgeois. It is not hard to see why the country should have found in the outbreak of war, that apparent thunderbolt from a cloudless sky, something very like an act both of fulfilment and deliverance.

3: Poets I

Brooke, Grenfell, Sorley

The impact of war on 4 August 1914 has often been described and the details are familiar: cheering crowds outside Buckingham Palace, a surge of patriotic fervour throughout the country, the rush to the recruiting offices. One young man who volunteered, J.B. Priestley, left a vivid account of his motives:

> There came, out of the unclouded blue of that summer, a challenge that was almost like a conscription of the spirit, little to do really with King and Country and flag-waving and hip-hip-hurrah, a challenge to what we felt was our untested manhood. Other men, who had not lived as easily as we had, had drilled and marched and borne arms – couldn't we? Yes, we too could leave home and soft beds and the girls to soldier for a spell, if there was some excuse for it, something at least to be defended. And here it was.[1]

In the opening weeks of the war many poems appeared in the press which were impeccably patriotic in sentiment and thoroughly wretched as literary art. Thomas Hardy's 'Men Who March Away', dated 5 September 1914, is a good deal better than the average run of these. It reflects the dominant mood unpretentiously, with obvious sincerity and the kind of baffled clumsiness that characterizes so much of Hardy's writing:

> Nay. We well see what we are doing,
>   Though some may not see –
>   Dalliers as they be –
>   England's need are we;
> Her distress would leave us rueing:
> Nay. We well see what we are doing,
>   Though some may not see!

---

[1] *Margin Released*, (London, 1962), p.82.

Another poem written at about the same time is Kipling's 'For All We Have and Are', which, in J.I.M. Stewart's words, 'is adequate to its grave occasion':

> For all we have and are,
> For all our children's fate,
> Stand up and take the war.
> The Hun is at the gate!
> Our world has passed away,
> In wantonness o'erthrown.
> There is nothing left today
> But steel and fire and stone!

Kipling combines his grim acceptance of war with a certain degree of relish about the overthrow of that 'wantonness' which he had so often condemned in his slack fellow-countrymen. In the second stanza Kipling seems to be echoing the poem that Henley had dedicated to him over twenty years before:

> Once more we hear the word
> That sickened earth of old:
> 'No law except the Sword
> Unsheathed and uncontrolled.'
> Once more it knits mankind,
> Once more the nations go
> To meet and break and bind
> A crazed and driven foe.

It was to be expected that Tory patriots like Kipling would share the popular enthusiasm for the war and would urge universal support for it. What was less inherently probable was that progressive and radical writers, the idols of the Left, would be equally wholehearted in supporting the war; but H.G. Wells offers a curious and instructive example. He had not long published *The World Set Free*, which exposed the futility and horror of war, and showed the nations resolving never to undertake it again. Wells's convictions, as revealed in that novel, were pacifist; but when the war against Germany broke out he rapidly wrote a series of newspaper articles, soon afterwards published in book form as *The War That Will End War*, which urged full support for the struggle against Prussian militarism, so that, once Germany was defeated, war itself might be abolished. Wells justified British participation – in defence of Belgium – by seeing the war as a real-life enactment of the 'The Last War' that he had described in *The World Set Free*. He did not expect it to last long, and was confident that France would defeat Germany within three months: he could even permit himself such confident observations as: 'a Russian raid is far more likely to threaten Berlin than a German to reach Paris'. (This, of course, was written before the battle of Tannenburg.)

Wells's support for the war earned him derisive comments from both Left and Right. T.E. Hulme ironically retailed an anecdote about a man suddenly taken ill who was examined by a vet, and was told, 'I don't know what's the matter with you, but I can give you something that will bring on blind staggers, and I can cure that all right.' Hulme continued:

> Now Mr Wells had never taken the possibility of an Anglo-German war seriously – he was pacifist by profession. It was not exactly his subject then, and last August may have found him somewhat baffled as to what to say. So he gave it blind staggers, he turned it into a 'war to end war', and there you are. Such writers, in dealing with a matter like war, alien to their ordinary habits of thought, are liable to pass from a fatuous optimism to a fatuous pessimism, equally distant from the real facts of the situation.[2]

On the other hand, Douglas Goldring sharply attacked Wells soon after the war (Goldring had volunteered at the outbreak of war, then fallen seriously ill and been discharged; two years later he was called up, and by that time had become a conscientious objector):

> When war broke out, while many of Mr Wells' disciples were keeping alight the flame of those principles which by his eloquence he had instilled into their minds, Mr Wells himself, like the majority of us, completely lost his head.[3]

Outright pacifists were few at the beginning of the war, though they included a number of intellectuals: Bertrand Russell, the Bloomsbury group, and other members of Lady Ottoline Morrell's circle. But for the most part the nation had no doubts that the war against Germany was both necessary and just; fanned by atrocity stories from Belgium, hatred of the Germans grew to an intensity greater than anything that arose in the Second World War. Disenchanted innocence turned savagely sour. The feelings of diffused patriotic fervour, heightened by the painful news during August of

---

[2] *Further Speculations*, p.175.
[3] *Reputations*, (London, 1920), p.90.

the long retreat of the British Expeditionary Force from Mons, needed a focus, a dominating myth that could give coherence to these strong but scattered emotions. One was to arise in extraordinary fashion. On 29 September 1914 Arthur Machen published a short story called 'The Bowmen' in the *Evening News*: Machen was a professional journalist who had made his début in the nineties with a number of short stories of the occultist, consciously bizarre kind that were popular at that time. 'The Bowmen' was, as he admitted, a very slight piece; it described the stand made by a company of British troops during the retreat from Mons. They were hard pressed by numerically stronger German forces, and though they fought back energetically were on the point of being overrun. At that moment one of them, more educated than the rest, murmured an invocation to St George, '*Adsit Anglis Sanctus Georgius*':

> His heart grew hot as a burning coal, it grew cold as ice within him, as it seemed to him that a tumult of voices answered to his summons. He heard, or seemed to hear, thousands shouting: 'St George! St George!'
> 'Ha! messire; ha! sweet Saint, grant us good deliverance!'
> 'St George for merry England!'
> 'Harrow! Harrow! Monseigneur St George, succour us.'
> 'Ha! St George! Ha! St George! a long bow and a strong bow.'
> 'Heaven's Knight, aid us!'
> And as the soldier heard these voices he saw before him, beyond the trench, a long line of shapes, with a shining about them. They were like men who drew the bow, and with another shout their cloud of arrows flew singing and tingling through the air towards the German hosts.

The fight turns in favour of the British, aided by these heavenly forces, and the Germans leave ten thousand dead on the field: a disastrous break-through has been averted.

The reception given to this frankly pot-boiling piece seems to have amazed Machen, and with good reason. Within a short time of its publication he was being asked if the story were founded on fact, and was pressed for details of its source. Despite his energetic assertion that the story was pure invention, the mythopoeic imagination of the public insisted otherwise. Rumours spread declaiming that the story was based on a genuine incident during the British retreat and Machen's denials were ignored. Before long the legend was elaborated so that the bowmen were described as 'angels' – no doubt because of the reference to 'a long line of shapes, with a shining about them' –

and thus was born the extraordinary myth of the 'Angels of Mons', which was firmly believed in by a great many people during the early years of the war. And if no one had actually seen them, there were innumerable second- or third-hand accounts, allegedly from soldiers involved in the retreat. The legend died hard and passed into the popular mythology of the war: there can be no doubt that it served as a genuine mythic focus for the anguish aroused by the British retreat during the early weeks of the war.

Yet of all the myths which dominated the English consciousness during the Great War the greatest, and the most enduring, is that which enshrines the name and memory of Rupert Brooke: in which three separate elements – Brooke's personality, his death, and his poetry (or some of it) – are fused into a single image. Brooke was the first of the 'war poets'; a quintessential young Englishman; one of the fairest of the nation's sons; a ritual sacrifice offered as evidence of the justice of the cause for which England fought. His sonnet, 'The Soldier', which brings together all these aspects, is among the most famous short poems in the language.

Brooke's personal legend was first embodied in Frances Cornford's epigram, written whilst he was still an undergraduate:

> A young Apollo, golden-haired,
> Stands dreaming on the verge of strife,
> Magnificently unprepared
> For the long littleness of life.

This already contains the essentials of the myth which was to develop during Brooke's life and then to burgeon luxuriantly after his death in April 1915. Already, during the poet's life, it seems to have been self-perpetuating: the image of the 'young Apollo, golden-haired' was given physical reality in the photograph taken by Sherril Schell in 1913, showing Brooke with bare shoulders and flowing locks, which formed the frontispiece of *1914 and other poems* (1915). Brooke's biographer Christopher Hassall records that this photograph was not well received by his friends, who referred to it as 'Your Favourite Actress'; one of them suggested that he might as well be photographed completely in the nude. The extravagances in the legend were played down in Edward Marsh's posthumous memoir, which fixed the public image of the dead poet: handsome, talented, theatrical, with a rather frenetic gaiety; a product of the Cambridge milieu which when transported to London produced the Blooms-bury ethos: Brooke disliked its upholders but shared many of their ideals – the cult of personal relations, in particular. There was also the social idealism which made him an enthusiastic Fabian, and the hints, scattered through many of his poems, of an energetic but rather soulful amorist. Hassall's biography fills in the picture about aspects of Brooke's personality which Marsh left in tactful silence. It's interesting to know, for instance, that Brooke was psychologically unstable, with a paranoid streak, and for quite long periods was on the edge of a nervous breakdown: for several years he was involved in a gruelling love affair that brought him little happiness. As his life becomes part of history, Brooke's legend is losing some of its glamour. But his life will continue to be fascinating, and will never lack some kind of archetypal quality, if only because he was such a perfect symbol of the doomed aspirations of Liberal England: a figure from an unwritten novel by his friend E.M. Forster.

To extricate Brooke's poetry from the personal legend in which it played a merely contributory role is not at all easy. The poetry can best be understood by placing it in its proper context in the Georgian movement: Brooke was one of the most admired contributors to Edward Marsh's first volume of *Georgian Poetry* when it appeared in 1912. Poetically, the Georgians were an ambiguous group. It has long been customary to regard them as no more than a remnant of late-Victorian romanticism, a poetic nadir before the advent of the modernists, Eliot and Pound. And there is some truth in this; there are good reasons for seeing the Georgians as the end of an era, as George Dangerfield does:

> Until the very outbreak of war, the poets stayed unresponsive to the changing times; stubborn, sweet, unreal, they were the last victims and the last heroes of Liberal England. And in the midst of them, a little in front of them, as one who takes his place before an effective background, there stands the engaging figure of Rupert Brooke.[4]

This is a persuasive notion: but it is too simple. A more discriminating view was advanced in C.K. Stead's *The New Poetic*. No matter how remote and old-fashioned the Georgians may seem now, at the time they regarded themselves, and were regarded, as somewhat revolutionary. Their comparative bluntness of language, and liking for 'ordinary', unpretentious subjects, was not to everyone's taste; and Brooke found himself in a good deal of trouble over one of his early poems, 'A Channel Passage', which deals with love and sea-sickness in a self-consciously brutal fashion:

---

[4] *The Strange Death of Liberal England 1910-1914*, (London, 1961), p.430.

Do I forget you? Retchings twist and tie me,
    Old meat, good meals, brown gobbets, up I throw.
Do I remember? Acrid return and slimy,
    The sobs and slobber of a last year's woe.
And still the sick ship rolls. 'Tis hard, I tell ye,
    To choose 'twixt love and nausea, heart and belly.

It is not difficult to sympathize with the original critics of the poem. Such excursions are not, to be sure, typical of Georgian poetry, but they can serve to modify both the received picture of the Georgian movement and (in those not very familiar with his work) of Brooke's poetic personality.

Technically, the Georgians were much less innovating than they thought: nothing they wrote approached the originality of the early Eliot. But ideologically they can be seen as participating in the post-Victorian mood of revolt, which was manifested in such literary monuments as Galsworthy's *The Man of Property* (1906) as well as, later, in the avant-gardism of Wyndham Lewis and the other 'men of 1914'. As Stead has indicated, the Georgians, in turning to a simple patriotism centred on images of rural England – the country cottage, the cricket match, the genial pub – were in reaction against the loud-mouthed but vague poetic imperialism associated with Kipling, and with less talented late-Victorian and Edwardian versifiers such as William Watson, Henry Newbolt, and Alfred Noyes, who dwelt heavily on the splendours of Empire and heroes like Drake and Nelson. In comparison, the Georgians were Little Englanders. Stead sums the matter up succinctly: 'The dominant images of three decades of poetry, even when they spring initially from a literary concern, carry accurately the mood, and in a sense the history, of England during that time: Drake and Nelson; rural England; fear in a handful of dust.'[5] In one of Brooke's most famous poems, 'The Old Vicarage, Grantchester', we have a lucid instance of the Georgian concentration on rural England; this poem was written in Berlin, and Hassall observes that Brooke originally intended to call it 'The Sentimental Exile', and suggests that the public might in that case have read it less solemnly. Such a reading may have been closer to Brooke's intention; the fact remains that the whole poem displays a kind of switchback irregularity of tone, alternatively satirizing the Cambridge landscape (and by implication the poet) and idealizing it. Such uncertainty is a perhaps inevitable concomitant of Georgian Little Englandism: it

----

[5] *The New Poetic* (London, 1964), p.87.

was difficult for the retreat to a rural fastness, no matter how delectable, to be entirely whole-hearted. At the same time as he wrote 'The Old Vicarage' Brooke was concerned about the possible advent of a European war.

What we think of as the characteristic 'war poetry' of 1914-18 was in fact, a continuation of the Georgian movement by poets who, volunteering in defence of the England they had written about so lovingly, found themselves thrust into the melting pot which Forster had envisaged at the conclusion of *Howards End*. Arthur Waugh, a critic of conservative tastes, remarked, 'the Victorian poets wrote of war as though it were something splendid and ennobling; but as a matter of fact they knew nothing whatever about it. The Georgian poets know everything there is to know about war, and they come back and report it to us as an unspeakable horror, maiming and paralysing the very soul of man.'[6] Brooke was denied such knowledge, for he saw practically no fighting, save for a brief skirmish outside Antwerp in the autumn of 1914. In a prose piece he indicates the state of mind of innumerable young men like himself at the start of the war: 'An Unusual Young Man', published in the *New Statesman* on 29 August 1914, supposedly describes a friend on the outbreak of war, though this figure is clearly a vehicle for Brooke's own opinions. He thinks about Germany, a country he knows and likes, and is incredulous at the idea of an armed conflict between England and Germany:

> But as he thought 'England and Germany' the word 'England' seemed to flash like a line of foam. With a sudden tightening of his heart, he realized that there might be a raid on the English coast. He didn't imagine any possibility of it *succeeding*, but only of enemies and warfare on English soil. The idea sickened him.[7]

The notion of a foreign invasion of England, already played on by Tory publicists like Kipling and Saki, evoked a ready response in the consciousness of the young Fabian. Brooke continues the essay with a rhapsodic description of the Southern English landscape in a passage recalling the similar descriptions in *Howards End*. This passage was subjected to a withering analysis by Cyril Connolly in *Enemies of Promise*: ' "England has declared war," he says to himself, "what had Rupert Brooke better feel about it?" ' His equipment

---

[6] *Tradition and Change* (London, 1919), p.150.
[7] *The Prose of Rupert Brooke*, ed. C. Hassall (London, 1956), p.195.

is not equal to the strain and his language betrays the fact...' As a critical judgement this is penetrating. And yet it is not the most interesting thing that one can say about this piece of writing: Brooke was having to fake an emotional attitude precisely because the experience of England being involved in a major war was so alien and ungraspable. There was, too, a curious interplay between the literary cult of rural England fostered by the Georgians, and the degree of patriotism that it is traditionally proper to feel when one's country goes to war: Brooke's feelings are very literary in their mode of expression, but are not thereby prevented from being genuine. As Connolly says, Brooke's equipment was unequal to the strain; but so was that of every other writer in those days. The literary records of the Great War can be seen as a series of attempts to evolve a response that would have some degree of adequacy to the unparalleled situation in which the writers were involved.

Brooke's '1914' sonnets were written during November and December of that year, and were published in a miscellany called *New Numbers*; they were not widely read at first, but on Easter Sunday 1915, Dean Inge, preaching in St Paul's, quoted 'The Soldier' from the pulpit; the poem was reprinted in *The Times* and aroused immense interest. And in a week or so there came the news of Brooke's death in the Aegean (unglamorously, from blood poisoning, on the way to the Gallipoli campaign): the juxtaposition of the poem in which Brooke had reflected on the possibility of his death – 'If I should die...' – and the news of his actual death was sufficient to give him the status of a hero and martyr. The sonnets themselves are not very amenable to critical discussion. They are works of very great mythic power, since they formed a unique focus for what the English felt, or wanted to feel, in 1914-15: they crystallize the powerful archetype of Brooke, the young Apollo, in his sacrificial role of the hero-as-victim. Considered, too, as historical documents, they are an index to the popular state of mind in the early part of the war. But considered more narrowly as poems, their inadequacy is evident. Such a judgement needs qualification. It is, for instance, a common critical gesture to compare Brooke's sonnets with the work of later war poets, notably Wilfred Owen. This seems to me to prove very little, except, in a purely descriptive way, that poets' attitudes changed profoundly as they learned more about the war. Beyond this one might as well attempt to compare the year 1914 and the year 1918. A more useful comparison is with Brooke's own earlier poetry, and with contemporary works that express a broadly similar state of mind. Brooke's poetic gifts were never robust, and he was very far from being the most talented of the Georgian group, but at his best he had a certain saving irony and detachment of mind, which, very naturally, were absent from the 1914 sonnets. At the same time, the negative aspects of his poetry, a dangerous facility of language and feeling, are evident. To compare like with like, the sonnets seem to me inferior to Kipling's 'For All We Have and Are' and to Julian Grenfell's 'Into Battle', both products of the opening phase of the war.

One difficulty in reading these sonnets is that elements that can be called representative, expressing currents of popular feeling, are closely interwoven with others which are purely personal to Brooke himself. Thus, to take the octet of the first sonnet, 'Peace':

> Now, God be thanked Who has matched us with His hour,
>   And caught our youth, and wakened us from sleeping,
> With hand made sure, clear eye, and sharpened power,
>   To turn, as swimmers into cleanness leaping,
> Glad from a world grown old and cold and weary,
>   Leave the sick hearts that honour could not move,
> And half-men, and their dirty songs and dreary,
>   And all the little emptiness of love!

The lines are lax in movement and facile in much of their detail; in a phrase like 'old and cold and weary' the words seem to be thrusting ahead of the sense. Yet there can be no doubt that they expressed quite closely a dominant state of mind, the attitude which, for instance, J.B. Priestley describes in the passage previously quoted: a turning aside from the stalely familiar, and an eager acceptance of new and unknown experience. Nor indeed was this attitude confined to English poets; Maurice Bowra has noted in a lecture on the poetry of the First World War how there were comparable manifestations at the outbreak of war by various Continental poets;[8] even such an unbellicose figure as Rilke could write:

> We are others, changed into resemblance; for each
> there has leapt into the breast
> suddenly no more his own, like a meteor, a heart.
> Hot, an iron-clad heart from an iron-clad universe.

Nevertheless, Brooke was also expressing certain wholly personal preoccupations. D.J. Enright, in a sharp comment on these poems,

---

[8] *Poetry of the First World War* (Taylorian Lecture; Oxford, 1961).

has asked of the line 'the little emptiness of love', 'whose love?'[9]
On the level of intention, at least, the love in question seems to be
Brooke's long and painful affair with 'Ka'.

   This self-regarding element is very much in evidence in the poems,
cutting across their apparent glad transcendence of the merely
personal; the result can be called theatrical, and it is this, rather than
Brooke's blank ignorance of things that no one else at that time knew
much about either, that makes the sonnets hard to take. In the most
famous of them, 'The Soldier', Brooke uses the Georgian concentra-
tion on rural England as a focus for a meditation on his own possible
death. He identifies his own body and the soil of England in an
almost mystical fashion:

> If I should die, think only this of me:
>   That there's some corner of a foreign field
> That is for ever England. There shall be
>   In that rich earth a richer dust concealed;
> A dust whom England bore, shaped, made aware,
>   Gave, once, her flowers to love, her ways to roam,
> A body of England's, breathing English air,
>   Washed by the rivers, blest by suns of home.

The oratorical tone of this seems to be part of the poem's essential
intention: not for nothing did it become a set-piece for recitation at
school prize-givings and similar public occasions. Yet though the
poem aims at oratorical impersonality, there is an unresolved con-
flict between a subjective lyric impulse, not at all sure of its language,
and the assumed decorum of patriotic utterance. As Enright puts it,
'The reiteration of England and "English" is all very well; but an odd
uncertainty as to whether the poet is praising England or himself –
"a richer dust" – remains despite that reiteration.'

   A similar criticism was made soon after the poems were published
by a younger and better poet than Brooke, Charles Hamilton Sorley,
who was killed in October 1915 at the age of twenty. In a letter of
April 1915 Sorley observed:

> I saw Rupert Brooke's death in *The Morning Post. The Morning
> Post*, which has always hitherto disapproved of him, is now loud
> in his praises because he had conformed to their stupid axiom of
> literary criticism that the only stuff of poetry is violent physical
> experience, by dying on active service. I think Brooke's earlier

---

[9] *The Modern Age*, ed. B. Ford, (Harmondsworth, 1961), p.155.

poems – especially notably *The Fish* and *Grantchester*, which you can find in *Georgian Poetry* – are his best. That last sonnet-sequence of his which you sent me the review of in the *Times Lit. Sup.*, and which has been so praised, I find (with the exception of that beginning 'These hearts were woven of human joys and cares, Washed marvellously with sorrow' which is not about himself) over-praised. He is far too obsessed with his own sacrifice, regarding the going to war of himself (and others) as a highly intense, remarkable and sacrificial exploit, whereas it is merely the conduct demanded of him (and others) by the turn of circumstances, where noncompliance with this demand would have made life intolerable. It was not that 'they' gave up anything of that list he gives in one sonnet: but that the essence of these things had been endangered by circumstances over which he had no control, and he must fight to recapture them. He has clothed his attitude in fine words: but he has taken the sentimental attitude.[10]

By any standard, this is a remarkably acute criticism of Brooke; all the more so, as it was made by one who had every right to make it and who could not be accused of being wise after the event.

Had Brooke survived and undergone the experiences of later poets on the Western Front – Sorley himself, Graves and Sassoon, Owen and Rosenberg – it is very probable that he would have tried to respond as they did to those experiences and achieved a correspondingly more profound mode of expression. In Edmund Blunden's words, 'That Brooke, if he had lived to march into the horrifying battlefield of the River Ancre with his surviving companions of the Hood Battalion in the deep winter of 1916, would have continued to write sonnets or other poems in the spirit of the 1914 Sonnets, is something that I cannot credit.' As Blunden suggests, the piece called 'Fragment', written by Brooke on a troopship not long before his death in April 1915, is a sign that he was beginning to have a firmer imaginative grasp of the reality of war:

> I strayed about the deck, an hour, to-night
> Under a cloudy moonless sky; and peeped
> In at the windows, watched my friends at table,
> Or playing cards, or standing in the doorway,
> Or coming out into the darkness. Still
> No one could see me.

---

10 *The Letters of Charles Sorley*, (Cambridge, 1919), p.263.

                              I would have thought of them
— Heedless, within a week of battle — in pity,
Pride in their strength and in the weight and firmness
And link'd beauty of bodies, and pity that
This gay machine of splendour'ld soon be broken,
Thought little of, pashed, scattered...
                                    Only, always,
I could but see them — against the lamplight — pass
Like coloured shadows, thinner than filmy glass,
Slight bubbles, fainter than the wave's faint light,
That broke to phosphorus out into the night,
Perishing things and strange ghosts — soon to die
To other ghosts — this one, or that, or I.

The only other poem to have been written by a combatant in the opening phase of the war, expressing a similar idealizing attitude to it, which has achieved anything like the surviving reputation of Brooke's sonnets, is Julian Grenfell's 'Into Battle'. Grenfell died of wounds in France on 27 May 1915, a month after Brooke's death. He was an equally glamorous figure and in some respects of more conventionally heroic stature: he was born in 1888, the eldest son of Lord Desborough, and educated at Eton and Balliol, where he was part of the legendary pre-war generation, so many of whom perished in France. Like others of those brilliant, semi-mythical young men, Grenfell seems to have excelled at everything. He was an accomplished classicist, a dedicated sportsman and, by all accounts, a superb athlete. He displayed, too, considerable talents at drawing and writing verse; despite his passion for physical activity — notably for riding and boxing — his letters made it clear that Grenfell also had an alert and lively intelligence. After Oxford, he went into the regular army, which he enjoyed immensely — he wrote in one letter, 'I'm so happy here. I love the Profession of Arms, and I love my fellow officers and all my dogs and horses' — and for several years served in India and South Africa.

For all his many talents, and the clear devotion to his family expressed in his letters, Grenfell seems to have been an enigmatic figure, even to his friends. A Balliol contemporary, Raymond Asquith, who was himself to be killed in France, has left an account of Grenfell which curiously depersonalizes him, turning Grenfell (despite Asquith's intentions) into a Renaissance statue, an emblematic embodiment of abstract heroic virtue:

It was easy to idealize Julian, because superficially he seemed to be built on very simple lines. One might have set him up in a public place as a heroic or symbolic figure of Youth and Force. In reality he was far too intelligent and interesting to be a symbolic figure of anything. His appetite for action was immense, but it was a craving of his whole nature, mind no less than body. His sheer physical vigour, as everyone knows, was prodigious. Perfectly made and perpetually fit he flung himself upon life in a surge of restless and unconquerable energy. Riding, or rowing, or boxing, or running with his greyhounds, or hunting the Boches in Flanders, he 'tired the sun with action' as others have with talk. His will was persistent and pugnacious and constantly in motion. His mind, no less, was full of fire and fibre; lively, independent, never for a moment stagnating, nor ever mantled with the scum of second-hand ideas, violent in its movements but always moving, intemperate perhaps in its habit but with 'the brisk intemperance of youth'.[11]

Grenfell was unique among the poets of the Great War in being a professional soldier rather than a volunteer from civilian life, and his response to war was different from his contemporaries' in a number of ways. For instance, Grenfell, having served in different parts of the Empire, manifested a genuine enthusiasm for the imperialist ideal, as opposed to the England-centred patriotism of the Georgians. On 6 August 1914 he wrote from South Africa:

> And don't you think it has been a wonderful and almost incredible, rally to the Empire; with Redmond and the Hindus and Will Crooks and the Boers and the South Fiji Islanders all aching to come and throw stones at the Germans. It reinforces one's failing belief in the Old Flag and the Mother Country and the Heavy Brigade and the Thin Red Line, and all the Imperial Idea, which gets rather shadowy in peace time, don't you think? But this has proved a real enough thing.[12]

Grenfell was quickly in action and proved an extremely intrepid fighter, delighting in single-handed raiding exploits in No Man's Land: during his short wartime life, he was awarded the DSO and twice mentioned in despatches. Grenfell represents the purest embodiment of the romantic, Hotspurian ideal that the Great War

---

[11] *Pages from a Family Journal 1888-1915*, (privately printed, 1916), p.37.
[12] This and subsequent extracts from Grenfell's letters are from *Pages from a Family Journal*, pp.452-526.

produced, at least among British writers; unlike the belligerent arm-
chair patriots at home, and unlike an innocent such as Brooke, he
was well acquainted with the nature of battle. He saw war, however,
in the terms that came most immediately to him, as a game, and it
was this that prompted him to write from Flanders in October 1914:

> I *adore* War. It is like a big picnic without the objectlessness of a
> picnic. I have never been so well or so happy. Nobody grumbles at
> one for being dirty. I have only had my boots off once in the last
> 10 days, and only washed twice. We are up and standing to our
> rifles by 5 a.m. when doing this infantry work, and saddled up by
> 4.30 a.m. when with our horses. Our poor horses do not get their
> saddles off when we are in trenches.

This letter has been taken, reasonably enough, as evidence of a
certain cheery callousness on Grenfell's part; but he adds, in the
following paragraph,

> The wretched inhabitants here have got practically no food left. It
> is miserable to see them leaving their houses, and tracking away,
> with great bundles and children in their hands. And the dogs and
> cats left in the deserted villages are piteous.

Although mostly fighting in infantry conditions Grenfell was a
cavalryman, and had an appropriately traditional and anachronistic
attitude to the war; his letters are full of a desire to see the cavalry go
dashing into action. Yet Grenfell was soon experiencing something
of the nature of technological war and was reluctantly sensing a
certain insufficiency in traditional heroic attitudes:

> About the shells, after a day of them, one's nerves are really abso-
> lutely beaten down. I can understand now why our infantry have
> to retreat sometimes; a sight which came as a shock to me at first,
> after being brought up in the belief that the English infantry
> cannot retreat.

Yet such an awareness, which was to prove central to the experience
of Sassoon and Owen, was here no more than a dent in Grenfell's
conventional though genuine assurance. Although a romantic, he
was not lacking in a sense of humour, as his 'Prayer for Those on the
Staff' might suggest:

> Fighting in mud, we turn to Thee,
>   In these dread times of battle, Lord,
> To keep us safe, if so may be,
>   From shrapnel, snipers, shell, and sword.

But not on us, for we are men
   Of meaner clay, who fight in clay,
But on the Staff, the Upper Ten,
   Depends the issue of the Day.

The staff is working with its brains,
   While we are sitting in the trench;
The Staff the universe ordains
   (Subject to Thee and General French)

God help the Staff – especially
   The young ones, many of them sprung
From our high aristocracy;
   Their task is hard, and they are young.

Lord, who mad'st all things to be,
   And madest some things very good,
Please keep the extra A.D.C.
   From horrid scenes and sight of blood.

See that his eggs are newly laid
   Not tinged as some of them – with green;
And let no nasty draughts invade
   The windows of his Limousine.

When he forgets to buy the bread,
   When there are no more minerals,
Preserve his smooth well-oiled head
   From wrath of caustic Generals.

O Lord, who mad'st all things to be,
   And hatest nothing thou has made,
Please keep the extra A.D.C.
   Out of the sun and in the shade.

This neat composition is good-humoured in its satire, but it points forward to Siegfried Sassoon's savage verses which expressed the front-line soldier's resentment at the imbecilities of the Staff.

   'Into Battle', written in April 1915, is the one poem that demands a place for Grenfell in any discussion of the poets of 1914-18. It is made up of a variety of constituent elements: the soldier's sense of dedication to a cause, his excitement in battle, and a strain of nature mysticism, all combined in a vein of Shelleyan exaltation. The opening lines of the poem offer a traditional lyric in praise of spring, and then make a large but seemingly inevitable transition to the soldier's

own spirit rising like the sap around him and to a sense of sacrifice
as rebirth:

> The naked earth is warm with spring,
>   And with green grass and bursting trees
> Leans to the sun's gaze glorying,
>   And quivers in the sunny breeze;
> And life is Colour and Warmth and Light,
>   And a striving evermore for these;
> And he is dead who will not fight;
>   And who dies fighting has increase.
>
> The fighting man shall from the sun
>   Take warmth, and life from the glowing earth;
> Speed with the light-foot winds to run,
>   And with the trees to newer birth;
> And find, when fighting shall be done,
>   Great rest, and fullness after dearth.

The sentiments are those traditional in the idealistic literature of
war, and the diction of these lines is not particularly original. Never-
theless, their quality, which seems to me real, comes largely from
their rhythm and syntax, in which a major element is the very high
concentration of verbs, conveying a sense of dynamic movement,
derived no doubt from Grenfell's own celebrated energy of mind and
body. One feels that he is at one with what he is saying: there isn't the
sense of theatricality and of the poet uncertainly striking an attitude
that is so evident in Brooke's sonnets. Later sections of the poem are
quieter and less rhetorical than the opening, as in the stanzas which
suggest a degree of identification with nature rather closer than that
habitually achieved by the Georgians:

> The woodland trees that stand together,
>   They stand to him each one a friend;
> They gently speak in the windy weather;
>   They guide to valley and ridge's end.
>
> The kestrel hovering by day,
>   And the little owls that call by night,
> Bid him be swift and keen as they,
>   As keen of ear, as swift of sight.

The concluding stanza is undoubtedly vulnerable, with its personified
abstractions portentously intruding, but even here I think the poem

is saved from mere neo-classical inertness by the placing of verbs and the resultant sense of energy:

> The thundering line of battle stands,
> And in the air Death moans and sings;
> But Day shall clasp him with strong hands,
> And Night shall fold him in soft wings.

('Thundering' and 'clasp' carry much of the force of these lines.)

The attitudes expressed in 'Into Battle' are almost unimaginably remote now; but they came naturally enough to an aristocratic young cavalry officer of great courage, with a passion for sport and a talent for writing verse, who had not wholly discovered the way the war was shaping by the time he died. But he had already sensed that heavy artillery and the machine-gun were driving out the traditional, romantic and chivalric view of war; after the Somme it could seem only an obscene mockery. 'Into Battle' is the last memorable verbal enactment of that attitude in English literature: the poetic equivalent of some final, anachronistic battle in which cavalry (etymologically close to chivalry) played a dominant part. When Maurice Baring came to commemorate Grenfell in a memorial sonnet which began, 'Because of you we will be glad and gay;/ Remembering you, we will be brave and strong...', such assurance was already sounding more than a little hollow.

A third poet who died in 1915 was Charles Sorley, killed in October at the Battle of Loos. Sorley's upbringing was fairly conventional: the son of an academic family at Cambridge, he attended Marlborough College, where he was happy, high-spirited and popular, with the attributes of a good all-rounder of unusually acute intelligence. But perhaps the most formative period of Sorley's life was the time from January to July 1914, which he spent in Germany, acquiring some knowledge of the language and the country, before, as he intended, going up to Oxford that autumn. A full account of his stay there is contained in Sorley's letters, which are fascinating: he had the rare gift of conveying, simply and unselfconsciously, the essential quality of his mind and personality in letters, in a way that makes one think of the great letter writers amongst English authors: Keats, Hopkins, D.H. Lawrence. It is scarcely an exaggeration to say that Sorley fell in love with Germany. Soon after his arrival he wrote about hearing German soldiers singing on the march, 'Then I understood what a glorious country it was: and who would win, if war came.' In another letter he remarked of the same experience:

And when I got home, I felt I was a German, and proud to be a German: when the tempest of the singing was at its loudest, I felt that perhaps I could die for Deutschland – and I have never had an inkling of that feeling about England, and never shall. And if the feeling died with the cessation of the singing – well I had it, and it's the first time I have had the vaguest idea what patriotism meant – and that in a strange land. Nice, isn't it?

Yet despite his admiration for the German spirit, Sorley remained critical of some of its manifestations – like the aggressiveness and anti-semitism of the corps students at the University of Jena, where he spent a term: 'the students with whom I mostly go about are Jews, and so perhaps I see, from their accounts of the insults they've had to stand, the worst side of these many coloured reeling creatures.' But with unhappily misplaced optimism – he was writing in July 1914 – Sorley claimed that the militaristic spirit was declining. When war broke out he was still in Germany, but he was able to return to Britain, where he joined up in a spirit of dutiful but unenthusiastic patriotism.

The letters written by the nineteen-year-old Sorley during his weeks in training in the autumn of 1914 are remarkable for their detachment and maturity of mind; all the more so, when one realizes the mood of hysteria and anti-German racialist nonsense that had descended on the country and infected public life. Their spirit is apparent in such a passage as this:

For the joke of seeing an obviously just cause defeated, I hope Germany will win. It would do the world good and show that real faith is not that which says 'we *must* win for our cause is just,' but that which says 'our cause is just: therefore we can disregard defeat.' All outlooks are at present material, and the unseen value of justice as justice, independent entirely of results, is forgotten. It is looked upon merely as an agent for winning battles.

Very few people, in the weeks after Britain entered the war, were capable of such lucid insights. Above all, Sorley refused to accept the current abuse and hatred of Germany, the country he had grown to love (he was even able to write sympathetically about the Kaiser, whom he saw as 'not unlike Macbeth, with the military clique in Prussia as his Lady Macbeth, and the court flatterers as the three weird sisters'):

I regard the war as one between sisters, between Martha and Mary, the efficient and intolerant against the casual and sympathetic.

Each side has a virtue for which it is fighting, and each that virtue's supplementary vice. And I hope that whatever the material result of the conflict, it will purge these two virtues of their vices, and efficiency and tolerance will no longer be incompatible.

At times, Sorley's impatience with the platitudes of conventional patriotism, and his capacity for painful self-knowledge, rose to an angry intensity:

England – I am sick of the sound of the word. In training to fight for England, I am training to fight for that deliberate hypocrisy, that terrible middle-class sloth of outlook and appalling 'imaginative indolence' that has marked us out from generation to generation. Goliath and Caiaphas – the Philistine and Pharisee – pound these together and there you have Suburbia and Westminster and Fleet Street. And yet we have the impudence to write down Germany (who with all their bigotry are at least seekers) as 'Huns', because they are doing what every brave man ought to do and making experiments in morality. Not that I approve of the experiment in this particular case. Indeed I think that after the war all brave men will renounce their country and confess that they are strangers and pilgrims on the earth. 'For they that say such things declare plainly that they seek a country.' But all these convictions are useless for me to state since I have not had the courage of them. What a worm one is under the cart-wheels – big clumsy careless lumbering cart-wheels – of public opinion. I might have been giving my mind to fight against Sloth and Stupidity: instead, I am giving my body (by a refinement of cowardice) to fight against the most enterprising nation in the world.

Sorley spent four months as an officer at the Front, and his letters written on active service preserve the same note of detached, often ironic, and always unillusioned commentary:

All patrols – English and German – are much averse to the death and glory principle; so, on running up against one another in the long rustling clover, both pretend that they are Levites and that the other is a Good Samaritan – and pass by on the other side, no word spoken. For either side to bomb the other would be a useless violation of the unwritten laws that govern the relations of combatants permanently within a hundred yards of distance of each other, who have found out that to provide discomfort for the other is but a roundabout way of providing it for themselves:

until they have their heads banged forcibly together by the red-
capped powers behind them, whom neither attempts to under-
stand.

With this humorously anti-Hotspurian description we seem very
remote from Julian Grenfell's passionate heroics, and not too far
away from the attitudes of Captain Yossarian. In another letter
written at about the same time Sorley wryly remarked: 'why the term
"slackers" should be applied to those who have not enlisted, God
knows. Plenty of slackers here, thank you. I never was so idle in my
life.'

But Sorley was well aware that any calm was likely to be short-
lived. In one of his last letters, written in August 1915, there is a grim-
mer note, and an anticipation of that concern with the brutalizing
effect of constant exposure to violence which was to be central for
Sassoon and Owen:

> Looking into the future one sees a holocaust somewhere: and at
> present there is – thank God – enough of 'experience' to keep the
> wits edged (a callous way of putting it, perhaps). But out in front
> at night in that no-man's land and long graveyard there is a free-
> dom and a spur. Rustling of the grasses and grave-tapping of
> distant workers: the tension and silence of encounter, when one
> struggles in the dark for moral victory over the enemy patrol: the
> wail of the exploded bomb and the animal cries of wounded men.
> Then death and the horrible thankfulness when one sees that the
> next man is dead: 'We won't have to *carry* him in under fire,
> thank God; dragging will do': hauling in of the great resistless
> body in the dark, the smashed head rattling: the relief, the relief
> that the thing has ceased to groan: that the bullet or bomb that
> made the man an animal has now made the animal a corpse. One
> is hardened by now: purged of all false pity: perhaps more selfish
> than before. The spiritual and the animal get so much more
> sharply divided in hours of encounter, taking possession of the
> body by swift turns.

Sorley's surviving poetry was published in a small posthumous
volume in 1916, *Marlborough and Other Poems*. A good deal of it
is pleasant juvenilia, written whilst Sorley was still at school, but in
some of the poems written before the outbreak of war the signs of an
individual talent are already plain. In 'Rooks', for instance, which
is dated 21 June 1913, we have what is on the face of it a fairly
straightforward piece of Georgian nature observation; nevertheless,
it is technically adroit, being based on two rhymes only, and has

some imaginative touches, such as the curious and vivid phrase, 'the evening makes the sky like clay', and the transformation, in the final stanza, of the aimlessly flapping rooks to the soul flying hopelessly 'from day to night, from night to day':

> There, where the rusty iron lies,
>   The rooks are cawing all the day.
> Perhaps no man, until he dies,
>   Will understand them, what they say.
>
> The evening makes the sky like clay.
>   The slow wind waits for night to rise.
> The world is half-content. But they
>
> Still trouble all the trees with cries,
>   That know, and cannot put away,
> The yearning to the soul that flies
>   From day to night, from night to day.

But it was the war that caused Sorley's rapid development towards the full artistic maturity that he had still not altogether reached at the time of his death. There is a sense in which Sorley, though not apparently influenced by the experiments of Pound and the Imagists, seems a more fundamentally 'modern' poet than his contemporaries who wrote about the war in its opening phase. A central attribute of literary modernism is the attempt to combine and fuse together separate or even contradictory elements of experience, rather than concentrate on only one element to the exclusion of others. Rightly or wrongly, 'complex' has become a major term of approbation in twentieth-century criticism (though the underlying attitude goes back to Coleridge). In this respect, Sorley's poems about the war are complex, lacking the single-mindedness of Brooke or Grenfell.

His steadfast refusal to adopt conventionally patriotic attitudes is evident in the sonnet 'To Germany', of which the octet runs:

> You are blind like us. Your hurt no man designed,
> And no man claimed the conquest of your land.
> But gropers both through fields of thought confined
> We stumble and we do not understand.
> You only saw your future bigly planned,
> And we, the tapering paths of our own mind,
> And in each other's dearest ways we stand,
> And hiss and hate. And the blind fight the blind.

Sorley saw the war as a tragic paradox, rather than as a simple cause.
In a number of other sonnets he explores an even larger and more
intimate paradox, death, which is at once the greatest possible
experience and the cessation of all experience:

> Saints have adored the lofty soul of you.
> Poets have whitened at your high renown.
> We stand among the many millions who
> Do hourly wait to pass your pathway down.

In one sonnet he seems to be alluding directly to Rupert Brooke's
'The Dead':

> When you see millions of the mouthless dead
> Across your dreams in pale battalions go,
> Say not soft things as other men have said,
> That you'll remember. For you need not so.
> Give them not praise. For, deaf, how should they know
> It is not curses heaped on each gashed head?
> Nor tears. Their blind eyes see not your tears flow.
> Nor honour. It is easy to be dead.
> Say only this, 'They are dead.' Then add thereto,
> 'Yet many a better one has died before.'
> Then, scanning all the o'ercrowded mass, should you
> Perceive one face that you loved heretofore,
> It is a spook. None wears the face you knew.
> Great death has made all his for evermore.

Unlike poets who were concerned with some kind of community
linking the dead with the living, Sorley's preoccupation is with the
absolute 'otherness' of death, a totally alien experience which
destroys all the distinctions that had been so important to the living:

> Such, such is Death: no triumph: no defeat:
> Only an empty pail, a slate rubbed clean,
> A merciful putting away of what has been.

One of Sorley's best poems, and one of the most often reprinted,
is 'All the Hills and Vales Along' (sometimes printed under the title
of 'Route March'), about a company of soldiers singing on the
march (once, not long before, Sorley had been excited by seeing
German soldiers in such a situation; but now the troops were British
and marching, many of them, to death). It is a good example of
Sorley's ability to unify disparate elements of experience: the physical
exhilaration of the marching men and his own underlying absorption

in the idea of death. The opening lines might, at a casual glance, suggest a clear-cut rousing song by one of the lesser Georgians:

> All the hills and vales along
> Earth is bursting into song,
> And the singers are the chaps
> Who are going to die perhaps.

But the third and fourth lines, juxtaposing the Housmanesque 'chaps' with the throwaway casualness of 'going to die perhaps' to considerable ironic effect, should make it clear that Sorley was writing with his characteristic subtlety and ambivalence. The second stanza of the poem seems to demand an indifference in the face of life or death simlar to that which Yeats was to attribute to his Irish airman:

> Cast away regret and rue,
> Think what you are marching to.
> Little live, great pass.

The following lines anticipate the harsh, laconic utterance of Yeats's later style (though the dominant influence on the poem is certainly Housman's):

> Jesus Christ and Barabbas
> Were found the same day.
> This died, that went his way.

In the next, penultimate stanza, Sorley asserts the total indifference of nature to human deeds and aspirations – unlike Grenfell, who saw heroic energy as part of the natural process – in a manner that looks forward to the existentialist stress on the alienation of man from his environment:

> Earth that never doubts nor fears,
> Earth that knows of death, not tears,
> Earth that bore with joyful ease
> Hemlock for Socrates,
> Earth that blossomed and was glad
> 'Neath the cross that Christ had,
> Shall rejoice and blossom too
> When the bullet reaches you.
> > Wherefore, men marching
> > On the road to death, sing!
> > Pour your gladness on earth's head,
> > So be merry, so be dead.

With 'so be merry, so be dead' the contradictions in the situation – to some extent already dramatized in the conflict between the poem's lilting form and its reflective content – are brought into deliberate collision.

Dennis Welland has remarked in his book on Wilfred Owen that 'a reliable guide to war poetry could be written in terms of changes in poetic attitudes to death'. In this and other poems Sorley seems to me to have adopted a strikingly individual attitude; unlike, on the one hand, the uninformed acceptance of Brooke and the more informed but still romantic acceptance of Grenfell; or, on the other hand, the angry rejection of Sassoon or the burning pity of Owen. Sorley's view of death seems to regard it as an act of existential assertion of human values in the face of an alien universe. One can find something similar in a fine poem written during the Second World War which looks back to the First, Herbert Read's 'To a Conscript of 1940' (whose epigraph, from Georges Bernanos, reads, '*Qui n'a pas une fois désespéré de l'honneur, ne sera jamais un héros*'):

> But one thing we learned: there is no glory in the deed
>   Until the soldier wears a badge of tarnished braid;
> There are heroes who have heard the rally and have seen
>   The glitter of a garland round their head.
>
> Theirs is the hollow victory. They are deceived.
>   But you, my brother and my ghost, if you can go
> Knowing that there is no reward, no certain use
>   In all your sacrifice, then honour is reprieved.

Save in a few lines here and there, Sorley did not achieve uniquely memorable verbal expression; his language was not always adequate for what he wanted to say – but there can be no doubt that it would have become abundantly so had he lived longer. Every death is an absolute loss: but Sorley's, at such an early age and when he had already given evidence both in his verse and in his letters of such remarkable powers of intelligence and feeling, was a tragedy for English letters. One can only quote, in a spirit of seriousness, the possibly ironical concluding lines of one of his sonnets to death:

> But a big blot has hid each yesterday
> So poor, so manifestly incomplete.
> And your bright Promise, withered long and sped,
> Is touched, stirs, rises, opens and grows sweet
> And blossoms and is you, when you are dead.

4: Poets II
Graves, Blunden, Read, and others

As the months passed, the war, prolonged now far beyond the expectations of most people in August 1914, continued to be commemorated in verse, both at home and amongst the forces overseas. Indeed, for many civilian writers the production of poems with an exhortatory note was a substantial part of their war effort. Most of these efforts, even by quite accomplished poets, are now better forgotten, though they can provide all hour or so of painful diversion for a reader who browses through one of the popular anthologies of the period, such as G.H. Clarke's *A Treasury of War Poetry* (1917). This process perhaps reached its nadir in the grotesque verses of Sir William Watson. Here is the sestet of his sonnet 'The Three Alfreds', written in honour of Lord Northcliffe:

> Last – neither King nor bard, but just a man
> Who, in the very whirlwind of our woe,
> From midnight till the laggard dawn began,
> Cried ceaseless, 'Give us shells – more shells,' and so
> Saved England; saved her not less truly than
> Her hero of heroes saved her long ago.

One or two civilian poets attempted, unwisely, to reproduce from imagination, or at second-hand, the experiences of the fighting man. Thus W.W. Gibson, one of the best of the Georgians, essayed a bogus toughness in passages like this:

> This bloody steel
> Has killed a man.
> I heard him squeal
> As on I ran
> ('The Bayonet')

The one poem by a civilian that has had more than a passing fame is Laurence Binyon's 'For the Fallen', first published in *The Times* on

21 September 1914. This is a rhetorical piece with a certain decent
gravity; one of its stanzas has become familiar in commemorations
of the dead of the Great War:

> They shall grow not old, as we that are left grow old:
> Age shall not weary them, nor the years condemn.
> At the going down of the sun and in the morning
> We will remember them.

By 1916 the alienation of the soldiers in France from the Home
Front had become very pronounced: V. de Sola Pinto has referred to
a separation between the 'Two Nations', divided by far more than
the mere physical expanse of the channel.[1] And as the soldier poets
developed new modes of expression corresponding with their
experience of trench warfare, while the civilians continued unthink-
ingly to uphold traditional attitudes, this alienation was given sharp
expression in literature – most notably by Siegfried Sassoon. But for
about a year many young poets in uniform were content to repro-
duce the attitudes of Rupert Brooke's 1914 sonnets – an elementary
sense of dedication and a love of England – and many of them didn't
survive to do more. But in those who did survive one can trace an
interesting development of sensibility.

Throughout the war, poetry, and in particular poetry from the
Front, was in great demand. Douglas Goldring wrote a sardonic
account of the phenomenon from a belligerently pacifist standpoint,
in an essay 'The War and the Poets', published in *Reputations* (1920):

> Lying about in every smart London drawing-room you would find
> the latest little volume, and at every fashionable book-shop the half-
> crown war poets were among the 'best selling lines'.... An atmos-
> phere was quickly and easily created favourable to the sale of verse,
> and the always gullible English public, flattered by the remarks in
> the Press about its 'revived interest in poetry', disbursed its shillings
> with a lavishness only equalled by its lack of discrimination.

These remarks were echoed by Richard Aldington, who wrote in
Death of a Hero of:

> the alleged vogue for 'war poets', which resulted in the parents of
> the slain being asked to put up fifty pounds for the publication
> (which probably cost fifteen) of poor little verse which should
> never have passed the home circle.

---

[1] *Crisis in English Poetry*, (London, 1951), p.142.

Goldring describes the pathetic verse of young men just out of school
who (for a time, at least) continued to write what was expected of them:

> Many of these Public Schoolboy soldiers must have gone straight
> from the cricket-field and the prefect's study to the trenches, in a
> kind of waking dream. Their mental equipment for withstanding
> the shock of experience was as useless as the imitation suit of
> armour, the dummy lance and shield of the actor in a pageant. It
> was their false conception of life, their inability to look at facts
> except through tinted glasses of one particular colour, which
> rendered the poems of so many of these young subalterns so value-
> less as literature, so tragic and accusing as human documents.

As an example of what he is referring to Goldring quotes these lines
(they are from a poem called 'Without Shedding of Blood...' by
Geoffrey Johnson):

> Malvern men must die and kill,
> That wind may blow on Malvern Hill;
> Devonshire blood must fall like dew,
> That Devon's bays may yet be blue;
> London must spill out lives like wine,
> That London's lights may ever shine.

This is not only feeble as poetry but false in sentiment: Sorley had
achieved a deeper insight when he posited the indifference of nature
to human affairs. Devon's bays would be equally blue in a German-
occupied England. Goldring comments on these lines:

> This is precisely the doctrine of the 'You-go-first' or 'Comb-them-
> all-out-except-me' press, accepted with a blind and touching
> credulity, and it is certainly not intended to be the scarifying satire
> which, in effect, it is.

The most popular English poet during the later years of the war
was a figure now little remembered, Robert Nichols, who whole-
heartedly accepted the role of a professional 'war poet' after a very
brief experience of the Front. Nichols was a conceited and theatrical
figure – Wilfred Owen referred to him as 'so self-concerned and
vaniteux in his verse' – and Robert Graves has left a sharp account
of Nichols as he appeared shortly after the war:

> Another poet on Boar's Hill was Robert Nichols, one more
> neurasthenic ex-soldier, with his flame-opal ring, his wide-brimmed
> hat, his flapping arms, and a 'mournful grandeur in repose' (the

phrase comes from a review by Sir Edmund Gosse). Nichols
served only three weeks in France, with the gunners, and got
involved in no show; but, being highly strung, he got invalided out
of the army and went to lecture on British war-poets in America
for the Ministry of Information. He read Siegfried's poetry and
mine, and started a legend of Siegfried, himself and me as the new
Three Musketeers, though the three of us had never once been
together in the same room.

Nichols's first book, *Invocation: War Poems and Others* (1915),
consisted largely of the Brooke-pastiche so prevalent in the first year
of the war, rendered with more than ordinary mawkishness:

> Begin, O guns, and when ye have begun
> Lift up your voices louder and proclaim
> The sick moon set, arisen the strong sun,
> Filling our skies with new and noble flame.
> The Soldier and the Poet now are one
> And the Heroic more than a mere name.

Nichols's next collection, *Ardours and Endurances*, the product
of his brief glimpse of active service, was something of a best-seller
in 1917. For this reason, it deserves a moment of attention for its
historical interest, though its intrinsic poetic merits are nil. One can
see why the book was such a success, for Nichols provided a formula
well calculated to appeal to civilian taste, which combined the stir-
ring but ignorant heroics of 1914-15 with a degree of mild realism
about the actual fighting, though without anything so embarrassing
as Sassoon's and Owen's emphasis on physical horror and the
brutalizing effect of combat. One section that was particularly
admired was 'The Assault', in which Nichols abandons his customary
sedate formality and launches into an essay in impressionistic free
verse in the manner of Vachel Lindsay:

> I hear my whistle shriek,
> Between teeth set;
> I fling an arm up,
> Scramble up the grime
> Over the parapet!
> I'm up. Go on.
> Something meets us.
> Head down into the storm that greets us.
> A wail.
> Lights. Blurr.

Gone.
On. On. Lead. Lead. Hail.
Spatter. Whirr! Whirr!
'Toward that patch of brown;
Direction left.' Bullets a stream.
Devouring thought crying in a dream.
Men, crumpled, going down...
Go on. Go.
Deafness. Numbness. The loudening tornado.
Bullets. Mud. Stumbling and skating.
My voice's strangled shout:
'Steady pace, boys!'
The still light: gladness.
'Look sir. Look out!'
Ha! Ha! Bunched figures waiting.
Revolver levelled quick!
Flick! Flick!
Red as blood.
Germans. Germans.
Good! O good!
Cool madness.

Once more, Douglas Goldring offers a trenchant comment: 'It was characteristic of our war-time criticism that this masterpiece of drivel, instead of exciting derision, was hailed as a work of genius and read with avidity.' Nichols's most useful contribution to the literature of the Great War is perhaps the long introduction in dialogue form to his *Anthology of War Poetry 1914-18*, published in 1943, in which he takes a retrospective look at the attitudes of 1914 and discusses, from a strongly traditionalist point of view, some of the later writing about the war.

There were many better poets than Nichols who fought and wrote about the war as they knew it: the two finest, Isaac Rosenberg and Wilfred Owen, were killed in 1918; they will be discussed subsequently. Of the poets who survived, most returned to their experiences in prose works, often of great distinction, published during the 1920s and 1930s.[2] Three of them, Robert Graves, Edmund Blunden and Herbert Read, all came to manhood, if not to artistic maturity,

---

[2] Patrick J. Quinn in *The Great War and the Missing Muse* (London and Toronto, 1994) gives a good account of the psychological and literary processes that led Graves and Sassoon to recreate their wartime experience in prose rather than verse.

during the war: in 1914, Graves was nineteen, Blunden, eighteen, and Read, twenty-one.

Graves's wartime poems were printed in two small volumes, *Over the Brazier* (1916) and *Fairies and Fusiliers* (1917), both of which he subsequently suppressed in his customary spirit of rigorous self-criticism. In many respects, Graves, in his early work, was a quintessential Georgian, with a taste for ballad-like forms, unpretentious, small-scale subjects with a rural flavour, and a particular inclination to folk-lore and fairy-tale. But Graves's Irish background gave his work a quality that separated him from the more conventional love of rural England of the other Georgians. His attachment to myth was a constant element in his poetry, whether it was the prettified fairy-stories of his earliest verse, or the powerful myths, dominated (and generated) by the White Goddess, that occur in his mature work. There is a successful example in *Fairies and Fusiliers*, 'Goliath and David', which retells the story of the biblical encounter; in this version, David's attempt fails and Goliath moves in for the kill:

> Loud laughs Goliath, and that laugh
> Can scatter chariots like blown chaff
> To rout; but David, calm and brave,
> Holds his ground, for God will save.
> Steel crosses wood, a flash, and oh!
> Shame for beauty's overthrow!
> (God's eyes are dim, His ears are shut.)
> One cruel backhand sabre-cut –
> 'I'm hit! I'm killed!' young David cries,
> Throws blindly forward, chokes... and dies.
> And look, spike-helmeted, grey, grim,
> Goliath straddles over him.

If it were not for the specific, placing detail in the penultimate line, this could be a poem of generalized nightmare, a pure symbol akin to, say, Edwin Muir's 'The Combat'. As it is, the symbolism and the homely rhythm and down-to-earth diction serve, in a partial way, to hold back the full despairing horror of the situation (the poem was dedicated to a friend of Graves's, killed in action).

Douglas Goldring admired Graves's war poems and wrote of him, 'Mr Graves has a gentle voice, naturally gay and cheerful, and always his own. He does not probe or question; when the actual becomes unbearable he flies away on the wings of his fancy.' In 1920, this was a fair judgement: Graves was certainly not alone in seeking a retreat from unbearable actuality in a measure of fancy or myth-making. The collapse of the patriotic myth-patterns of 1914-15 left all the best poets of that time disorientated and in search of a more valid frame of reference. In another poem about the war Graves counterpoints 'fancy', remembered or imagined, with the trenches – 'It's a Queer Time' (actually written, in a spirit of anticipatory speculation, some weeks before Graves saw any action):

> Or you'll be dozing safe in your dug-out –
> A great roar – the trench shakes and falls about –
> You're struggling, gasping, struggling, then...hullo!
> Elsie comes tripping gaily down the trench,
> Hanky to nose – that lyddite makes a stench –
> Getting her pinafore all over grime.
> Funny! because she died ten years ago!
>   It's a queer time.
>
> The trouble is, things happen much too quick;
> Up jump the Bosches, rifles thump and click,
> You stagger, and the whole scene fades away:
> Even good Christians don't like passing straight
> From Tipperary or their Hymn of Hate
> To Alleluiah-chanting, and the chime
> Of golden harps...and...I'm not well today...
>   It's a queer time.

The understatement of the refrain, 'It's a queer time', indicates the habitual stance that Graves adopted, or tried to adopt, to the realities of war: basically, an attitude of 'stiff upper-lip' reserve, lightened with gaiety and backed by the always-possible retreat into myth. In some of Graves's poems we see the visible crack-up of the Brooke-Grenfell attitude, and in recording this with horrified fascination Graves loses some of his customary detachment. As in 'Big Words', a monologue spoken by a young soldier telling himself he is not afraid to die; it ends:

> '...I know I'll feel small sorrow,
> Confess no sins and make no weak delays
> If death ends all and I must die tomorrow.'
>
> But on the firestep, waiting to attack,
> He cursed, prayed, sweated, wished the proud words back.

On those occasions when Graves confronts the horror around him without obliquity, the fascination – which Sassoon refers to in

Memoirs of an Infantry Officer – is apparent; but Graves is unable
to do anything with the experience itself; it doesn't provoke either
the anger of Sassoon or the pity of Owen:

> Where, propped against a shattered trunk,
>   In a great mass of things unclean,
> Sat a dead Boche; he scowled and stunk
>   With clothes and face a sodden green,
> Big-bellied, spectacled, crop-haired,
> Dribbling black blood from nose and beard.
>
> ('Dead Boche')

Graves spent longer in the front line than most of his contemporaries
– on the Somme he was already a veteran of Loos – and miraculously
survived until the Armistice, although he was at one point officially
reported killed. But the experiences of war obsessed Graves for a
long time, and his post-war poetry was romantic, trivial and overtly
escapist: not until he had come to terms with his wartime past in
Goodbye to All That was he able to feel some degree of emotional
liberation. Indeed, there is probably much truth in A. Alvarez's
assertion that Graves never wholly recovered from the Great War
and the long ensuing period of spiritual shell-shock. A good deal
about his poetic personality suggests this: he has a superb technical
equipment which is often directed at marginal subjects or variations
on already familiar themes – characteristically the vicissitudes of
tormented love, treated with great honesty and narrowness; there is
also Graves's physical exile from England and his deliberate alienation
from the life and ideas of his age; and the evasive use of mythology.

Edmund Blunden, like Graves, has every claim to be regarded as a
Georgian. He, too, was absorbed in country scenes and folk-lore,
into which the reality of war made a violent intrusion; and, like
Graves, he precipitated his experience in a memorable prose work,
Undertones of War. Yet if there is one quality which distinguishes
Blunden from the other Georgians it is the intensity of his absorption
in the countryside. When dealing with Blunden it is hardly appropriate
to talk of the 'rural scene' with all that that implies of a background
or mere setting; he knows the country with a deep knowledge and a
deep love and it pervades the whole structure of his mind and feel-
ings. Blunden's world of nature is not particularly wild or wayward
in a Romantic fashion; it is ordered and in harmony with man, and
it offers, above all, the image of a pastoral, pre-industrial society. It
goes a good deal deeper than the weekend-cottage view of nature of
the typical Georgian. That this was an anachronistic, even primitivistic

view to hold in the opening decades of the twentieth century goes without saying: Blunden's poetry, traditional in themes, language and feeling, is entirely naked to any attacks that the modern sensibility cares to make upon it. But I am not now concerned with defending his poetic procedures, merely with pointing out that it was his particular cast of mind and feeling that enabled him to stand up to the experiences of the Front with remarkable firmness.

Blunden, in short, was less fundamentally affected by the trenches – though his experiences there were as harrowing as many others' – than some of his contemporaries. His sensibility was modified, certainly, but it was not entirely shattered and remade. He himself has remarked:

> Among the multitudes of us shipped to the Pas de Calais a few months before the Great Push (or Drive) of the British Army in 1916, I was a verse-writer; my interests were not yet changed from what life had formed before all this chaos. Lurking in the trenches by day or prowling out of them at night, I would perforce know what a bedevilled world is, and yet to make poems about it was a puzzle. In May and June 1916, in my note-books, the grimness of war began to compete as a subject with the pastorals of peace. By the end of the year, when madness seemed totally to rule the hour, I was almost a poet of the shell-holes, of ruin and of mortification. But the stanzas then written were left in the pocket-book: what good were they, who cared, who would agree?[3]

He is indeed capable of providing a direct description of the mechanical nightmares of war suppressing the ordered world of nature, as in ' "Transport Up" at Ypres', which concludes:

> And so they go, night after night, and chance the shrapnel
>   fire,
> The sappers' waggons stowed with frames and concertina wire,
> The ration-limbers for the line, the lorries for the guns:
> While overhead with fleering light stare down those withered
>   suns.

'Withered suns', makes its point effectively. But more often Blunden places the destruction and disorder of war within an existing frame of reference rooted in rural values. 'The Unchangeable', dated 1917, offers a good example of this:

[3] *War Poets 1914-1918* (London, 1958), pp.26-7.

Though I within these two last years of grace
Have seen bright Ancre scourged to brackish mire,
And meagre Belgian becks by dale and chace
Stamped into sloughs of death with battering fire —
Spite of all this, I sing you high and low,
My old loves, Waters, be you shoal or deep,
Waters whose lazy and continual flow
Learns at the drizzling weir the tongue of sleep.
For Sussex cries from primrose lags and brakes,
'Why do you leave my woods untrod so long? ...'

Poems such as this inevitably direct at Blunden the charge of escapism, of retreating from the reality of battle into a pastoral dream-world. One might say, initially, that in so far as writing poetry under fire was for Blunden to some extent a therapeutic activity, his 'retreat' to the familiar may have been justified in the process of preserving his wholeness of mind. Again, Blunden was very aware of his limitations, and one of the things that he was not often capable of expressing was the sense of scandal, of outrage at the moral enormities of war, that characterized the response of Sassoon and Owen. He simply accepted the war as one of the basic data of experience that could not be evaded, even though it was always fundamentally less 'real' than the sights and sounds of rural England. It is an axiom of modern literary consciousness that painful experiences are more intrinsically authentic than pleasant ones, that a mutilated man is more 'real' than a sound one, that fighting is more 'real' than taking a country walk. But reality deflects such assumptions.

In a perceptive note on Blunden's war poetry Ian Carr has written:

His best poems, with only one or two exceptions, are about the tiny breathing spaces or static moments between one action and the next. His themes are: self-preservation and how to offset madness; the devastation of nature by war; the fears and imaginings of a war-sodden mind; order and chaos.[4]

Unlike Graves, Blunden continued to write poems about the war once it was over: he returned thankfully to the contemplation and celebration of the countryside, its creatures and its lore, but his feelings were played upon, though not distorted, by the memory of war — as, for instance, in '1916 Seen From 1921':

---

[4] *Stand* (iv, 3), p.50.

Tired with dull grief, grown old before my day,
I sit in solitude and only hear
Long silent laughters, murmurings of dismay,
The lost intensities of hope and fear;
In those old marshes yet the rifles lie,
On the thin breastwork flutter the grey rags,
The very books I read are there – and I
Dead as the men I loved, wait while life drags

Its wounded length from those sad streets of war
Into green places here, that were my own...

Undertones of War contains a sizeable 'Supplement of Poetical Inter-
pretations and Variations': one of these poems, 'Third Ypres', had
previously been published in a collection called *The Shepherd* in 1922:
Blunden described it as one of his most comprehensive and particular
attempts to render war experience poetically. In it Blunden makes
the direct confrontation of violent experience that characterized
Rosenberg, Owen and Sassoon; it is, without a doubt, his finest war
poem. It is an autobiographical fragment in blank verse; Blunden
sticks to the slightly archaic diction and phrasing that he habitually
employs, but he nevertheless achieves an impressive strength and
starkness; in these lines one notices his use of a pastoral image – the
ploughman – stressing the traditional, 'right' use of the land, con-
trasting with its present occupants who have ploughed it up to no
useful end:

The hour is come; come, move to the relief!
Dizzy we pass the mule-strewn track where once
The ploughman whistled as he loosed his team;
And where he turned home-hungry on the road,
The leaning pollard marks us hungrier turning.
We crawl to save the remnant who have torn
Back from the tentacled wire, those whom no shell
Has charred into black carcasses – Relief!
They grate their teeth until we take their room,
And through the churn of moonless night and mud
And flaming burst and sour gas we are huddled
Into the ditches where they bawl sense awake,
And in a frenzy that none could reason calm,
(Whimpering some, and calling on the dead)
They turn away: as in a dream they find
Strength in their feet to bear back that strange whim
Their body.

In a subsequent passage we have a clear example of Blunden's use of
the manifestations of nature not as 'escape' or marginal illustration,
but in a deliberately sanative way:

> And while I squeak and gibber over you,
> Look, from the wreck a score of field-mice nimble,
> And tame and curious look about them; (these
> Calmed me, on these depended my salvation).

Blunden's major contribution to the literature of the Great War was
in prose. Yet his war poems contain the same qualities of mind and
feeling that were displayed in *Undertones of War* – above all, the
concrete presence of physical environment and awareness of detail.
If they are neither traditionally heroic nor radically anti-heroic, they
are the products of a gentle mind intent upon preserving its defences;
not, in such conditions, an ignoble aim.

Another writer whose finest literary memorial to the war was in
prose is Herbert Read: his *In Retreat* is a classic of its kind, worthy
to rank with the longer achievements of Graves and Blunden. Perhaps
because he wrote so much prose, in so many different fields, Read's
poetry has never been given the attention it deserves. But during the
First World War and subsequently he wrote some of the best poems
about it by any English writer. Read – an anarchist knight in later
years – was always a paradoxical, even contradictory figure, and the
letters from the Front included in *The Contrary Experience* (1963)
show that this was already true of the young officer of 1915-18. At
the outbreak of war Read considered himself a pacifist – though
'politically', not 'ethically' – but he was also, without any great sense
of contradiction, a member of the Leeds University Officers' Train-
ing Corps. At the same time, like many ardent young men of those
days, he was a disciple of Nietzsche. In 1915 he was commissioned,
and his letters from France reveal an odd mixture of idealism and
non-conformism; in one letter written in January 1917 he ranges, in
a single short paragraph, through the whole gamut of possible
attitudes to the war:

> But war is a tragic paradox: it destroys that which it should pre-
> serve. To any right-minded person life is sacred: so that the ques-
> tion of war becomes a question of values: is such an ideal *which
> can only be attained by war*, of more value than life? Modern war
> is largely actuated by economic aggression. And that 'ideal' can
> hardly be compared with life. But a war for justice, for liberty, he
> who loses his life in such a war shall find it.

Read was not conventionally patriotic, but he had his own reasons, rooted in Nietzschean individualism, for his commitment. In April 1917 he wrote: 'I don't want to die for my king and country. If I do die, it's for the salvation of my own soul, cleansing it of all its little egotisms by one last supreme egotistic act.' Although Read appreciated the comradeship of army life, he came increasingly to hate the military machine; and yet, at the Armistice, he seriously considered applying to stay on in the army.

As a poet Read is unlike the other writers I have so far discussed in that his literary affiliations were defiantly modern. If he classed himself with a group it would be with the Imagists, not the Georgians, and the poems in his books *Naked Warriors* and *Eclogues* (both 1919) are avant-garde in technique, employing free verse and precise, disjointed images. *Naked Warriors* is starkly realistic in its methods, but Read wrote of it:

> It isn't exactly a joyful book: it is a protest against all the glory camouflage that is written about the war: It means I have to be brutal and even ugly. But the truth should be told, and though I'm not quite conceited enough to imagine that I can do it finally, I think my voice might get a hearing. But I'd rather write one 'pastoral' than a book of this realism. My heart is not in it; it is too objective.

Naked Warriors, which did not appear until the war had ended, is indeed brutal in its realism. One of the poems in it, 'The Happy Warrior', parodies the pious Wordsworthian ideal by showing the soldier reduced to a state of brutish insensibility:

> I saw him stab
> And stab again
> A well-killed Boche.

Here and in other pieces in this brief collection Read is striking a note of straightforward protest, in the manner of Sassoon, though his reliance on the imagistic mode of presentation and abstention from overt comment leads to remoteness rather than immediacy. But in some of the poems Read's philosophical interests provide an additional dimension. 'Fear' is an example:

> Fear is a wave
> Beating through the air
> And on taut nerves impinging
> Till there it wins
> Vibrating chords.

All goes well
So long as you tune the instrument
To simulate composure.

(So you will become
A gallant gentleman.)

But when the strings are broken,
Then you will grovel on the earth
And your rabbit eyes
Will fill with the fragments of your shatter'd
      soul.

This has the bleakness and surgical precision of Read's other war poems, and though free in form is unified in imagery: the nerves of the body are seen as the strings of a highly-tuned instrument, played on by fear; then, in the last stanza, they are transformed into the strings of a marionette. When they are broken the toy collapses, and this image works backward to take in the neat, parenthetically enclosed 'gallant gentleman', and suggests that he too is no more than a puppet. The final image becomes concrete with the phrase, 'rabbit eyes', suggesting not only the traditional emblem of cowardice, but also the piteous condition of a wounded, terrified rabbit crawling on the ground. Read is here confronting the ever-present possibility of cowardice in battle – the overthrow of Hotspur by Falstaff – which is conventionally a crime but which is, often, purely biological, the revolt of the organism against the directives of the ethical intelligence.

He explores this question at greater length in 'The Execution of Cornelius Vane', a narrative poem in clipped, laconic, free verse about a soldier who runs away from battle, is captured and shot for cowardice. The man is presented as a simple manifestation of the desire to live, a desire which underlies the whole of burgeoning nature but which is an insufficient basis for the complexities of human civilization:

Cornelius perceived with a new joy
Pale anemones and violets of the wood,
And wished that he might ever
Exist in the perception of these woodland flowers
And the shafts of yellow light that pierced
The green dusk.

Two days later
He entered a village and was arrested.
He was hungry, and the peace of the fields
Dissipated the terror that had been the strength of his will.

Condemned to death for desertion, he continues to the end to pro-
claim the biological virtue of cowardice, the desire to be part of the
natural rather than the human order:

He saw a party of his own regiment,
With rifles, looking very sad.
The morning was bright, and as they tied
The cloth over his eyes, he said to the assembly:
'What wrong have I done that I should leave these:
The bright sun rising
And the birds that sing?'

Read's finest contribution to the poetry of the Great War was not
written until several years afterwards; this is *The End of a War*,
published in 1933, which Allen Tate has described as 'not only a
great war poem but a great poem on a great subject: the impact upon
the contemplative mind of universal violence, whether the violence
be natural or man-made'. In this striking poem Read uses a bizarre
incident from the closing hours of the war: on 10 November 1918,
a battalion of British soldiers was advancing in pursuit of the retreat-
ing German army, harrassed by machine-gun fire. Towards dusk
they find a wounded German officer lying on the outskirts of a
village; he tells them that the Germans have evacuated the place.
The British march into the village and are ambushed by concealed
Germans with machine-guns and many of them are shot down. The
enraged survivors seek out the hidden German soldiers and bayonet
them, and the wounded officer who had betrayed them is similarly
treated. Later the mutilated body of a murdered girl is discovered in
a cottage; the British officer in charge of the unit can do nothing at
that hour, and, exhausted, he retires to bed. The next day when he
wakes the Armistice has been declared and the war is over.

Read does not attempt to articulate these incidents into a dramatic
unity; the poem is a triptych whose separate sections are headed,
'Meditation of the Dying German Officer', 'Dialogue Between the
Body and the Soul of the Murdered Girl', and 'Meditation of the
Waking English Officer'. Read's intentions are contemplative, not
dramatic or narrative; his verse is subtle and austere, low-pitched
and muscular. By a remarkable feat of imaginative sympathy Read,

who had previously shown such a deep understanding of the nature
of cowardice, presents in the dying German's monologue a fervent
statement of the case for traditional patriotism and militarism:

> Faith in self comes first, from self we build
> the web of friendship, from friends to confederates
> and so to the State. This web has a weft
> in that land we live in, a town, a hill
> all that the living eyes traverse. There are lights
> given by the tongue we speak, the songs we sing,
> the music and the magic of our Fatherland.
> This is a tangible trust. To make it secure
> against the tempests of inferior minds
> to build it in our blood, to make our lives
> a tribute to its beauty – there is no higher aim.
> This good achieved, then to God we turn
> for a crown on our perfection: God we create
> in the end of action, not in dreams.

He accepts his imminent death as inevitable:

> I die, but death was destined. My life was given
> my death ordained when first my hand
> held naked weapons in this war. The rest
> has been a waiting for this final hour.
> In such a glory I could not always live.
>
> My brow falls like a shutter of lead, clashes
> on the clench'd jaw. The curtain of flesh
> is wreathed about these rigid lines
> in folds that have the easy notion of a smile.
> So let them kiss earth and acid corruption:
> extinction of the clod. The bubble is free
> to expand to the world's confines or to break
> against the pricking stars. The last lights shine
> across its perfect crystal: rare ethereal glimmer
> of mind's own intensity.

As so often in Read's verse, the isolated images are all the more
effective for the apparent flatness of their context; and the verse
movement has a remarkable distinction.

In the second section the two voices of soul and body alternate
with an imagistic concentration that is not easy to paraphrase; there
are hints of Marvell's 'Dialogue between Body and Soul', but the

opposition is less absolute. The murdered girl is seen as an embodi-
ment of the life-principle, but her spiritual aspirations are stuff from
which the passions which lead to war may spring; once more the
insufficiency of the purely 'natural' is cruelly underlined:

SOUL

War has victims beyond the bands
bonded to slaughter. War moves with armoured wheels
across the quivering flesh and patient limbs
of all life's labile fronds.

BODY

France was the garden I lived in.
Amid these trees, these fields, petals fell
flesh to flesh; I was a wilder flower.

SOUL

Open and innocent. So is the heart
laid virgin to my choice. I filled
your vacant ventricles with dreams
with immortal hopes and aspirations that exalt
the flesh to passion, to love and hate.
Child-radiance then is clouded, the light
that floods the mind is hot with blood
pulse beats to the vibrant battle-cry
the limbs are burnt with action.

The Wordsworthian theme of the obscuring of early innocence was
always fundamental to Read and inspired some of his most beautiful
writing in prose and verse.

The third section sets against the hard certainties and assertions of
the dying German officer the hesitations and confusions of the
Englishman, which echo the sentiments of many British war poets
and which may be seen as typifying the educated young English-
man's response to the war once the exaltation of 1914 had passed.
As against the German's belief in an immanent God revealing himself
in action, the Englishman clings to a belief, despite the horror around
him, in a God who is love, who is, in fact, the Christian God:

Now I see, either the world is mechanic force
and this the last tragic act, portending
endless hate and blind reversion
back to the tents and healthy lusts

of animal men: or we act
God's purpose in an obscure way.

There is no reason to suppose that Read endorses any one of the
views he imaginatively enacts and juxtaposes: they are attempts at
completeness of contemplation. Read is not a moralist in the ordi-
nary sense; in this poem, at least, he is attempting to unfold the
possible diversities of human response to a tragic event. In a note at
the end of the poem he writes: 'It is not my business as a poet to con-
demn war (or, to be more exact, modern warfare). I only wish to
present the universal aspects of a particular event. Judgment may
follow, but should never precede or become embroiled with the act
of poetry.' Such a view of poetry seems, at first glance, to be quite
contradictory to that of someone like Owen, but it is truer to say that
it complements it. Like Owen, Read wrote poems of protest during
the war; but after it, when enough years had passed, he was able to
replace the poetry of protest with a poetry of contemplation whose
sympathies were impartially distributed and which did not contain
directives for action. Owen was denied such an opportunity. *The
End of a War* is Read's major poetic statement about the Great
War; but it is not quite his final word: he returned to the topic, very
movingly, in the context of the Second World War when he wrote
'To a Conscript of 1940'.

There were a number of other writers whose principal contribu-
tion to the literature of the Great War was made in prose some years
after it ended, but who also wrote poems which recorded their
immediate reactions and impressions and which, though not of out-
standing merit, deserve some attention. Perhaps the most prominent
was Ford Madox Ford – known until 1919 as Ford Madox Hueffer
– whose *Parade's End*, published in 1924-8, is the greatest English
novel to come out of the war. In 1914 Ford was forty-one and
already an established writer in many genres: his fine novel *The
Good Soldier* – not a war story – appeared in 1915. Despite his
partly German origins, and the fact that a few years earlier he had
made an attempt to claim German nationality in order to obtain a
divorce in Germany, Ford responded to the war in a wholeheartedly
patriotic fashion; indeed, there may have been an element of com-
pensation for his previous inclinations towards Germany. Under the
auspices of a Government propaganda scheme Ford produced two
books of a somewhat didactic kind, one attacking Prussia and the
other praising France. He also wrote a poem called 'Antwerp' about
the wretched plight of the Belgian refugees arriving in London in the

autumn of 1914. Ford had written a substantial amount of poetry since his youth, but not much of it was of enduring merit; he himself did not take the business of writing poetry seriously – he always considered prose to be his proper element, and in this he was surely right – but Ezra Pound said some generous things about Ford's poems. 'Antwerp' is clearly the product of intense and laudable feelings, but it exhibits the characteristic faults of most of Ford's poetry: it is rhythmically inert, with lax, intermittently rhyming lines, and little interest in the verbal texture. There are one or two passages, however, that achieve a certain power:

> This is Charing Cross;
> It is midnight;
> There is a great crowd
> And no light.
> A great crowd, all black that hardly whispers aloud.
> Surely, that is a dead woman – a dead mother!
> She has a dead face;
> She is dressed all in black;
> She wanders to the bookstall and back,
> At the back of the crowd;
> And back again and again back,
> She sways and wanders.

In 1915, Ford, though over military age, volunteered for the army and was commissioned as a subaltern in the Welch Regiment. He had a simple patrotic motive in doing so, but as his biographer Douglas Goldring admits Ford may have also had a secondary motive in wishing to get away from his entanglement with the novelist Violet Hunt. Although he was not long in the front lines, he suffered from gas and shell-shock and endured a good deal of ill health, as well as the further provocation of getting on badly with his superior officers (who considered him too old for his duties). He spent most of the war on semi-administrative duties, first in France and then in England; but his experience of the fighting was reflected in a number of poems which were published in *On Heaven* in 1918. Most of them are written in the semi-free verse which Ford favoured, with lines of irregular length and emphatic rhymes, often feminine. The poems are loosely meditative, tending to be sentimental, reflecting a seemingly anachronistic – for 1917-18 – mood of simple devotion to England, recalling the aspirations of 1914; or commemorating dead comrades:

> Poor little Arnott – poor little lad...
> And poor old Knapp,
> Of whom once I borrowed a map – and never returned it,
> And Morris and Jones and all the rest of the Welch,
> So many gone in the twenty-four hours of a day....

In some places Ford attempts to write about the actualities of battle in a ballad-measure which, in effect, prevents them being realized at all; unlike Sorley's poems of a superficially similar kind, which set up an ironic tension between form and content:

> Dust and corpses in the thistles
> Where the gas-shells burst like snow,
> And the shrapnel screams and whistles
> On the Bécourt road below...

Not until he wrote *Parade's End* was Ford able to confront such experiences without evasion. But in places he catches something of the sardonic note that characterizes the war poetry of his younger comrades, as in the flat, ironic reflections of 'That Exploit of Yours', which anticipates some images in Owen's 'Strange Meeting':

> I meet two soldiers sometimes here in Hell
> The one, with a tear in the seat of his red pantaloons
> Was stuck by a pitchfork,
> Climbing a wall to steal apples.
>
> The second has a seeming silver helmet,
> Having died from the fall of his horse on some tram-lines
> In Dortmund.
>
> These two
> Meeting in the vaulted and vaporous caverns of Hell
> Exclaim always in identical tones:
> 'I at least have done my duty to Society and the Fatherland!'
> It is strange how the cliché prevails...
> For I will bet my hat that you who sent me here to Hell
> Are saying the selfsame words at this very moment
> Concerning that exploit of yours.

Like Ford, Richard Aldington was better known as a novelist than as a poet; his *Death of a Hero* was one of the most discussed war novels of 1929. But he was also a prolific poet who wrote a good many poems on active service, collected in *Images of War* in 1919. Also like Ford, Aldington had been a friend and associate of Ezra

Pound in the years before 1914; they had both appeared in Pound's
Des Imagistes anthology and had contributed to *Blast*. But Alding-
ton, as a much younger man – he was born in 1893 – was more
actively a protegé of Pound's, who claimed Aldington and Hilda
Doolittle (who wrote as 'H.D.' and became Aldington's wife) as the
original members of the Imagist school in 1912. Aldington's pre-war
Imagist poems were graceful but slight, and very literary in their
orientations; he had had a classical education, and inclined towards
the recreation of classical legend rather than the precise delineation
of the physical world around him.

His war poems are still Imagist in form, and they move uneasily
between retreats into Greek legend and idealized Mediterranean
imagery, and determined attempts to face the present facts of mass
slaughter. Aldington was at best a loose, casual versifier, and his
Imagist war poems lack the concentration and tautness of those by
Herbert Read. But here and there he effectively pinned down a
moment of experience:

> Dusk and deep silence...
>
> Three soldiers huddled on a bench
> Over a red-hot brazier,
> And a fourth who stands apart
> Watching the cold rainy dawn.
>
> Then the familiar sounds of birds –
> Clear cock-crow, caw of rooks,
> Frail pipe of linnet, the 'ting! ting!' of chaffinches,
>
> And over all the lark
> Outpiercing even the robin...
>
> Wearily the sentry moves
> Muttering the one word: 'Peace.'
>
> ('Picket')

The tension between realism and aestheticism in Aldington's verse is
evident in a pair of poems, 'Soliloquy 1' and 'Soliloquy 2'; the former
contains brutal images of death, but the latter ends with a serene
description of a dead soldier:

> More beautiful than one can tell,
> More subtly coloured than a perfect Goya,
> And more austere and lovely in repose
> Than Angelo's hand could ever carve in stone.

In a rather longer poem, 'The Blood of the Young Men', Aldington
expresses the feeling, which is central to Owen and Sassoon, that
young men are being uselessly sacrificed in large numbers for the
good of those at home – women and old men – and emphasizes the
division between the Two Nations which had become so marked by
the middle of the war:

> Old men, you will grow stronger and healthier
> With broad red cheeks and clear hard eyes –
> Are not your meat and drink the choicest?
> Blood of the young, dear flesh of the young men.

In dealing with such a pressing but intractable theme, Aldington
shows little of Owen's delicacy and control and tends to collapse
into bathos and hysteria, with overtones of *fin de siècle* vampirism,
though the poem does have a certain harsh force. In general, Alding-
ton is revealed in his war poems as a self-regarding writer, with a
purely personal revulsion from the scenes of war, concerned solely
with registering his sensations, whether of disgust or aesthetic
revery: he is scarcely capable of transcending his personal situation
and achieving the generalized states of feeling of his better contem-
poraries.

In 1930 (a few weeks after *Death of a Hero*) Frederic Manning's
novel of trench life, *Her Privates We*, was also acclaimed; both were
part of the wave of war books, whether memoirs or novels, pub-
lished in 1928-30, which I discuss in a later chapter. Manning was
not, in fact, acknowledged as the author of *Her Privates We*, which
was published under the pseudonym of 'Private 19022', but by the
time of his death in 1935 the fact of his authorship was fairly well
known. Nothing in Manning's previously literary career would have
prepared one for the tough colloquial realism of this novel. Like
Ford and Aldington, he had been a friend of Pound in pre-war days;
he was a rather shadowy figure, born in Australia, who had been
something of a cultivated wanderer between London and the Conti-
nent. In 1910 he published a collection of elegant essays on historical
and mythological topics, *Scenes and Portraits*, and, in the same year,
Poems, which had a strong flavour of the 1890s. In his second collec-
tion, *Eidola* (1917), where the poems are mostly in precisely written
free verse and classical and literary in inspiration, Manning makes
some reference to his war experiences:

> These are the damned circles, Dante trod,
> Terrible in hopelessness,
> But even skulls have their humour.

An eyeless and sardonic mockery:
And we,
Sitting with streaming eyes in the acrid smoke,
That murks our foul, damp billet,
Chant bitterly, with raucous voices
As a choir of frogs
In hideous irony, our patriotic songs.

('Grotesque')

And in 'The Face' Manning writes about death with a delicacy that
shows up the comparative crudeness of Aldington's treatment:

Out of the smoke of men's wrath,
The red mist of anger,
Suddenly,
As a wraith of sleep,
A boy's face, white and tense,
Convulsed with terror and hate,
The lips trembling...
Then a red smear, falling...
I thrust aside the cloud, as it were tangible,
Blinded with a mist of blood.
The face cometh again
As a wraith of sleep:
A boy's face delicate and blonde,
The very mask of God,
Broken.

The poets discussed in this chapter survived the war. So did Edgell
Rickword who was born in 1898, and whose service in the last year
of the war produced a small number of good poems, including 'The
Soldier Addresses His Body' and 'Trench Poets', showing his early
dedication to Donne; and 'Winter Warfare', in which he uses an
ironically jaunty ballad-measure and a delicate, exact fancy to
capture the quality of winter in the Line:

Those who watched with hoary eyes
    saw two figures gleaming there;
Hauptman Kalte, Colonel Cold,
    gaunt in the grey air.

Stiffly, tinkling spurs they moved,
    glassy eyed, with glinting heel
Stabbing those who lingered there
    torn by screaming steel.

An interesting figure among the victims was Arthur Graeme West, whose literary remains were published in 1919 as *The Diary of a Dead Officer*. He was born in 1891, was a Balliol graduate, and was killed in April 1917. West's diary is a particularly melancholy book; no one, after the initial stage of exaltation, enjoyed the war very much, but West shows little of the tough-mindedness of Graves or Blunden or Read, who were, one imagines, men of equally acute sensibilities. He goes in for cloudy Paterian philosophizing about death: 'What midges we all are, what brief phantoms in a dream – a dream within a dream, this truly is my life, and how gladly would I end it now.' West came to reject all traditional values, comradeship, patriotism, religion, and aspired first towards stoicism and then towards nihilism. He was haunted by an impulse to desert and commit suicide, but was unable to bring himself to the point of action: he saw himself as a Hamlet-figure:

> I do ill to go. I ought to fight no more. But death, I suppose, is the penalty, and public opinion and possible misunderstanding... You see how complicated it gets...I am *almost* certain I do wrong to go – not quite certain, and anyhow, I question if I am of martyr stuff.

Like Sassoon, he became convinced that the war was being unnecessarily prolonged, but his response to this realization had nothing of Sassoon's moral clarity and courage. He was unable to transcend a purely personal despair and irascibility.

Nevertheless, some of West's poems are impressive. 'God! How I hate you, you young cheerful men' shows a savage reaction against the heroics of the early phase of war poetry:

> Hark how one chants –
> 'Oh happy to have lived these epic days' –
> 'These epic days'! And *he'd* been to France,
> And seen the trenches, glimpsed the huddled dead
> In the periscope, hung on the rusty wire:
> Choked by their sickly foetor, day and night
> Blown down his throat: stumbled through ruined hearths,
> Proved all that muddy brown monotony
> Where blood's the only coloured thing.

West's best poem is certainly 'The Night Patrol', a piece of bleak, faithful description in blank verse which shows the early dominance – it is dated March 1916 – of the mode of extreme realism, and conveys an anti-heroic attitude all the more effectively for being implicit:

And we placed
Our hands on the topmost sand-bags, leapt and stood
A second with curved backs, then crept to the wire,
Wormed ourselves tinkling through, glanced back
        and dropped.
The sodden ground was splashed with shallow pools,
And tufts of crackling cornstalks, two years old,
No man had reaped, and patches of spring grass,
Half-seen, as rose and sank the flares, were strewn
With the wrecks of our attacks: the bandoliers,
Packs, rifles, bayonets, belts, and haversacks,
Shell fragments, and the huge whole forms of shells
Shot fruitlessly – and everywhere the dead.
Only the dead were always present – present
As a vile sickly smell of rottenness;
The rustling stubble and the early grass,
The slimy pools – the dead men stank through all,
Pungent and sharp; as bodies loomed before,
And as we passed, they stank; then dulled away
To that vague factor, all encompassing,
Infecting earth and air.

This is very effective in the expressive rhythms and syntax, and the firm but unhysterical insistence of its realistic detail. Here West achieves the control that is missing in the more directly personal writing of his letters and diary entries; 'The Night Patrol' ensures West a place among the poets of the Great War.

5: Poets III
Thomas and Gurney

A patriotic love of England dominated the writing of the first phase of the war, whether by civilians or by fighting men, and was most famously expressed in Rupert Brooke's *1914* sonnets. In poetry it represented an intensification of the pre-war Georgian spirit. The 'England' in question was sometimes elastic enough to include the more attractive parts of Scotland, Ireland and Wales, but it excluded the large cities, and the industrial North and Midlands. For poets at the Front England represented an ideal to cherish in memory, in contrast to the shattered battlefields of Northern France. This deeply English pastoral mode, treasuring the beauty of the countryside and the regular patterns of rural life, struck a sympathetic chord with many readers and still has the power to do so. It ignored many social and historical realities, as a modern historian has pointed out: 'It would be hard to guess, for example, from the writings or verse of Sassoon, Blunden or Graves that the English landscape they loved in fact represented British agriculture in distress and decay.'[1] But myth has the power to transcend history, particularly social history.

Two poets with a peculiarly intense devotion to rural England, going beyond conventional patriotic sentiment or the Georgian weekend cottage, were Edward Thomas and Ivor Gurney. Their achievement has become more apparent in recent years, in part because of the dedicated work of biographers and editors.[2] Thomas

---

[1] Correlli Barnett, *The Collapse of British Power* (London, 1972), p.430.
[2] R. George Thomas has edited Thomas's *Collected Poems* (Oxford, 1978); John Pikoulis has expressed serious reservations about aspects of this edition in 'On Editing Edward Thomas', *PN Review*, 103 (May-June 1995). R.G. Thomas has also written a biography, *Edward Thomas: A Portrait* (Oxford, 1985). Michael Hurd's *The Ordeal of Ivor Gurney* (Oxford, 1978) is an excellent life. Gurney's *Collected Letters* are edited by R.K.R. Thornton (Manchester, 1991), and his *Collected Poems* by P.J. Kavanagh (Oxford, 1982); Thornton has also edited *Severn and Somme and War's Embers* (Manchester, 1987).

was an artilleryman of thirty-nine when he was killed in France in 1917, and he had only begun writing poetry at the start of the war. Before that he had been a hard-pressed professional man of letters who had published many books of travel, biography and belle-lettres. Thomas's first book, which appeared in his teens, was called *The Woodland Life*, and it had successors with such titles as *Beautiful Wales, The Heart of England, The Book of the Open Air, The South Country, The Country*, and *A Literary Pilgrim in England*. Thomas's earlier literary career is interesting for its symptomatic and represen-tative nature. He came of age at the turn of the century, and his dominant literary influences were Victorian: Pater, who left him the legacy of an excessively mannered prose, until he managed after much effort to shake it off; and Ruskin, who remained a positive inspiration and model for Thomas's observation of nature.

Thomas loved rural England and English poetry; David Garnett said that he 'admired and appreciated *all* the poets of the past that I had ever heard of'. He wrote about literature in the discursive manner of Lamb or Hazlitt, and in 1907 he edited *The Pocket Book of Poems and Songs for the Open Air*, saying in the introduction that he had included 'about sixty of the sweetest songs that a wise man would care to sing or hear sung, in the fields, at the inn, on the road at dawn or nightfall, or at home'. This is the note of the hearty Edwardian bookman, but there was a good deal more to Thomas than that. He was sensitive and intelligent, moody and subject to severe depressions and psychosomatic illnesses, which in 1908 were diagnosed by a perceptive doctor as having their origins in what Thomas referred to as his 'elaborate self-consciousness'. His friend the American poet Robert Frost, who was then living in England, perceived that Thomas had more potentialities as a writer than turn-ing out pleasing pot-boilers on acceptable themes. He believed that Thomas was half-way to being a poet in his prose, and that he should take the plunge and become one properly. The influence of Frost, together with the new consciousness and personal circumstances which followed the outbreak of war, turned Thomas into a poet. His biographer R. George Thomas remarks that 'the two-way traffic between ordinary speech and the writer's craft had absorbed his attention from early 1908'. Frost helped him to find his own way of bringing poetry and everyday speech together – which had become a necessity in the early twentieth century – though by a different route from that taken by Frost's countrymen Pound and Eliot. Frost wrote to Lascelles Abercrombie in 1915 that the war 'had made some sort of new man and a poet out of Edward Thomas'. It was also making a new world; Thomas was swept by history out of the regressive, late-Romantic atttitudes of the Edwardian years, though he still made creative use of the Victorian heritage, notably in his Ruskinian perceptions. In poetry he achieved the concentration which his prose lacked.

The war made Thomas a poet and it ended his life, so there are good reasons for regarding him as a war poet. But his poetry was all written before he went to France as an over-age volunteer at the beginning of 1917. The only literary records of his service at the Front are in the terse diary entries that he made until he was killed by an exploding shell on 9 April 1917. Only one of Thomas's poems, and not one of his best, directly addresses the war. 'This is no case of petty right or wrong' begins by decently distancing the poet from patriotic hysteria:

> This is no case of petty right or wrong
> That politicians or philosophers
> Can judge. I hate not Germans, nor grow hot
> With love of Englishmen, to please newspapers.
> Beside my hate for one fat patriot
> My hatred of the Kaiser is love true...

After some tormented reflections, the poem ends with a love of England that is familiar and conventional, though certainly sincere:

> But with the best and meanest Englishmen
> I am one in crying, God save England, lest
> We lose what never slaves and cattle blessed.
> The ages made her that made us from the dust:
> She is all we know and live by, and we trust
> She is good and must endure, loving her so:
> And as we love ourselves we hate her foe.

For the most part the war appears occasionally in Thomas's poetry as a destructive power in the background that disrupts the continuities of rural life. Some of his poems are in the mode of Wordsworthian pastoral where the poet meets and ponders on the lives of tramps and other simple rustics; and as with Wordsworth, they are open to the charge of turning human beings into symbols. This may be true of one of Thomas's most admired poems, 'Lob'. In 'A Private' he commemorates a dead countryman, perhaps a little too neatly:

> This ploughman dead in battle slept out of doors
> Many a frosty night, and merrily

Answered staid drinkers, good bedmen, and all bores:
'At Mrs Greenland's hawthorn bush,' said he,
'I slept.' None knew which bush. Above the town,
Beyond 'The Drover', a hundred spot the down
In Wiltshire. And where now at last he sleeps
More sound in France – that, too, he secret keeps.

The more impressive 'As the team's head brass', is also in this Wordsworthian mode; the poet meets a ploughman and talks to him about the war and about a tree that has fallen and cannot be moved until the war is over and men return from the army. But the poet refrains from generalizing reflections, and ends by simply describing what he sees in the field in front of him:

'Only two teams work on the farm this year.
One of my mates is dead. The second day
In France they killed him. It was back in March,
The very night of the blizzard, too. Now if
He had stayed here we should have moved the tree.'
'And I should not have sat here. Everything
Would have been different. For it would have been
Another world.' 'Ay, and a better, though
If we could see all all might seem good.' Then
The lovers came out of the wood again:
The horses started and for the last time
I watched the clods crumble and topple over
After the ploughshare and the stumbling team.

Thomas has come a long way from Edwardian geniality and sentimentality about the countryside. In bare and direct lines he evokes both the permanence of human love and human labour, and, in the pregnant words, 'for the last time', the transience of the moment. In Thomas's best poems the features of the landscape, though described with Ruskinian precision and fidelity, take on a symbolic quality. This is true of 'The Owl', which is a kind of war poem:

Downhill I came, hungry, and yet not starved;
Cold, yet had heat within me that was proof
Against the North wind; tired, yet so that rest
Had seemed the sweetest thing under a roof.

Then at the inn I had food, fire, and rest,
Knowing how hungry, cold and tired was I.
All of the night was quite barred out except
An owl's cry, a most melancholy cry

Shaken out long and clear upon the hill,
No merry note, nor cause of merriment,
But one telling me plain what I escaped
And others could not that night, as in I went.

And salted was my food and my repose,
Salted and sobered, too, by the bird's voice
Speaking for all who lay under the stars,
Soldiers and poor, unable to rejoice.

Thomas often sounds in his poems the elegiac, wistful note that
has been common in English lyric poetry for the past two hundred
years, reinforced by his personal melancholy. Most of them do not
directly refer to the war, but the sense of transience, of a loved way
of life being under threat, is frequently felt. And apart from the war,
Thomas was aware of the decay that had resulted from the long
depression in English agriculture. He writes in 'Tall Nettles':

Tall nettles cover up, as they have done
These many springs, the rusty harrow, the plough
Long worn out, and the roller made of stone:
Only the elm butt tops the nettles now.

And in 'The Mill-Water':

Only the sound remains
Of the old mill;
Gone is the wheel;
On the prone roof and walls the nettle reigns.

The Georgian poets did not care for such observations, but they were
to be keenly picked up by the young W.H. Auden. The exquisite
four-line poem, 'The Cherry Trees', expresses transience in entirely
natural images, fusing personal feeling, an immediate historical
sense of loss, and the ancient conviction, *sunt lacrimae rerum*:

The cherry trees bend over and are shedding
On the old road where all that passed are dead,
Their petals, strewing the grass as for a wedding
This early May morn when there is none to wed.

Ivor Gurney was a good deal younger than Thomas, being born in
1890, and was less formally educated, but he showed a similar devo-
tion to English landscape and English literature. He came from a
lower middle-class family of very limited resources – his father was
that proverbial figure, a tailor of Gloucester – and became what

would be known in later years as a 'scholarship boy'. He early showed great talent as a musician, and after attending the Cathedral Choir School and King's School in Gloucester he won a scholarship to the Royal College of Music in London. Gurney volunteered early in the war and served in the Gloucestershire Regiment. He was slightly wounded and suffered mildly from the effects of gas; in 1918 he underwent a form of nervous breakdown and was invalided out of the army. Gurney was both a composer and a poet. In the former capacity he is still highly esteemed; in particular, he is remembered as one of the finest English song-writers of this century. As a poet, he published only two collections in his lifetime, *Severn and Somme* (1917) and *War's Embers* (1919).

A few years after the war Gurney went mad. It is too simple to say that this was entirely because of his experiences at the Front, for he had shown signs of mental instability before the war, but there can be no doubt that his condition was exacerbated by it. He was confined to a mental hospital from 1922 until his death from tuberculosis in 1937. He left behind a large number of unpublished poems; after some earlier and unsatisfactory editions, they were scrupulously edited by P.J. Kavanagh in *The Collected Poems of Ivor Gurney* in 1982. Kavanagh's edition is not, however, complete, since he does not include all the contents of Gurney's two published volumes; it needs to be complemented by R.K.R. Thornton's annotated edition of these, *Severn and Somme and War's Embers* (1987). Thornton has also edited Gurney's substantial *Collected Letters* (1991), a major work of scholarship which reveals Gurney as a wonderful letter-writer, in the vein of Keats or Hopkins. As Thornton says of the letters, 'It is no surprise that there should be such an interest in the letters since not only do they substantially tell the story of Gurney's mature life and development, but they are intrinsically attractive; witty, generous, playful, committed, informative, and above all reflective of Gurney's enormous creative talent.'[3]

The title of Gurney's first book, *Severn and Somme*, is emblematic of the contrast expressed by many poets between English memories and French actualities. Gurney shared the dominant passion for England, and throughout the war remained an admirer of Brooke's sonnets. But, more than for most poets at the time – more, even, than for Edward Thomas with his deep love of Hampshire – 'England', for Gurney, was the region where he grew up: the city of Gloucester

---

[3] Gurney, *Letters*, p.vii.

and its cathedral, the Cotswold and Malvern hills, and the villages whose names recur like a litany in his poems:

> God, that I might see
> Framilode once again!
> Redmarley, all renewed
> Clear shining after rain.

Writing to Edmund Blunden in 1922, Gurney suggests that Blunden's poems, which he admired, were rather too generalized in their rural reference: 'It is true you have not written of so lovely a county as this is – Had you lived in Gloucestershire more than the general background of green leafage-stuff would seem to appear to me.'[4]

Gurney's letters show intelligence, humour, and a keen intellectual curiosity. Above all, they illustrate Paul Fussell's claim that for the English the Great War was a very literary war. The letters are a tissue of allusions and half-buried quotations, most often from Romantic and Victorian poets, but frequently from Shakespeare, and not just from the major plays. He often refers to the poets he is reading; he is impressed with *Paradise Lost*, but still finds Milton a lesser figure than Bach (Gurney often cross-refers between literature and music): 'Milton is one of the great men not worth crossing the street to speak to. Bach was worth a hungry pilgrimage to see.'[5] The omissions, though, are significant; he never once refers to Donne, whom both Rupert Brooke and Isaac Rosenberg read with fascination. Gurney was very interested in contemporary poets and he comments shrewdly on the work of those he came across, but his horizons, both in his reading and his own poetry, are limited by the Georgian movement; Ralph Hodgson and John Masefield were the two poets he most admired. Gurney does not attempt anything like the imagistic proto-modernism of Aldington or Read, or the expressionistic experiments of Rosenberg, or even the transformed traditionalism which conveys a sense of dissolution and crisis that we find in Edward Thomas.

Within these limitations Gurney is a poet of great accomplishment. His first volume contains pastiche of Brooke and Grenfell, but Gurney's own voice is evident in the songs and poems in ballad metre, which show the musician's finely attuned ear. 'Carol', though insubstantial, is marvellously *cantabile*. So, too, is 'Song', where the longing for England is expressed in a delicate lyric, comparable to Christina Rossetti or Paul Verlaine:

---

4 Ibid., p.538.
5 Ibid., p.40.

Only the wanderer
    Knows England's graces,
Or can anew see clear
    Familiar faces.

And who loves joys as he
    That dwells in shadows?
Do not forget me quite
    O Severn meadows.

'he Strong Thing' shows Gurney's ability to write powerful openings:

I have seen Death and the faces of men in fear
    Of Death, and shattered, terribly ruined flesh,
Appalled; but through the horror, coloured and clear
    The love of my county, Gloster, rises afresh.

The contrast between present death and violence and a remem-
ered, beloved landscape, expressed in smooth, musical verse, recurs
ı *Wars Embers*. But there is a new, more forceful note in some of the
oems, such as 'The Target':

I shot him, and it had to be
One of us! 'Twas him or me.
'Couldn't be helped,' and none can blame
Me, for you would do the same.

My mother, she can't sleep for fear
Of what might be a-happening here
To me. Perhaps it might be best
To die, and set her fears at rest.

For worst is worst, and worry's done
Perhaps he was the only son...
Yet God keeps still, and does not say
A word of guidance any way.

Well, if they get me first, I'll find
That boy, and tell him all my mind,
And see who felt the bullet worst
And ask his pardon, if I durst.

All's a tangle. Here's my job.
A man might rave, or shout, or sob;
And God He takes no sort of heed.
This is a bloody mess indeed.

Gurney's theme of the two dead enemies encountering each other after death was most deeply expressed in Owen's 'Strange Meeting'. In 'The Target' and elsewhere, Gurney, like Sorley, shows himself aware of the ironic potentialities in Housman's terse manner. The poem reflects the puzzlement of the private soldier, for whom the war was an incomprehensible muddle, whatever those in authority might make of it. This note runs through the wartime letters, which are full of poignant guesses and calculations about how long the war might last, all of which fell well short of its actual duration (at least until March 1918, when Gurney wrote, 'The War looks good for another two years yet!'). At the same time, they are quietly but unfalteringly patriotic, with a firm assumption that Germany has to be defeated. Gurney nowhere approaches an attitude of out-and-out protest, or even the detached existentialist commitment that is evident in Sorley or Read; although in a letter of July 1917 he shows a degree of sharp disillusionment:

> though I am ready if necessary to die for England, I do not see the necessity; it being only a hard and fast system which has sent so much of the flower of England's artists to risk death, and a wrong materialistic system; rightly or wrongly I believe myself able to do work which will do honour to England. Such is my patriotism, and I believe it to be the right kind.[6]

But when the German army broke through on the Western Front in March 1918 Gurney wrote, 'The fighting last year sickened all the B.E.F. Everyone was fed up and said the rudest things about the King, Lloyd George, our War aims and Capitalism, bitter things about the hopelessness of trying to move Fritz, the bullying out of the line, etc etc. But now all this has changed. They'll fight like heroes.'[7]

Gurney's post-war poetry, which is much more extensive than the contents of his two published volumes, is very difficult to assess. In 1919-20 he had collected enough poems for a third book, which the publisher rejected. During this period Gurney was trying to pick up the threads of his normal life and returning to his musical studies, but within a year or so his mental disturbance had defeated him. It is increasingly evident in his late letters, which make distressing reading; Thornton ends his edition in 1922, when Gurney entered the asylum in Kent where he would spend the rest of his life. In the poems Gurney wrote after 1919 I see two contradictory aspects. He had

---

[6] Ibid., p.288.
[7] Ibid., p.417.

greatly gained in emotional power after his experiences of war, which he was able to look back on and try to order. This is evident in the opening of 'Mist on Meadows', written some time between 1919 and 1922:

> Mist lies heavy on English meadows
> As ever on Ypres, but the friendliness
> Here is greater in full field and hedge shadows,
> And there is less menace and no dreadfulness
> As when the Verey lights went up to show the land stark.

This is effective and memorable, but the poem seems to me to collapse into banality in the concluding lines. Gurney's control of what he is writing has become become hit-and-miss, in contrast to the delicate, assured technique of his earlier poems. His rhymes become forced and he is given to long lines in alexandrines and fourteeners, metres which it is almost impossible to use in English for serious ends. The ghost of William McGonagall hovers over some of Gurney's later poems. Yet there are still a good many which work and which are moving and rewarding, even if I find fewer of them than does Gurney's editor, P.J. Kavanagh. 'The High Hills' and 'The Songs I Had' have the lyrical purity that is one of Gurney's strengths, with a new note of sadness added. And 'The Silent One' matches anything in Sassoon and Owen in its terrible directness:

> Who died on the wires, and hung there, one of two –
> Who for hours of his life had chattered through
> Infinite lovely chatter of Bucks accent:
> Yet faced unbroken wires; stepped over, and went
> A noble fool, faithful to his stripes – and ended.

In 'War Books', written after Gurney had been confined, he writes with pain and anger about his experiences, and those of his comrades; at the same time, it shows his characteristic self-consciousness about being a poet:

> What did they expect of our toil and extreme
> Hunger – the perfect drawing of a heart's dream?
> Did they look for a book of wrought art's perfection,
> Who promised no reading, nor praise, nor publication?
> Out of the heart's sickness the spirit wrote
> For delight, or to escape hunger, or of war's worst anger,
> When the guns died to silence and men would gather sense
> Somehow together, and find this was life indeed,
> And praise another's nobleness, or to Cotsworld get hence.

Another poem of this period is in fact called 'War Poet', and this is a role that Gurney accepted for himself, as is suggested by the titles of his published books. During the war, when he was keenly reading such recent poetry as came his way, he was particularly interested in those who already had a claim to the title. In August 1917 he reads poems by Sassoon, with rapidly waning enthusiasm; within a few days he goes from finding him 'a poet', to 'one who tries to tell Truth, though not perhaps a profound truth', to 'the half-poet, the borrower of magic', and then, after making comments on specific poems, to 'the half-poet, the borrower of magic'. The following year he says of Robert Graves – who was five years younger than Gurney – 'he is a poet, and I'm not'; in 1922 he makes a brief favourable reference to Owen's 'Strange Meeting'.

But Edward Thomas is the poet in whom Gurney had the greatest interest and for whom he felt the greatest affinity. When he starts reading him in 1917 he says of Thomas's poems, 'Very interesting they are; nebulously intangibly beautiful. But he had the same sickness of mind I have – the impossibility of serenity for any but the shortest space.'[8] Thereafter his admiration for Thomas rose steadily; he called him 'a very poetic soul indeed, and English at the core' and in 1919 he wrote 'E.T. grows more dear to me as the days pass'. Gurney felt that his poems might be influenced by Thomas, and in his later work he may well have been imitating Thomas's descriptive poems in running-on couplets. He also wrote musical settings for at least eighteen of Thomas's poems. The two men never met, but in the 1930s Thomas's widow Helen paid several visits to Gurney in the dismal asylum where he was confined, as she describes in an extraordinarily moving account quoted by Michael Hurd in *The Ordeal of Ivor Gurney*:

The next time I went with Miss Scott I took with me one of Edward's own well-used ordinance maps of Gloucester where he had often walked. This proved to have been a sort of inspiration, for Ivor Gurney at once spread them out on the bed and he and I spent the whole time I was there tracing with our fingers the lanes and byeways and villages of which he knew every step and over which Edward had walked. He spent that hour in re-visiting his beloved home, in spotting a village or a track, a hill or a wood and seeing it all in his mind's eye, a mental vision sharper and more actual for his heightened intensity. He trod, in a way we who were

---

[8] Ibid., p.375.

sane could not emulate, the lanes and fields he knew and loved so well, his guide being his finger tracing the way on the map. It was most deeply moving, and I knew that I had hit on an idea that gave him more pleasure than anything else I could have thought of. For he had Edward as his companion in this strange perambulation and he was utterly happy, and without being over-excited.

This way of using my visits was repeated several times and I became for a while not a visitor from the outside world of war and wireless, but the element which brought Edward back to life for him and the country where the two could wander together.[9]

Gurney, in his later years, is one of the saddest figures in modern literature. It seems peculiarly cruel, as Helen Thomas, noted, that he could not be returned to his native Gloucestershire, where he longed to be more than anywhere else, but it was believed that he might try to take his life if he went back there. Perhaps, as his biographer suggests, his condition might have been alleviated, even cured, by modern methods of treatment. He lives, though, in the five posthumously published volumes of his songs, and in his poems and letters.

Closely associated with Gurney was his friend, F.W. Harvey, another Gloucestershire poet, who had an attactive but much slighter gift. Gurney commemorated him in a number of poems, and briefly thought that Harvey had been killed; but he had been captured and spent the last two years of the war in a German prison camp. Like so many poets, including Gurney himself, Harvey went in for pastiche of Rupert Brooke; the Byronically sardonic vein of 'To the Devil on his Appalling Decadence', has worn rather better:

> But you were called familiarly 'Old Nick' –
> The Devil, yet a gentleman you know!
> Relentless – true, yet courteous to a foe.
> Man's soul your traffic was. You would not kick
> His bloody entrails flying in the air.
> Oh, 'Krieg ist Krieg,' we know, and 'C'est la guerre!'
> But Satan, don't you feel a trifle sick?

The poets discussed in the last two chapters, who were writing after the initial phase of war poetry represented by the dead of 1915 – Brooke, Grenfell, and Sorley – show marked differences in talent and seriousness. But most of them, apart from Robert Nichols, represent one of two possible attitudes: either the poetry, traditionalist

---

[9] Hurd, *Ordeal*, pp.168-9.

in its orientations, which found strength when confronting the realities of battle in the idea and the images of rural England, amongst whose practitioners one can class Blunden, Thomas, Gurney, Harvey, and to some extent Ford; or the poetry of anti-heroic protest, using rather than evading the conditions of the Front and applying a deliberate technique of realism; here one would include Read, Aldington, and West. Robert Graves moves, in his wartime poems, rather uncertainly between the two. Most of these poets were very young and not well known at the time (Ford and Thomas were older and more established) though *Severn and Somme* went into a second edition, and Wilfred Owen said in a letter, 'I have ordered several copies of *Fairies and Fusiliers*, but shall not buy all, in order to leave the book exposed on the Shrewsbury counters.' Owen's letter was addressed to Siegfried Sassoon, his friend and mentor of 1917-18, and it is in Sassoon's poetry that we discover the most radical progress from early patriotic idealism through to ironic realism and then to the angry extremes of anti-heroic protest.

6: Poets IV
Sassoon

Most of the 'trench poets' who were popular during the war, like Robert Nichols and E.A. Mackintosh, author of *A Highland Regiment* and *War, the Liberator*, are now forgotten. The major exception is Siegfried Sassoon. In 1917 his *The Old Huntsman* made an impact on civilians because of the originality of its subjects, and on soldiers because of their authenticity. Wilfred Owen said of it, 'Nothing like his trench-life sketches has ever been written or ever will be written'. And in the following year, the searing poetic manifesto of *Counter-Attack* attracted a large number of admiring readers, among them – rather disconcertingly for Sassoon – Winston Churchill.

There was nothing in Sassoon's early life and background to suggest a potential rebel and a defier both of public opinion and military authority. In *Memoirs of a Fox-Hunting Man*, the first of the volumes of fictionalized autobiography that make up the 'Sherston' trilogy, and in two books of direct autobiography, *The Old Century* (1938) and *The Weald of Youth* (1942), Sassoon left a full and evocative account of his pre-war life (he was older than most of the other poets of the war, being already twenty-eight in 1914), which can, not unfairly, be described as one of cultivated idleness: his energies were largely taken up with hunting and cricket, with collecting old books (rather more for their bindings than their contents), and with the composition of exquisite countrified verses that denoted a poetic talent minor to the point of debility. Sassoon typified an *echt*-Georgian state of mind: whatever radicalism he manifested during the war was forced upon him by events, not temperamental; and in his moments of most bitter anger his poetic methods remained traditional, however startling his sentiments. Like so many poets who were caught up in the war, Sassoon began with an exercise in the Brookian mode, 'Absolution':

> The anguish of the earth absolves our eyes
> Till beauty shines in all that we can see.
> War is our scourge; yet war has made us wise,
> And, fighting for our freedom, we are free.

Sassoon himself commented, in *Siegfried's Journey*, 'The significance of my too nobly worded lines was that they expressed the typical self-glorifying feelings of a young man about to go to the Front for the first time. The poem subsequently found favour with middle-aged reviewers, but the more I saw of war the less noble-minded I felt about it.' In *Goodbye to All That* Robert Graves left a spirited account of his first meeting in France with Sassoon:

> At this time I was getting my first book of poems, *Over the Brazier*, ready for the press; I had one or two drafts in my pocket-book and showed them to Siegfried. He frowned and said that war should not be written about in such a realistic way. In return, he showed me some of his own poems. One of them began:
>
> > Return to greet me, colours that were my joy,
> > Not in the woeful crimson of men slain...
>
> Siegfried had not yet been in the trenches. I told him, in my old-soldier manner, that he would soon change his style.

(The wartime friendship of Graves and Sassoon has been entertainingly documented in their respective autobiographies; Graves appears in *Memoirs of an Infantry Officer* as 'David Cromlech', a provocatively opinionated and argumentative young man, who, though several years younger than Sassoon, seems to have been the dominant personality). Sassoon's statement continues with an account of his change of style and attitude:

> This gradual process began, in the first months of 1916, with a few genuine trench poems, dictated by my resolve to record my surroundings, and usually based on the notes I was making whenever I could do so with detachment. These poems aimed at impersonal description of front-line conditions, and could at least claim to be the first things of their kind.

One of Sassoon's early war poems is 'The Kiss', a rhapsodic address to a bayonet which concludes:

> Sweet Sister, grant your soldier this:
> That in good fury he may feel
> The body where he sets his heel
> Quail from your downward darting kiss.

According to Graves, Sassoon, having originally written this poem in a state of genuine bellicose fervour, later offered it as a satire. If one compares the states of mind that would enable one to read the poem as, respectively, serious and satirical, one finds not merely a contrast between two traditional attitudes to fighting, but an indication of the radical way in which attitudes to the Great War shifted during the course of it. In order to read the poem seriously one would need to see the horror of stabbing and shooting men (whether intensely realized or not) as [a] necessary, and [b] strictly subsidiary to the end of achieving victory – which represented the absolute value underlying the poem. When one reads the poem satirically these values are reversed: the absolute value is seen as *not* stabbing and shooting men in any circumstances – and the notion of doing so is exposed as selfevidently wicked – and to this all other questions, including that of achieving victory, are strictly subsidiary. This was, of course, a matter of emotional rather than narrowly intellectual conviction. It became an axiom in the war poetry of Sassoon and Owen, and later in the wave of anti-war literature that swept through Britain and other countries in 1928-30, that to expose with sufficient fidelity the nature of death and mutilation in battle was a sufficient argument against war; the life-ethic which T.E. Hulme had condemned became dominant. (But this was not universally so; for instance, the memoirs of Ernst Jünger, *The Storm of Steel*, contain passages as grim as anything in Barbusse or Owen, and yet Jünger wrote as a convinced German patriot and militarist.)

As Sassoon indicated, the impulse behind the war poems in *The Old Huntsman* was strictly realistic, even naturalistic, a desire to show things as they were without any haze of patriotic sentiment. In some ways Sassoon was not particularly well equipped for the role of ruthless realist; his basic, strongly Georgian sensibility and background were very inclined to see man and his surroundings in some kind of harmony, no matter how precarious. In such a poem as 'At Carnoy', for instance, he traces this harmony on the very edge of its imminent dissolution.

> Down in the hollow there's the whole Brigade
> Camped in four groups: through twilight falling slow
> I hear a sound of mouth-organs, ill-played,
> And murmur of voices, gruff, confused, and low.
> Crouched among thistle-tufts I've watched the glow
> Of a blurred orange sunset flare and fade;
> And I'm content. Tomorrow we must go
> To take some cursed Wood...O world God made!

The poem is dated 'July 3rd 1916', two days after the start of the
Somme offensive. It was circumstances rather than temperament
that made Sassoon a realist; unlike other soldier poets he could not
be content with using scenes of rural English life as a compensation
and balance for the brutality of life at the Front: in 'The One-Legged
Man' Sassoon thrusts the two together in angry and shocking juxta-
position. The poem begins as a deceptive pastoral piece:

> Propped on a stick he viewed the August weald;
> Squat orchard trees and oasts with painted cowls;
> A homely, tangled hedge, a corn-stooked field,
> With sound of barking dogs and farmyard fowls.

But in the final couplet the unexpected point is hammered home with
unsubtle force: 'He hobbled blithely through the garden gate,/And
thought: "Thank God they had to amputate!" '
   In other, similarly epigrammatic poems Sassoon directs an impulse
of pure anger across the constantly growing gulf that separated the
unthinking civilian world of the Nation at Home with its jingoistic
slogans from the embattled Nation Overseas. One example is 'They',
with its devastating thrust at a platitudinous bishop – as D.J. Enright
has remarked, rather a sitting bird; another is ' "Blighters" ':

> I'd like to see a Tank come down the stalls,
> Lurching to rag-time tunes, or 'Home, sweet Home,' –
> And there'd be no more jokes in Music-halls
> To mock the riddled corpses round Bapaume.

Sassoon recalls in *Siegfried's Journey* how this poem was written
after a visit to the Liverpool Hippodrome: 'it was my farewell to
England, and as such it was the sort of thing I particularly wanted to
say.'
   Elsewhere in *The Old Huntsman* Sassoon made a more radical
onslaught on traditional attitudes than he may have realized; as in
'The Hero', summed up in his original notes as: 'Brother officer
giving white-haired mother fictitious account of her cold-footed
son's death at the front. "He'd told the poor old dear some gallant
lies which she would nourish all her days, no doubt." ' In this poem
– based all too probably on authentic happenings – the image of the
hero is undermined with the energy of a Thersites. Sassoon has
observed of this poem and 'The One-Legged Man': 'These perfor-
mances had the quality of satirical drawings. They were deliberately
written to disturb complacency.' This sums up very well the quality
of Sassoon's war poetry; it has the deliberate simplicity and hard

outline of good poster art. He is usually regarded as a smaller, because less compassionate and universal, poet than Owen; and this is certainly true. Satire does not reach the heights achieved by Owen's generalized lyric pity; but within the limitations of his satirical mode Sassoon is a brilliant performer. In those poems, however, in which he attempts something closer to Owen's manner, his treatment is less assured. One example is 'Died of Wounds':

> His wet, white face and miserable eyes
> Brought nurses to him more than groans and sighs:
> But hoarse and low and rapid rose and fell
> His troubled voice: he did the business well.
>
> The ward grew dark; but he was still complaining,
> And calling out for 'Dickie'. 'Curse the Wood!
> 'It's time to go. O Christ, and what's the good? –
> 'We'll never take it; and it's always raining.'
>
> I wondered where he'd been; then heard him shout,
> 'They snipe like hell! O Dickie, don't go out'...
> I fell asleep...next morning he was dead;
> And some Slight Wound lay smiling on his bed.

The desperate pathos of the first two stanzas is effectively maintained; but Sassoon seems to flinch away from too direct a confrontation with the actual death, and the assertive irony of the final line is something of a retreat.

In *The Old Huntsman* one can follow the transformation of Sassoon's war poetry from early conventional idealism to the severe realism of the poems based on his notebook entries; and here the tone is often didactic rather than realistic in any detached documentary fashion: Saasoon was increasingly dominated by the desire to use poetry as a means of forcibly impressing on the civilian world some notion of the realities of front-line life. In *Counter-Attack*, which appeared in the summer of 1918, we find Sassoon's most powerful and memorable war poetry. But between the publication of the two books Sassoon underwent the experience that he described in detail in *Memoirs of an Infantry Officer*, and which Graves gave his own account of in *Goodbye to All That*: his revolt against military authority, his one-man campaign against the continuation of the war.

Sassoon had joined up at the beginning of the war, been commissioned, fought in France with exceptional bravery, even ferocity – he was known to his company as 'Mad Jack' – had been awarded the MC and recommended for the DSO. But in the summer of 1917 he decided that the war was being unjustifiably prolonged when there was a possibility of a negotiated peace, and that the sufferings of the troops in France were correspondingly betrayed. He made a statement to his commanding officer which was reproduced in the press; it began:

> I am making this statement as an act of wilful defiance of military authority, because I believe that the war is being deliberately prolonged by those who have the power to end it.
>
> I am a soldier, convinced that I am acting on behalf of soldiers. I believe that this war, upon which I entered as a war of defence and liberation, has now become a war of aggression and conquest. I believe that the purposes for which I and my fellow-soldiers entered upon this war should have been so clearly stated as to make it impossible to change them, and that, had this been done, the objects which actuated us would now be attainable by negotiation.
>
> I have seen and endured the sufferings of the troops, and I can no longer be a party to prolong these sufferings for ends which I believe to be evil and unjust.

Sassoon had hoped that he would be court-martialled, and that his protest would receive publicity and have a certain propaganda value; but the outcome was rather different, mainly, it appears, because of Graves's forceful intervention. He describes in his autobiography how shocked he was by Sassoon's pronouncement; not because he disagreed with the sentiments but because he felt that it would do no good and might have a disastrous result for Sassoon personally. So he made use of such influential friends as he could muster to get the authorities to play down the protest and treat Sassoon gently; Sassoon was invited to appear before a medical board who would enquire into his state of mind. He declined to do so, but Graves finally persuaded him to appear before a second board: in Sassoon's account the 'persuasion' took the form of a flat lie, in which Graves assured Sassoon that even if he did not attend the second medical board the military authorities would still refuse to court-martial him; instead he would be confined in a lunatic asylum for the remainder of the war. Sassoon wrote, in *Memoirs of an Infantry Officer*: 'I was unaware that David had, probably, saved me from being sent to prison by telling a very successful lie. No doubt I should have done the same for him if our positions had been reversed.' Graves, in his account, merely states, 'At last, unable to deny how ill he was, Siegfried consented to appear before the medical board.'

The board agreed that he should be treated as a shell-shock case, and Sassoon was sent as a patient to Craiglockhart military hospital near Edinburgh, where he was a patient of the neurologist and anthropologist, W.H.R. Rivers, and where be formed a crucial friendship with a young fellow-patient – Wilfred Owen. Sassoon had been disposed of tactfully enough; in his own later writings his accounts of the episode are a little ambiguous. Writing as 'Sherston' in *Memoirs of an Infantry Officer* (1931), he gives the impression of an unsophisticated figure, bitterly affected by his experiences at the Front and a little out of his depth in the intellectual pacifist circles that he began to frequent, whose protest was a rational act, even though 'Sherston' seems to have been not wholly single-minded in his convictions. In a later account, written in his own person, *Siegfried's Journey* (1945), Sassoon does not contradict his earlier narrative but implies that his own mental condition played a larger part in forcing his protest than he had previously suggested. He denies, however, the bland official contention that he had been suffering from a nervous breakdown: 'people in such a condition don't usually do things requiring moral courage'.

Whatever his precise motives, there can be no doubt about Sassoon's courage; and many other young officers would have shared his sentiments even though they might have doubted the wisdom and efficacy of making his kind of gesture. By 1917 there was a spreading mood of revolt against the war; Graves refers in *Goodbye to All That* to 'Osbert and Sacheverell Sitwell, Herbert Read, Siegfried, Wilfred Owen, myself, and most other young writers of the time, none of whom believed in the war'. Some of Osbert Sitwell's poems savagely expressed a feeling of protest akin to Sassoon's, though in a less concise and memorable form. One of the best of them, 'The Trap', uses the symbolism of a rabbit caught and bleeding in a trap to refer to the habit of the press in dismissing all suggestions for a negotiated peace – such as the Pope's and Lord Lansdowne's – as 'traps'. In 'Hymn to Moloch' Sitwell dramatizes the familiar alienation between the generations: the young men at the Front and their seniors safely at home.

> Eternal Moloch, strong to slay,
> Do not seek to heal or save.
> Lord, it is the better way
> Swift to send them to the grave.

> Those of us too old to go
> Send our sons to face the foe,
> But, O lord! *we* must remain
> Here, to pray and sort the slain.

In *Siegfried's Journey*, Sassoon continued to uphold his protest, referring to it as 'a course of action that I have never regretted and for which there was no apparent alternative'. But a page or so later he disconcertingly states:

> I must add that in the light of subsequent events it is difficult to believe that a Peace negotiated in 1917 would have been permanent. I share the general opinion that nothing on earth would have prevented a recurrence of Teutonic aggressiveness.

This is a distinct shift of ground on Sassoon's part, no doubt conditioned by the fact that he was writing during the Second World War. If a negotiated peace in 1917 would not have succeeded, then, in retrospect, the generals and politicians who urged a fight to the finish regardless of the cost were right; and all those lonely voices, the Pope's as well as Sassoon's, who urged a truce, were objectively wrong; and his brave gesture of protest had no point.

The evidence of history suggests that a true negotiated peace during the course of the war was not a real possibility. Nevertheless, young officers like Graves and Sassoon believed that it was and that the Government was criminal in not following up the possibility. That remained the opinion of Graves, who wrote in an article in 1963: 'All the political and military blunders of the past forty years derive from a single one. It was the abandonment in the first world war of a well-tried British rule: namely never to fight beyond the point where victory will cost more than defeat'.[1] What would have happened if the more radical elements in the Liberal Government had succeeded in preserving British neutrality in August 1914 so the country had never become involved in a catastrophic Continental conflict is a matter for speculation. Neutrality may not have been an option; as Modris Eksteins has shown in *Rites of Spring* (1989) there was enthusiasm for war in all the combatant countries. But Britain lost a great deal by entering the war, and still more by pursuing a fight to the finish. The pressures in favour of going to the defence of Belgium against a clear act of German aggression were immensely strong: though Bertrand Russell was to make himself very unpopular

---

[1] 'The Fight to a Finish in 1914-1918', *Sunday Times*, 24 February 1963.

by coolly pointing out that the treaty guaranteeing Belgian neutrality was a rather loosely-phrased document and did not seem very rigidly binding on Britain. He showed that in the 1880s, when Britain was more friendly towards Germany than towards France, the idea was freely put forward in Britain that the Belgian guarantee did not require British intervention if the Germans entered Belgium simply in order to secure a passage for their troops to invade France (this, of course, was precisely the German claim in August 1914). In fact, Russell argued, the Belgian guarantee was invoked as an excuse for war rather than the other way round. In August 1914 no one had any notion of the duration or the consequences of the struggle that was so enthusiastically embarked on. But by 1917 people knew only too well. Graves may have been right in his utopian claim: 'Our rulers blundered criminally by not accepting that German peace offer as a basis for negotiation. Once an armistice had been arranged, nothing would have prevented the rival forces from fraternising, and nothing could have made them fight again'. But in Eliot's words, 'What might have been is an abstraction/ Remaining a perpetual possibility/ Only in a world of speculation'.

To return to Sassoon's poetry, and in particular to *Counter-Attack*: in these poems he completes the transformation of documentary realism into an angry didactic outcry. Although he was never a poetic modernist or even, like Owen, a conscious experimenter Sassoon was forced by the need for exactness in registering front-line experience into a degree of colloquial language and a conversational tone that was still uncommon in contemporary verse. The quality of his realism, in language and subject-matter, is evident in the first stanza of the title-poem:

We'd gained our first objective hours before
While dawn broke like a face with blinking eyes,
Pallid, unshaved and thirsty, blind with smoke.
Things seemed all right at first. We held their line,
With bombers posted, Lewis guns well placed,
And clink of shovels deepening the shallow trench.
   The place was rotten with dead; green clumsy legs
   High-booted, sprawled and grovelled along the saps
   And trunks, face downward, in the sucking mud,
   Wallowed like trodden sand-bags loosely filled;
   And naked sodden buttocks, mats of hair,
   Bulged, clotted heads slept in the plastering slime.
   And then the rain began, – the jolly old rain!

There is an obvious contrast between the two parts of the stanza: in the opening lines the stress is on action; the attacking troops, though possibly exhausted, are alert and prepared: 'We held their line,/With bombers posted, Lewis guns well placed'. Tone and diction have a marked colloquial bareness: 'Things seemed all right at first.' But this patch of local military activity is seen to be literally resting on the dead; the larger point emerges that the war is being fought on a foundation of corpses. In the opening phrase of the second part, 'The place was rotten with dead', the colloquial tone is continued, with a suggestion that the dead are now equated with infesting vermin or some form of loathsome corruption. But then the manner changes, and the remaining extended description of the accumulated corpses is written in a complex, almost Miltonic syntax which creates a tension with the continued brutal realism of the diction and subject: the dead, the literal foundation of the activity of the living, are described with a kind of gruesome ritualism that sets them apart from the modest, brisk activity of the still-living. There is a sharp return to the colloquial in the final phrase, 'the jolly old rain!' Jon Silkin has remarked:

> One cannot speak the phrase 'jolly old rain' without evoking the hearty, almost lunatic, back-slapping camaraderie endemic in a society insensible to human pain, insensible therefore to the grotesque dead here. And thus, characteristically, Sassoon makes one of his lunges at the establishment he held responsible for the prolonged suffering of the soldiers.[2]

This is a plausible interpretation, though it is possible that Silkin is making these words bear too large a weight of meaning: the larger context is not satirical, and a phrase like 'the jolly old rain' may be no more than an instance of the soldier's inevitable tendency to reduce the phenomena of front-line life to something like acceptable proportions by the use of familiar and contemptuous terms; one can compare the song about corpses 'hanging on the old barbed wire'.

The description of the huddled corpses is also reminiscent of a work that must have had a certain influence on the poems in *Counter-Attack* – Henri Barbusse's *Le Feu*. This novel appeared in France in 1916, and the English translation, *Under Fire*, came out the following year. Barbusse is a realist in the tradition of Zola; his novel is a series of loosely connected sketches of trench life, based, it appears,

---

[2] *Stand* (iv, 3), p.39.

on his own diaries; it is a work of violent protest against the war
and the destruction of values that it involved, and it is marked by a
harrowing and emphatic stress on death, mutilation and corruption,
both moral and physical. Like the English war poets, Barbusse is
concerned to shatter the traditional image of the hero:

> 'How will they regard this slaughter, they who'll live after us, to
> whom progress – which comes as sure as fate – will at last restore
> the poise of their conscience? How will they regard these exploits
> which even we who perform them don't know whether one
> should compare them with those of Plutarch's and Corneille's
> heroes or with those of hooligans and apaches?'

Le Feu, being written so close to the experiences which inspired it,
is a novel of violent feeling and no detachment. In many respects, it
is a work of intensive documentary realism; but in some ways Bar-
busse seems to have distorted, or at least formalized, his narrative in
order to construct significant and didactic patterns. Unlike his
English contemporaries, he betrays a strong political commitment;
he was well to the Left, and in later years became an active Com-
munist. One should point out that a French critic, Jean Cru, sub-
sequently questioned much of the accuracy of Barbusse's detail, and
was very critical of the authenticity of the total picture conveyed by
the novel (see Cru's *Témoins*, Paris, 1929). Sassoon and Owen both
responded very favourably to *Le Feu* when they read it at Craig-
lockhart in 1917, and herein lies its significance for a study of English
war poetry. Sassoon lent the book to Owen, 'which set him alight as
no other war book had done', and a paragraph from the novel about
the brutalizing effect of war appears as an epigraph to *Counter-
Attack*.

In this collection Sassoon brought to perfection the hard, epigram-
matic style that had already served him as an apt instrument for
satire. We also see a certain extension of his range, as in the bitter
pathos of 'Does it Matter?'

> Does it matter? – losing your sight?
> There's such splendid work for the blind;
> And people will always be kind,
> As you sit on the terrace remembering
> And turning your face to the light.
>
> Do they matter? – those dreams from the pit?...
> You can drink and forget and be glad,
> And people won't say that you're mad;

> For they'll know that you've fought for your country,
> And no one will worry a bit.

Or consider, again, the blend of complex feelings in 'To Any Dead Officer':

> Good-bye, old lad! Remember me to God,
>   And tell Him that our Politicians swear
> They won't give in till Prussian Rule's been trod
>   Under the Heel of England...Are you there?...
> Yes...and the War won't end for at least two years;
> But we've got stacks of men...I'm blind with tears,
>   Staring into the dark! Cheero!
> I wish they'd killed you in a decent show.

There is a compelling use of colloquialism and the relaxed under-statements of casual conversation. One might mention, again, 'Repression of War Experience', where the movement of the verse enacts a collapse from precarious serenity to shell-shocked nightmare; or 'Suicide in the Trenches', in which Sassoon, like other war poets, discovers the possibilities for ironical effect in a Housmanesque vehicle:

> You smug-faced crowds with kindling eye
> Who cheer when soldier lads march by,
> Sneak home and pray you'll never know
> The hell where youth and laughter go.

Yet despite the extended range in *Counter-Attack*, Sassoon remains a poet of narrow but direct effects: his language is hard, clear, sharply defined, rather than suggestive or capable of the associative effects of a poet of larger resources. On the whole, Sassoon remained aware of his limitations and did not attempt a profundity that was beyond him: his gifts were, pre-eminently, those of a satirist, and it was in satire that he excelled; some of his epigrams have achieved a permanent status, like 'The General' – '"He's a cheery old card," grunted Harry to Jack....But he did for them both by his plan of attack.' The principal target for Sassoon's satire was the civilian population, and, in particular, figures like politicians and journalists, who issued exhortations or encouragements to the troops without having any real conception of what they were enduring. And in one harsh poem, 'Glory of Women', Sassoon seems to attack the female sex in general: 'You love us when we're heroes, home on leave,/ Or wounded in a mentionable place...' The feeling

of being alienated from the women at home, who were fixated in
civilian ignorance and conventional heroic responses, was expressed
by a number of writers who went through the war; they felt them-
selves thrown back on the deeper and more authentic camaraderie of
their fellows in arms. Sassoon's animus was given horrifying crisp
expression in 'Fight to a Finish':

> The boys came back. Bands played and flags were flying,
>   And Yellow-Pressmen thronged the sunlit street
> To cheer the soliders who'd refrained from dying,
>   And hear the music of returning feet
> 'Of all the thrills and ardours War has brought,
> This moment is the finest.' (So they thought.)
>
> Snapping their bayonets on to charge the mob,
>   Grim Fusiliers broke ranks with glint of steel,
> At last the boys had found a cushy job.
>
> I heard the Yellow-Pressmen grunt and squeal;
> And with my trusty bombers turned and went
> To clear those Junkers out of Parliament.

In this savage piece one comes up against the limits of Sassoon's (and
perhaps of any) satirical approach: the complexities of actual experi-
ence are reduced to a single satisfying gesture (and a phrase like 'the
soldiers who'd refrained from dying' suggests that the anti-heroic
mode, just as much as the heroic, can achieve its effects too easily).
In fact, although Sassoon's political sympathies at this time were
vaguely on the Left (but not in the committed manner of Barbusse),
this poem reveals a state of mind that could lead to fascism in its
early, idealistic phase: the Italian fascisti, after all, were disillusioned
ex-servicemen who considered that they had been betrayed by the
corrupt institutions of a decadent parliamentary society (their anti-
proletarian bias had been anticipated by the feelings of the English
Tommy that munition-workers were 'shirkers'; Graves remarked to
a shocked Bertrand Russell during the war that his men loathed
munition-workers and would be only too glad of the chance to shoot
a few).

Counter-Attack secured Sassoon's reputation as a poet. By 1918
the public mood was ready for what he had to say, and his attacks
on the Nation at Home were accepted with a possibly masochistic
fervour. It found admirers in unexpectedly high places; Winston
Churchill, at that time Minister of Munitions, was one: he learnt by

heart some of the poems in *Counter-Attack*, and approved of them because, he claimed, they would finally bring home to the civilian population what the troops at the Front had to endure. Thus, Sassoon's anti-war outcry had been transformed, by a more agile mind than he could have foreseen, into a subtler form of pro-war propaganda. The Establishment has always been adept at incorporating rebels, and Sassoon – now once more a serving officer – saw something of the process when he was invited to meet Churchill and goodhumouredly treated to a set speech on the militaristic virtues.

There is a significant passage in Henry Williamson's autobiographical novel, *A Test to Destruction*: the hero, Phillip Maddison, has heard *Counter-Attack* discussed by some other young officers whilst he was in hospital, and later he asks his Colonel about it:

> 'Have you read, by any chance, the poems called *Counter Attack*, sir?'
>
> 'Oh yes. I read them in course of duty. I'm Intelligence at the War House, for my sins.'
>
> 'What do you think of them, sir?'
>
> 'Oh, I think we've all felt like that, at one time or another. I'm no judge of poetry, but I heard Winston Churchill at White's talkin' about them the other day. "Cries of pain wrung from soldiers during a test to destruction", were his words.'

If the poems in *Counter-Attack* were, in fact, regarded as inspired shell-shock symptoms, as psychological evidence rather than moral statements, then it seems as if Sassoon's public protest was blunted, just as his attempt at a personal protest had been. Nevertheless these poems, expressing a mood of anti-heroic revolt with such fervour and harsh wit, strike a new and incisive note in the literature of war.

Throughout the 1920s, when he continued to have left-wing leanings, Sassoon wrote sharp, epigrammatic verses that sniped at authority and conventional attitudes. In this respect he was at one with his age (one can compare the more concentrated satirical observations of Edgell Rickword), and sometimes these poems rise to an unusual level of poetic intensity, as in 'On Passing the New Menin Gate':

> Here was the world's worst wound. And here with pride
> 'Their name liveth for ever,' the Gateway claims.
> Was ever an immolation so belied
> As these intolerably nameless names?
> Well might the Dead who struggled in the slime
> Rise and deride this sepulchre of crime.

As with other writers who narrowly survived the Great War, it was to remain Sassoon's one authentic subject; it, or the emotions stemming from it, inspired his best poems, and his prose works. When Sassoon attempted to write straightforward poems on subjects remote from the war, he dwindled to the stature of a minor Georgian survival: the bulk of his later poetry, sententious or laxly pastoral, is carefully written and very dull. He continued to write pungently satirical poems into the 1930s, but in 1940 he commemorated the feelings of the time in one or two flatly conventional patriotic poems. 'Silent Service', for instance, begins,

> Now, multifold, let Britain's patient power
> Be proven within us for the world to see.
> None are exempt from service in this hour;
> And vanquished in ourselves we dare not be.

This has been aptly described by D.J. Enright as 'a dash of Winston Churchill in an ocean of water'; he makes the necessarily damaging comparison with Herbert Read's 'To a Conscript of 1940'.[3] (There were more reasons for *feeling* like this in 1940 than in 1914, but less excuse for writing like it.) In such pieces the mood is close to that of Sassoon's early exalted war poems of 1915; the wheel has swung full circle. But it is the poems of 1916-18 that count, and that represent Sassoon's major contribution both to English poetry and the records of the Great War.

---

[3] *The Modern Age*, p.161.

7: Poets V
Rosenberg and Owen

The British soldier-poet of 1914-18 was likely to be a young officer from a middle-class home with a public school education, whose imagination and sensibility had been nurtured by English rural life. Isaac Rosenberg, killed in action on 1 April 1918, was none of these things; but he was one of the finest of the war poets. Rosenberg, the child of a poor Jewish family, was born in 1890 in Bristol but grew up in the East End of London. He left school at fourteen, but soon displayed unusual talents both as a writer and painter, and in 1910 some wealthy friends paid for him to attend the Slade School of Art. In 1912 he published at his own expense a small pamphlet of poems, *Night and Day*. When war broke out Rosenberg was in South Africa – like, as it happens, a poet of very different background and temperament, Julian Grenfell – where his sister was living and where he had gone in search of an improvement in his health. In 1915 Rosenberg returned to England and joined the army, though not for the most obvious motives. He remarked in a letter:

> I never joined the army from patriotic reasons. Nothing can justify war. I suppose we must all fight to get the trouble over. Anyhow before the war I helped at home when I could and I did other things which helped to keep things going. I thought if I'd join there would be the separation allowance for my mother.[1]

Rosenberg never rose above the rank of private, and for physical and temperamental reasons he found army life more difficult than most; in his letters he speaks of being frequently punished for forgetfulness. But he was still able to find time for writing: in 1915 he published a second pamphlet of poems, *Youth*, and in 1916, a verse play, *Moses*;

---

[1] *Collected Works*, ed. G. Bottomley and D. Harding, (London, 1937), p.305.

his remaining poems written in the army were not published until
after his death.

Rosenberg was distinguished from the other war poets by his
Jewish origins and by his urban and working-class background,
which meant that he had no English pastoral nostalgia to set against
front-line experience. And since he went through the war as a private
he saw that experience in a different perspective from the junior
officers. But above all, Rosenberg is distinguished by the nature of
his poetic talent. Most of his contemporaries had been formed in the
Georgian mould, and had to adapt their basically conventional verse
forms to sustain a weight of new experience: one sees the process
very clearly in Sassoon; but Rosenberg was from the beginning an
experimenter, or perhaps an explorer, in his use of poetic language.
His pre-war poems are numerous enough to show his originality of
approach, and even if the war had not intervened there is every
reason to suppose that he would have continued his explorations.
Unlike some of his slightly younger contemporaries, Rosenberg was
not made into a poet by the war, but it both brought his gifts to a
sudden maturity and cut them short.

Siegfried Sassoon referred to the biblical and prophetic quality of
Rosenberg's work – Hebrew history and legend were one of his
prime sources of inspiration – and summed it up in this way:

> His experiments were a strenuous effort for impassioned expres-
> sions; his imagination had a sinewy and muscular aliveness; often
> he saw things in terms of sculpture, but he did not carve or chisel;
> he *modelled* words with fierce energy and aspiration, finding
> ecstasy in form, dreaming in grandeurs of superb light and deep
> shadow; his poetic visions are mostly in sombre colours and
> looming sculptural masses, molten and amply wrought.[2]

Rosenberg's exploratory habit of language has been more precisely
defined by D.W. Harding: 'Rosenberg allowed his words to emerge
from the pressure of a very wide context of feeling and only a very
general direction of thought. The result is that he seems to leave
every idea partly embedded in the undifferentiated mass of related
ideas from which it has emerged'.[3] One might, perhaps, gloss this by
saying that rather often Rosenberg wasn't at all sure what he wanted
to say when he was writing a poem: the comparison of a sculptor

---

[2] Foreword to *Collected Poems of Isaac Rosenberg* (London, 1949), p.vii.
[3] *Experience into Words* (London, 1963), p.100.

plastically working on his statue and letting the conception grow
accordingly isn't altogether exact, since clay and words are very
different media. Certainly, one is much more aware of *process*, of
composition as something continuous rather than a single act, in
reading Rosenberg's poetry than with any of his contemporaries.
Taking a less favourable view than Harding's, one can say that much
of Rosenberg's earlier work is marked by a quality that could be
called groping as much as exploration, and is often incoherent and
obscure. But this is no more than to say that it was the apprentice
work of a dedicated and potentially powerful talent.

The impact of the war had an immediately sharpening effect on
Rosenberg's poetry: his poem, 'On Receiving News of the War',
written in Cape Town in 1914, shows his capacity for linguistic
compression and for conveying meaning non-discursively through
symbolic images:

> Snow is a strange white word.
> No ice or frost
> Has asked of bud or bird
> For Winter's cost.
>
> Yet ice and frost and snow
> From earth to sky
> This Summer land doth know.
> No man knows why.
>
> In all men's hearts it is.
> Some spirit old
> Hath turned with malign kiss
> Our lives to mould.
>
> Red fangs have torn His face.
> God's blood is shed.
> He mourns from His lone place
> His children dead.
>
> O! ancient crimson curse!
> Corrode, consume.
> Give back this universe
> Its pristine bloom.

The rather cryptic final stanza suggests that Rosenberg, though
seeing the catastrophic nature of war much more clearly than most
of his contemporaries, was also inclined to regard it as a possibly

regenerative disaster; as Rilke, for instance, had in the *Fünf Gesang*. One recalls Rilke's image, 'Hot, an iron-clad heart from an iron-clad universe' (see page 37) in the final stanza of another of Rosenberg's poems, 'August 1914':

> Iron are our lives
> Molten right through our youth.
> A burnt space through ripe fields
> A fair mouth's broken tooth.

Here Rosenberg manipulates very skilfully the multiple associations of his images; each of them can be construed both literally and figuratively. War has transformed 'our lives' to iron by the imposition of a cruel and inexorable pattern; but the first two lines also suggest the slaughter by iron of 'our youth', namely the young soldiers engaged in fighting. Similarly, the 'burnt space through ripe fields' is both a literal picture of what must have been a common sight in France in the late summer of 1914, and a compressed image of the destruction wrought by war on the amenities and traditions of normal human behaviour. Again, 'a fair mouth's broken tooth' can be a slight but disfiguring physical mutilation resulting from battle, or more extensively a symbol of the brutalizing effect of war on any manifestations of human beauty.

Rosenberg is set apart from other poets of the Great War, in the first place, by a certain detachment and impersonality; in Harding's words, 'he tried to feel in the war a significance for life as such, rather than seeing only its convulsion of the human life he knew'. One might go further and say that there was always an element of aestheticism in Rosenberg's vision; whereas Owen aimed at fusing the poetry and the pity, Rosenberg kept them separate. There is a significant passage in one of his pre-war essays: 'It is a vain belief that Art and Life go hand in hand. Art is as it were another planet, which does indeed reflect the ways of life, but is, nevertheless, a distinct and separate planet.' The symbolist notion of a separate and self-contained world of art could not have been phrased more concisely.

There is a good example of Rosenberg's aestheticism in a poem called 'Louse Hunting', in which the focus is not on the misery of the lice-infested soldiers but rather on the grotesque visual patterns they make in trying to kill the lice (Rosenberg also treated this theme in a wryly ironical fashion in 'The Immortals'). The fact that he was also a painter influenced Rosenberg's development as a poet.

He had, above all, a twofold vision of the war: he was aware both of the human suffering it involved, and the unsurpassed human effort, which he regarded as a kind of absolute value, which it called forth. And this set him apart from traditional patriots and from the poets of anti-war protest. Although, as his letters show, Rosenberg could not regard the war as in any way justifiable, he accepted it imaginatively as a totally embracing way of life. There was nothing in his previous existence that could serve him as a sanative norm in the way that rural England did for many of his contemporaries (if anything, it was Jewish history and tradition that filled this role for Rosenberg); and as a private soldier he was more deeply immersed in the war than the officer-poets. At the same time, his detachment was unimpaired by the appalling sense of responsibility for others that they had to bear, and which is one of the dominant motives of Owen's poetry. The contrast is clearly brought out if one compares Rosenberg's 'Marching' with Sorley's 'All the Hills and Vales Along': in the latter there is an implicit separation between the speaker and the marching men – 'the chaps/Who are going to die perhaps' – who are enjoined, in a blend of compassion and irony, 'So be merry, so be dead'. Rosenberg's poem is written from the standpoint of one of the marching men:

> My eyes catch ruddy necks
> Sturdily pressed back –
> All a red brick moving glint.
> Like flaming pendulums, hands
> Swing across the khaki –
> Mustard-coloured khaki –
> To the automatic feet.
>
> We husband the ancient glory
> In these bared necks and hands.
> Not broke is the forge of Mars;
> But a subtler brain beats iron
> To shoe the hoofs of death
> (Who paws dynamic air now).
> Blind fingers loose an iron cloud
> To rain immortal darkness
> On strong eyes.

The precisely observed and isolated visual detail of the opening lines indicates the painter's eye. Then, in the second part, we have the packed, rapidly succeeding metaphors that characterize much of Rosenberg's verse. The poem allows for the viability of the heroic

mode, inasmuch as the men 'husband the ancient glory'; the mytho-
logical forge of Mars continues to function, but the changed nature
of modern war seems to be recognized, and the hovering impatient
presence of death is also acknowledged. In the richly complex closing
lines, which resist complete explication, Rosenberg combines a
number of diverse strands. The 'blind fingers' are blind because they
are Fate's; but also because of the muddle directing the course of the
war which is constantly sending men to death. The 'iron cloud',
incorporating one of Rosenberg's favourite eipthets, is both a
generalized symbol for war and a more exact indication of some
specific phenomenon, perhaps an artillery bombardment, which
rains 'immortal darkness'. This last phrase is deliberately ambigu-
ous: it may mean that death can bestow immortality; but also that
the darkness of death is itself 'immortal' (i.e. unending). In conjunc-
tion with the 'strong eyes' of the final line, one has both an idea of the
unseeing but defiant eyes of some heroic statue secure in its immortal
reputation, and of the 'strong' (that is, vigorous and active) eyes of
men prematurely closed by death: one may compare Ezra Pound's
'Quick eyes gone under earth's lid'. And 'blind' in the antepenulti-
mate line adds force to the juxtaposition of 'darkness' and 'eyes', and
suggests a further possibility, that the 'immortal darkness' fallen on
the 'strong eyes' is not that of death but of blindness.

Harding has referred to the way in which Rosenberg fuses two
apparently disparate attitudes, which as he puts it, 'express a stage of
consciousness appearing before either simple attitude has become
differentiated'. Certainly Rosenberg's imagination seems to have
functioned dialectically, and this may have been both cause and
effect of his great attachment to the poetry of Donne, of whom he
wrote before the war, 'I have certainly never come across anything
so choke-full of profound meaningful ideas. It would have been very
difficult for him to express something commonplace if he had to.'
The dialectical habit of mind, and the specific influence of Donne,
are very apparent in one of Rosenberg's best, and best-known,
poems, 'Break of Day in the Trenches', in which the dialectical move-
ment is objectified by the figure of the rat, moving freely between the
British and German trenches. The basic structure of the poem recalls
Donne's 'The Flea'. The soldier in the trench is juxtaposed between
two modest natural objects:

> The darkness crumbles away –
> It is the same old druid Time as ever.
> Only a live thing leaps my hand –

> A queer sardonic rat –
> As I pull the parapet's poppy
> To stick behind my ear.

Yet he does not employ them primarily for solace, as a means of escape from the destructive presence of war in the manner of Blunden. The rat's function is to emphasize by his very freedom the arbitrary separation between the two front lines, and by his low, ugly vitality to point up the fact of human death:

> It seems you inwardly grin as you pass
> Strong eyes, fine limbs, haughty athletes
> Less chanced than you for life....

(The carrying over of 'strong eyes' from 'Marching' is an instance of Rosenberg's practice of repeating his favourite phrases.) The poem returns to the poppy in the final lines:

> Poppies whose roots are in man's veins
> Drop, and are ever dropping;
> But mine in my ear is safe,
> Just a little white with the dust.

The poppies were to become a celebrated emblem of the British war dead, following the popularity of John McCrae's 'In Flanders Fields':

> If ye break faith with us who die
> We shall not sleep, though poppies grow
> In Flanders fields.

Here, Rosenberg is emphasizing their intimate connection with the dead; the magnificent image, 'Poppies whose roots are in man's veins', refers to the way in which the poppies are, as it were, growing out of the innumerable bodies of the dead, whose red blood seems to have flown out of their veins and into the flowers. Poppies were traditionally emblematic of sleep, and so of death. They are a short-lived flower – they 'drop, and are ever dropping' – but their tran-sience is scarcely more than that of the men who are constantly dropping in their midst. Nevertheless, the one poppy singled out for attention at the beginning of the poem is, for the moment, 'safe', in the precarious haven of the soldier's ear: they are, perhaps, destined to drop together. This is an unusual but effective alignment of man and nature, and shows Rosenberg's originality of insight. The poem ends with all the multiple associations of the pregnant word, 'dust';

the dust that whitens the poppy is the same dust that covers the dead and to which they will, in the end, turn.

Rosenberg's fullest and most complex crystallization of his experience of war is 'Dead Man's Dump'. Rosenberg described the genesis of this poem in a letter to Edward Marsh, dated 8 May 1917: 'Ive written some lines suggested by going out wiring, or rather carrying wire up the line on limbers and running over dead bodies lying about. I don't think what I've written is very good but I think the substance is, and when I work on it Ill make it fine...' Read without reference to the poem itself, this outline might indicate a piece of brutal realism, worked up from personal experience, rather in the manner of Sassoon's front-line sketches. But the finished achievement of 'Dead Man's Dump' is very different: realism is transformed into symbolism and, as in his other trench poems, Rosenberg does not dwell on the details of violent death and mutilation. In Harding's words, 'he thinks only in terms of death which comes quickly enough to be regarded as a single living experience'. 'Dead Man's Dump' is indeed an exploration of death as an absolute experience, which at the same time has something of the complexity and gradations of life. From the beginning, Rosenberg's language fuses realism and symbolism:

> The plunging limbers over the shattered track
> Racketed with their rusty freight,
> Stuck out like many crowns of thorns,
> And the rusty stakes like sceptres old
> To stay the flood of brutish men
> Upon our brothers dear.

The bleak phrase from his letter, 'carrying wire up the line on limbers', has been thoroughly transformed: the first two lines are direct, realistic observation, but in the third line, the comparison of the coils of barbed wire to 'crowns of thorns' is both visually apt and richly associative. In the reference to stakes 'like sceptres' which are supposed to stay the enemy flood one is, I think, meant to recall Canute, and no doubt, too, the fact that his attempt to stay the actual flood of the sea was fruitless: so too the wire may fail in its protective function. One sees at this point how Rosenberg has already moved farther away from the particular and the concrete, towards a generalized significance; it is, however, part of his strength that his perceptions are always rooted in the concrete, and he always returns to it:

> The wheels lurched over sprawled dead
> But pained them not, though their bones crunched,
> Their shut mouths made no moan.

> They lie there huddled, friend and foeman,
> Man born of man, and born of woman,
> And shells go crying over them
> From night till night and now.

If one compares this with the huddled corpses in the opening stanza of Sassoon's 'Counter-Attack', one can gauge how very different Rosenberg's intentions were. In the third stanza we find a remarkable statement of the idea glanced at in 'Break of Day in the Trenches', that there is a relation between man and nature which is brought to fruition when the dead return to the soil:

> Earth has waited for them,
> All the time of their growth
> Fretting for their decay:
> Now she has them at last!
> In the strength of their strength
> Suspended – stopped and held.

In the fifth stanza there is a kind of awe at the absoluteness of the experience of death combined with a sense of loss and pity; the last two lines recall some of the dominant images of 'August 1914', here used with greater freedom:

> None saw their spirits' shadow shake the grass,
> Or stood aside for the half used life to pass
> Out of those doomed nostrils and the doomed mouth,
> When the swift iron burning bee
> Drained the wild honey of their youth.

Harding has said of this stanza, 'It is noteworthy here that Rosenberg is able and content to present contrasted aspects of the one happening without having to resort to the bitterness or irony which are the easier attitudes to such a contrast.' If one believes the best war poetry is essentially a poetry of protest and revolt, Rosenberg's detachment and impersonality may seem disturbing, even a little inhuman. Whilst recognizing this, one must also point out that he moves to a degree of transcendence that takes him far away from his starting point in the realities of front-line activity; in such poetry we have a profound exploration of the concept of death, startling in its imaginative intensity, which goes beyond simple description, no matter how deeply felt, of the casualties of battle:

> They left this dead with the older dead,
> Stretched at the cross roads.

Burnt black by strange decay
Their sinister faces lie,
The lid over each eye,
The grass and coloured clay
More motion have than they,
Joined to the great sunk silences.

Here is one not long dead;
His dark hearing caught our far wheels...

In the middle stanza, Rosenberg shows both a painter's eye and an
ontological insight; the memorable phrase, 'Joined to the great sunk
silences', functions like an Arnoldian touchstone. The poem moves
towards the sombre paradox of its conclusion when the just dead try
to cry out to the living:

We heard his weak scream,
We heard his very last sound,
And our wheels grazed his dead face.

The last word, in the dialectical development of Rosenberg's poem,
rests with the anguish of both the living and the dead.

There is another poem in which Rosenberg attempts to penetrate
death as a self-contained and absolute way of life, transcending that
of the living – 'Daughters of War'. Here he abandons any attempt at
realism, and builds his poem on a symbolic structure which shows
the fallen swept up by the 'Daughters of War', who are seen as both
Amazons and Valkyries:

Even these must leap to the love-heat of these maidens
From the flame of terrene days,
Leaving grey ashes to the wind – to the wind.

Rosenberg believed this to be his best poem, and it contains some
characteristically fine lines and images; but it seems to me to lack the
unity and the exactness of 'Dead Man's Dump' or 'Break of Day in
the Trenches'. Above all, it suffers from being wholly in a symbolic
mode, instead of displaying the strength which comes from counter-
pointing the symbolic against the realistic.

Rosenberg's war poems are not numerous, and I think that those
I have referred to are the best of them, though there are others that
would require mention in a more extended discussion, such as 'In
War' and 'A Worm Fed on the Heart of Corinth'. Some critics, notably
Jon Silkin,[4] have seen signs of a major achievement in Rosenberg's

---

4 Ibid., p.538.

verse plays, *Moses* and the fragmentary *The Unicorn*. It is certainly
true that he had been feeling his way in these compositions towards
larger themes than he had so far attempted, but their language seems
to me obscure and clotted, typical of the groping effect that Rosen-
berg's poetry manifested when he was in less than full control of his
medium. Some of the individual speeches are impressive, but the
plays themselves fail to convince, above all, as drama. Because of the
nature of his approach to composition, which produced something
of a hit-or-miss effect, Rosenberg's successes are scattered, and his
failures to move into meaning and coherence are rather numerous.
But the quality of his successes is a sufficient sign of the talent that
the war destroyed. Above all, Rosenberg is distinguished from most
of his contemporaries who wrote about their experiences as com-
batants by seeming to have already mastered the war in poetic terms,
instead of being mastered by it. For most of the poets who survived,
the war remained the central experience of their lives, exercising pro-
foundly traumatic effects and continuing to influence their attitudes
in later years. This is true of Sassoon, and to a considerable extent of
Graves and Blunden; and, among novelists, of Henry Williamson. If
Rosenberg had survived, in all probability the war would have been
only one potential subject, and perhaps not the most important, in
his activity as a poet; I do not think it would have had the same
dominating effect on his imagination as it had on some of his con-
temporaries. At all events, he seems to me to have had the most
interesting potentialities, as opposed to realized achievements, of
any of the war's victims. As a poet of the front line his only peer is
Wilfred Owen. Rosenberg treated war intensely but impersonally as
a complex manifestation of values; Owen, with greater personal
engagement, in which compassion, anger and a desire to inform all
played a part. As he wrote in the fragmentary preface to the projected
book of poems that was never published in his lifetime, 'All a poet
can do today is warn.'

Owen's reputation has grown steadily since the first selection of
his poetry appeared under Siegfried Sassoon's editorship in 1920.
Over the years he has been the object of distinguished editorial, bio-
graphical and critical work.[5] He is, by common consent, the greatest

---

[5] There have been several editions of Owen's poems, all edited by poets: Edmund
Blunden's in 1931; C. Day Lewis's in 1963; and Jon Stallworthy's *Complete Poems
and Fragments* in 1983. The last of these is a magnificent work of scholarship in two
volumes, bringing together all of Owen's poems and manuscript drafts, with facsimile
reproductions. Harold Owen's life of his brother in the context of their family, *Journey*

English poet of the First World War. In view of this reputation, it is critically illuminating to consider one or two unfavourable judgements that were passed on him during the years when his reputation was becoming established. In 1924 the celebrated patriotic poet, Sir Henry Newbolt, said of Owen's poetry, 'I don't think these shell-shocked war poems will move our grandchildren greatly – there's nothing fundamental or final about them.' Newbolt could not have been more wrong; in time Owen came to replace Rupert Brooke as a culture-hero and symbolic victim of the war. But Newbolt's further comments provide a useful context for the discussion of Owen:

> [Sassoon] has sent me Wilfred Owen's poems, with an Introduction by himself. The best of them I knew already – they are terribly good, but of course limited, almost all on one note. I like better Sassoon's two-sided collection – there are more than two sides to this question of war, and a man is hardly normal any longer if he comes down to one. S.S. says that Owen pitied others but never himself: I'm afraid that isn't quite true – or at any rate not quite fair. To be a man one must be willing that others as well as yourself should bear the burden that must be borne. When I looked into Douglas Haig I saw what is really great, – perfect acceptance, which means perfect faith. Owen and the rest of the broken men rail at the Old Men who sent the young to die: they have suffered cruelly, but in the nerves and not the heart – they haven't the experience or the imagination to know the extreme human agony – 'Who giveth me to die for thee, Absalom my son, my son'. Paternity apart, what Englishman of fifty wouldn't far rather stop the shot himself than see the boys do it for him?[6]

This is an uncomfortably smug piece of writing, with its presumption to distinguish between degrees of suffering, and history has not

---

from Obscurity, appeared in three volumes between 1963 and 1965. With John Bell, Harold Owen edited the *Collected Letters* (London, 1967). Stallworthy published the standard biography, *Wilfred Owen* in 1974. There have since been two outstanding studies: Dominic Hibberd's *Owen the Poet* (London, 1986), which illuminatingly shows how Owen drew on the Aesthetic and Decadent traditions in his poetic response to war; and Douglas Kerr's *Wilfred Owen's Voices* (Oxford, 1993), which develops Hibberd's approach, and discusses Owen's work in terms of the related discourses derived from his family, from the Church, from the Army and from English poetry.

[6] *The Later Life and Letters of Sir Henry Newbolt*, ed. M. Newbolt (London, 1942), p.314. (Quoted by C.K. Stead in *The New Poetic*)

borne out Newbolt's judgement on Douglas Haig. He fails to realize that for many young officers the ultimate agony was precisely the sense of paternal responsibility they felt for their men, forced prematurely on them when they themselves were scarcely more than youths. Nevertheless, his honesty and sincerity are unmistakable. Newbolt expresses the pain and bafflement of those older civilians who were a regular target for the wrath of the soldier-poets. Undoubtedly, many older men would have taken part in the fight if they could; and the death of a son can hardly be anything other than a personal tragedy. Yet underlying Newbolt's remarks is the implicit and unexamined premise that the civilians accepted without question, and which the spokesmen of the Nation Overseas came increasingly to reject: namely, that the military continuation of the struggle was absolutely necessary and unavoidable; the war had to be fought to a finish and any suggestion of a negotiated peace was a 'trap'. The sense of alienation between Home Front and Army was most painfully felt when it divided the generations; when young soldiers were faced with the blank incomprehension of their fathers, secure in civilian ignorance, brain-washed by official propaganda and filled with Hun-hating hysteria.

This alienation has been vividly rendered by Henry Williamson in the wartime volumes of *A Chronicle of Ancient Sunlight*, in which young Phillip Maddison, on leave from the Front, is constantly at odds with his smug though well-meaning father. And from this feeling there stemmed the conviction that the young men at the Front were being offered as a blood sacrifice by the older civilians at home, which inspired such poems as Richard Aldington's 'The Blood of the Young Men', and Osbert Sitwell's 'Hymn to Moloch', and which was given passionate expression by Owen in 'The Parable of the Old Man and the Young':

> When lo! an angel called him out of heaven,
> Saying, Lay not thy hand upon the lad,
> Neither do anything to him. Behold,
> A ram, caught in a thicket by its horns;
> Offer the Ram of Pride instead of him.
> But the old man would not so, but slew his son, –
> And half the seed of Europe, one by one.

(The final line makes the point rather too explicit; it is omitted in one of the surviving manuscripts of the poem.)

In the face of such feelings, Newbolt and others of his generation could only reply that the charge was unfair, and return accusations of 'loss of nerve' or 'shell-shock'. For them, the Hotspurian categories of 'heroism' and 'honour' had become hardened, indeed fossilized, into unshakeable rigidities of mind. By contrast, the front-line fighters, for all their anguish of mind and body, were uttering a rational and traditional conviction: if war is the continuation of politics by other means, as Clausewitz had claimed, then it should be conducted for precise and limited aims, which should be clearly defined; and when the struggle for victory is costing more than defeat then some other means of achieving those ends should be sought. In fact, the British war aims were not clearly defined, and punishing Germany became an end in itself, as the Treaty of Versailles made evident. In the conviction that everything must be subjugated to the war, which had to be continued at whatever cost, we see the origins of the totalitarian state of mind which subjects all human activity to the overriding needs of the State.

But considered more narrowly as literary criticism, some of New-bolt's objections are worth considering. In particular, it is true that Owen's range is narrow, in some ways 'all on one note': his concern is with suffering, and he directs his energies to rendering it with as much power and fidelity as he can muster. This is deliberate – 'Above all I am not concerned with Poetry... My subject is War, and the pity of War' – but Owen's conscious restriction of range does, I think, count against him if he is being considered as a claimant for greatness. Rosenberg, though he wrote fewer war poems than Owen, was able, in the best of them, to master a larger area of experience. A celebrated criticism of Owen was levelled by W.B. Yeats in his last years: he had excluded him from the *Oxford Book of Modern Verse* (1936) on the grounds that 'passive suffering was not a proper subject for poetry', and he defended the exclusion in a letter to Dorothy Wellesley of 21 December 1936:

> When I excluded Wilfred Owen, whom I consider unworthy of the poets' corner of a country newspaper, I did not know I was excluding a revered sandwich-board man of the revolution, and that somebody has put his worst and most famous poem in a glass-case in the British Museum – however, if I had known it, I would have excluded him just the same. He is all blood, dirt and sucked sugar-stick (look at the selection in *Faber's Anthology* – he calls poets 'bards', a girl a 'maid', and talks about 'Titanic wars'). There is every excuse for him, but none for those who like him.

The venomous tone of Yeats's remarks is inexcusable, indicating rancour and, perhaps, jealousy. He was using Owen as a stick to beat

the Leftist poets of the 1930s, who had lately adopted Owen as a
progenitor of their own attitudes. Yet Yeats's assertions contain a
grain of truth (just as the harsh and unfair criticisms made of Keats
by Arnold and Hopkins do, in fact, isolate and highlight one aspect
of Keats's poetic personality). In particular, they point to the extreme
rapidity of Owen's development, and the unevenness of his finally
achieved maturity. It is well to remember that Owen, despite his
interest in poetic experiment and his technical curiosity, began as a
poet rooted in Romanticism, late as well as early, and the French and
English Decadence, and aspects of that origin persist, even in the
work produced in the great creative phase of his Keatsian *annus
mirabilis*, 1917-18.[7] 'The Kind Ghosts' (dated 30 July 1918), is a late
instance:

> She sleeps on soft, last breaths; but no ghost looms
> Out of the stillness of her palace wall,
> Her wall of boys on boys and dooms on dooms.

Owen was brought to a cruelly premature flowering in the hothouse
of the Western Front, and his work shows something of the fragility
as well as the brilliance of the forced product. Yeats's criticism of
Owen's diction points to the fact that his language was slower to
develop than his sensibility, and wasn't always equal to his demands
on it.

Having acknowledged these limitations, one can go on to point to
the magnitude of Owen's achievement. Within a few months he gave
the poetry of the anti-heroic attitude – prefigured by Byron and
Stendhal, and, more immediately, in the verse of Sassoon and the
prose of Barbusse – as absolute an expression as the traditional
heroic attitude had received in countless epics and dramas. Owen
caught a basic change in sensibility. It was the inability to realize that
such a change had taken place that caused the bafflement of New-
bolt. War was no longer the same; modern technology had seen to
that; and Owen ensured that it could no longer be seen as the same.
In theory, no doubt, to die in agony from a gas attack was no differ-
ent from dying 'cleanly' by the sword or a bullet in the traditional
manner; in practice, however, the discrepancy between ends and
means became too great, and the horror of the means discredited the
end:

---

[7] See Hibberd's discussion.

If you could hear, at every jolt, the blood
Come gargling from the froth-corrupted lungs,
Obscene as cancer, bitter as the cud
Of vile, incurable sores on innocent tongues, –
My friend, you would not tell with such high zest
To children ardent for some desperate glory,
The old Lie: Dulce et decorum est
Pro patria mori.

Owen's first poetic treatment of the war is a sonnet called '1914', which in C. Day Lewis's words is 'of interest both for its resemblances and its unlikenesses to the state of mind expressed in Rupert Brooke's *1914*':

War broke: and now the Winter of the world
With perishing great darkness closes in.
The foul tornado, centred at Berlin,
Is over all the width of Europe whirled,
Rending the sails of progress. Rent or furled
Are all Art's ensigns. Verse wails. Now begin
Famines of thought and feeling. Love's wine's thin.
The grain of human Autumn rots, down-hurled.

For after Spring had bloomed in early Greece,
And Summer blazed her glory out with Rome,
An Autumn softly fell, a harvest home,
A slow grand age, and rich with all increase.
But now, for us, wild Winter, and the need
Of sowings for new Spring, and blood for seed.

This sonnet is a rhetorical exercise, with a Keatsian note in the closing lines of the octet, but it is thematically interesting as a deflection from personal excitement and idealism to the generalized apocalyptic note sounded by European poets in 1914, Rosenberg among them.

The poems by which Owen will be remembered were written later, the majority of them between August 1917 and September 1918. It was in July 1917 that Owen had his crucial encounter with Siegfried Sassoon at Craiglockhart. Meeting Sassoon did not transform Owen's poetry, for he had already embarked on his mature poetic manner, but the older poet's encouragement and example were of immense help to Owen in confirming him in his path. In Sassoon he found the intellectual stimulus that he had so far lacked. Owen left an account of their friendship in a number of letters, and Sassoon described it in *Siegfried's Journey* and in a broadcast given in 1948, 'Wilfred Owen: A Personal Appreciation',[8] in which he said:

> I could see that this was the sort of poetry I liked. But at that time my critical perceptions were undeveloped, and I was slow in realising that his imagination worked on a larger scale than mine, and that in technical accomplishment and intellectual approach he was on a higher plane. My trench-sketches were like rockets, sent up to illuminate the darkness. They were the first thing of their kind, and could claim to be opportune. It was Owen who revealed how, out of realistic horror and scorn, poetry might be made. My judgement was to some extent affected by his attitude of devoted discipleship. I knew that I could write epigrammatic satires better than he could, and he was attempting, in a few of his pieces, to imitate them. This has sometimes caused my influence on him to be exaggerated. The truth of the matter was that I arrived just when he needed my stimulation and advice. It was my privilege to be in close contact with him while he was attaining a clear view of what he wanted to say and deploying his technical resources to a matured utterance.

In a few poems, such as 'The Chances' and 'The Letter', we see Owen attempting Sassoon's bitterly epigrammatic vein, and achieving a modest success; but it is evident that his real talents were best expressed in other kinds of writing.

Unlike other war poets, Owen rarely attempts a contrast, nostalgic or ironic, between the trenches and remembered English scenes. His absorption in the concrete realities of the Front is complete, and the only authentic England is in France:

> (This is the thing they know and never speak,
> That England one by one had fled to France,
> Not many elsewhere now, save under France.)
> ('Smile, Smile, Smile')

His poetry is also rooted in the despair springing from an awareness that the war might go on for an indefinite number of years, with no possible end in sight: the final German collapse in 1918 caught many people by surprise. Owen's dominant theme is the slaughter, or maiming, apparently endless, of young men; and it is marked by a concentration on what Webster's doomed Duchess called 'The thousand several doors where men may take their exits': gassing, in

[8] In *A Tribute to Wilfred Owen*, ed. T.J. Walsh (Birkenhead, 1964), pp.34-42.

'Dulce Et Decorum Est'; blinding, in 'The Sentry' and 'A Terre'; mutilation, in 'Disabled'; madness, in 'Mental Cases' and 'The Chances'; shell-shock, in 'The Dead-Beat'; and suicide, in 'S.I.W.'. Owen is distinguished from Rosenberg by his stress on the details of death and mutilation, and by his predominantly realistic manner of description. But in one of his most terrifying poems, 'The Show', he moves into symbolism, in a nightmare vision where the battlefield is seen as a mass of writhing caterpillars:

> I saw their bitten backs curve, loop and straighten,
> I watched those agonies curl, lift, and flatten,
> Whereat, in terror what that sight might mean,
> I reeled and shivered earthward like a feather.

> And Death fell with me, like a deepening moan.
> And He, picking a manner of worm, which half had hid
> Its bruises in the earth, but crawled no further,
> Showed me its feet, the feet of many men.
> And the fresh-severed head of it, my head.

But this kind of obliquity is not Owen's characteristic manner, which usually stays closer to the human end of the spectrum. One of his finest and most typical poems is 'Futility':

> Move him into the sun —
> Gently its touch awoke him once,
> At home, whispering of fields unsown,
> Always it woke him, even in France,
> Until this morning and this snow.
> If anything might rouse him now
> The kind old sun will know.

> Think how it wakes the seeds,
> Woke, once, the clays of a cold star.
> Are limbs, so dear-achieved, are sides,
> Full-nerved – still warm – too hard to stir?
> Was it for this the clay grew tall?
> – O what made fatuous sunbeams toil
> To break earth's sleep at all?

With considerable economy of means, Owen places the tragedy of an individual death on a plane of cosmic significance; or rather, this death, so futile in its finality, points to an ultimate futility in the whole order of things. The 'sowing' of the first stanza, with the multiple associations of rural activity, of a young man's unrealized potentialities, and of unachieved sexual fulfilment, is transformed in the second to an image of life itself, the germ awakened in the nascent earth by the action of light, leading, ultimately, to the emergence of human life – epitomized in the fine image, 'Was it for this the clay grew tall?'

The poem illustrates the constant preoccupation of Owen's major phase: the destruction of youth. The note here is mutedly sensuous; it is more overtly so in other poems. 'Greater Love' is a key example, in which Owen explores the ultimate sacrifice made by the dead; their devotion both resembles and transcends sexual love. I have already mentioned, in discussing Sassoon, the attitude which rejected women and feminine values, seeing in them manifestations of the uncomprehending civilian ethos; Sassoon gave it angry expression in 'Glory of Women'. Owen clearly shared this feeling, stressing the masculine self-sufficiency of the companionship of the trenches, as in 'Apologia Pro Poemate Meo':

> I have made fellowships –
>   Untold of happy lovers in old song.
>   For love is not the binding of fair lips
>   With the soft silk of eyes that look and long,
>
> By Joy, whose ribbon slips, –
>   But wound with war's hard wire whose stakes are strong;
>   Bound with the bandage of the arm that drips;
>   Knit in the webbing of the rifle-thong.

In 'Greater Love' Owen writes:

> Red lips are not so red
>   As the stained stones kissed by the English dead.
> Kindness of wooed and wooer
> Seems shame to their love pure.
> O Love, your eyes lose lure
>   When I behold eyes blinded in my stead!

The rejected 'red lips' are an emblem both of women and of normal sexuality; and in subsequent stanzas there are successive rejections, supposedly addressed to the personified 'Love' but in fact recalling various attributes of femininity:

> Your slender attitude
>   Trembles not exquisite like limbs knife-skewed...
>   Your dear voice is not dear,
>   Gentle, and evening clear,
>   As theirs whom none now hear...

Or consider these lines from 'The Send-Off':

So secretly, like wrongs hushed-up, they went.
They were not ours:
We never heard to which front these were sent.

Nor there if they yet mock what women meant
Who gave them flowers.

As Day Lewis remarks, 'Owen had no pity to spare for the suffering
of bereaved women'; there is, admittedly, the plangent line in 'Anthem
for Doomed Youth', 'the pallor of girls' brows shall be their pall',
but this is a visual detail rather than a profoundly compassionate
note. Male fellowship and self-sacrifice is an absolute value, and
Owen celebrates it in a manner that fuses the paternal with the erotic.
In the last year of his life, encouraged by Sassoon, he came to accept
his homosexuality and to meet people of the same inclination; a fact
which seems to have been a considerable factor in his rapid artistic
development. Owen's attitude in his poetry to the 'boys' or 'lads'
destined for sacrifice has affinities with Housman's.

One uses the word 'sacrifice' advisedly. Owen had early on aban-
doned orthodox Christianity, and marked his abandonment in 'At a
Calvary near the Ancre', which ends: 'But they who love the greater
love/ Lay down their life; they do not hate.' But at the same time he
identified the sufferings of his men with the passion of Christ; in a
letter of 1917 he wrote:

> Already I have comprehended a light which never will filter into
> the dogma of any national church: namely, that one of Christ's
> essential commands was: Passivity at any price! Suffer dishonour
> and disgrace, but never resort to arms. Be bullied, be outraged, be
> killed; but do not kill. It may be a chimerical and an ignominious
> principle, but there it is. It can only be ignored; and I think pulpit
> professionals are ignoring it very skilfully and successfully indeed
> ... And am I not myself a conscientious objector with a very seared
> conscience? ... Christ is literally in 'no man's land'. There men
> often hear his voice: Greater love hath no man than this, that a
> man lay down his life for a friend. Is it spoken in English only and
> French? I do not believe so. Thus you see how pure Christianity
> will not fit in with pure patriotism.

The aesthetic passivity of Owen's admired Keats was transformed
into an attitude of religious quietism. And in 1918 Owen wrote in a
letter to Osbert Sitwell:

> For 14 hours yesterday I was at work – teaching Christ to lift his
> cross by numbers, and how to adjust his crown, and not to imagine

he thirst till after the last halt; I attended his Supper to see that
there were no complaints; and his feet that they should be worthy
of the nails. I see to it that he is dumb and stands at attention
before his accusers. With a piece of silver I buy him every day, and
with maps I make him familiar with the topography of Golgotha.

It is the sense of the war as a ritual sacrifice, in which he was involved
as both priest and victim, that gives Owen's finest poems their
particular quality, far transcending the simple protest and rebellion
of Sassoon (or some of his own less ambitious pieces).[9]

Among Owen's finest poems is 'Strange Meeting': T.S. Eliot
described it as a poem 'which is of permanent value and, I think, will
never be forgotten, and which is not only one of the most moving
pieces of verse inspired by the war of 1914-18, but also a technical
achievement of great originality.'[10] That achievement lay particu-
larly in Owen's use of pararhyme, of which Blunden wrote, 'What
he made of it is felt at its fullest, perhaps, in the solemn music of
"Strange Meeting", but again and again by means of it he creates
remoteness, darkness, shock, emptiness, the last word.' Critics have
discussed the various influences on the poem, such as Shelley's
Revolt of Islam and Keats's *Endymion* and *Hyperion*, and the
familiar Romantic myth of the *Doppelgänger*, in which the poet
encounters his own *alter ego*. The poem imposes a double vision on
the reader:

> It seemed that out of battle I escaped
> Down some profound dull tunnel, long since scooped
> Through granites which titanic wars had groined
> Yet also there encumbered sleepers groaned,
> Too fast in thought or death to be bestirred.
> Then, as I probed them, one sprang up,and stared
> With piteous recognition in fixed eyes,
> Lifting distressful hands as if to bless.

The poet is caught up in a dream vision in which his surroundings –
the dug-out and his sleeping comrades – are transformed into some-
thing very different – a tunnel through granite – and are yet still
dimly recognizable. The scene is Hell, and he meets the enemy he has
lately killed (one of Owen's drafts reads, 'I was a German conscript,
and your friend').

---

[9] Kerr gives an excellent account of Owen's complex attitudes to religion.
[10] *Tribute to Wilfred Owen*, p.28.

The opening is magnificently dramatic, but later passages are obscure. Owen has created a powerful myth, but does not seem at all sure sure what, in detail, he wishes to do with it. Admittedly, one admires the proleptic insight of lines like:

> Now men will go content with what we spoiled,
> Or, discontent, boil bloody and be spilled.
> They will be swift with swiftness of the tigress.
> None will break ranks, though nations trek from progress.

Yet the immediately following lines show free-wheeling eloquence rather than the poetic concentration of other parts of the poem:

> Courage was mine, and I had mystery,
> Wisdom was mine, and I had mastery:
> To miss the march of this retreating world
> Into vain citadels that are not walled.

Geoffrey Hill has expressed unease about the poem's diction; quoting the line, 'With a thousand pains that vision's face was grained', he asks, 'is this the agony of the trenches transcended, or is it a half-reluctant acknowledgment of the overpowering music of *Hyperion*?'[11]

One of Owen's finest realistic poems, in which he is absorbed in the physical and moral desperation of the troops' condition, is 'Exposure'. And in 'Anthem for Doomed Youth' he gave a memorable form to his sense of the war as a prolonged ritual oblation. I would also agree with Jon Silkin's high valuation of 'Insensibility', which might be called Owen's 'Hollow Men': in this poem he achieved an unusual hardness of tone and a highly expressive verse movement:

> Happy are men who yet before they are killed
> Can let their veins run cold.
> Whom no compassion fleers
> Or makes their feet
> Sore on the alleys cobbled with their brothers.
> The front line withers,
> But they are troops who fade, not flowers
> For poets' tearful fooling:
> Men, gaps for filling:
> Losses who might have fought
> Longer; but no one bothers.

---

[11] *Stand* (vi, 4), p.7.

There is, perhaps, in the opening of this and subsequent sections of the poem an ironic echo of Du Bellay's *'Heureux qui, comme Ulysse, a fait un beau voyage'*. The harsh reference to 'Poets' tearful fooling' points directly to Owen's Preface to his poems: 'Above all I am not concerned with Poetry. My subject is War, and the pity of War.' (Although as Dominic Hibberd has shown, Owen was in fact intensely concerned, up to the moment of his death, with poetry as an art and a vocation.)

In one sense, however, Owen's poems need to be read together: they mutually illuminate each other and have a cumulative power. In their totality, as I have suggested, they have done more than any other work in English to form a sensibility that can grasp the nature of technological war. If Brooke and Binyon seem anachronistic, then that is largely because of what we have learnt from Owen. And he achieved this change in our perceptions by hammering hard at limited but intense areas of experience: for all his power, his emotional range is restricted. He wished it to be, as his 'Preface' makes clear. I find it hard to imagine how Owen might have developed had he survived: the war was his overwhelming subject, and the work of his great final year was, in more than one sense, a consummation. It seems to me that a total cessation of creative activity would have been as likely a result of the anti-climax of peace as the vein of Catullan love poetry that Day Lewis suggests he might have gone on to write.

8: Civilian Responses

Although my main concern is with the literary records of the Great War left by those who fought in it, I shall now look at the work of a few civilian writers, which may illuminate or establish a context for the poetry and prose of the combatants. Without any doubt, the most celebrated novel to describe reactions to the war on the Home Front was H.G. Wells's *Mr Britling Sees it Through*; published in September 1916, it quickly ran into many editions. As we have seen, Wells, although a socialist and a pacifist, accepted the war as a means of extirpating Prussian militarism and the militaristic spirit generally, and so helping to establish universal peace. The early facile optimism of his pamphlet *The War That Will End War* was soon dissipated by events, although Wells continued to believe to the ~~Wells~~ end that the war was a basically just conflict between the peace-loving powers – Britain and France – and the forces of militarism. As Peter Buitenhuis describes in *The Great War of Words*, Wells became one of the team of eminent writers whom C.F.G. Masterman got together to produce literary propaganda in support of the British and Allied war effort. In *Mr Britling Sees It Through* we see him pulling back from his propagandist activities to capture the life of the time in a novel. It is in fact a work of inspired journalism rather than of marked literary distinction, but it provides an absorbing account of the impact of war in August 1914 on a liberal, prosperous, professional family living in a comfortable house in Essex. Mr Britling is a scarcely disguised projection of Wells himself (seen, perhaps, as a modest representative of national attitudes, since 'Britling' can be interpreted as 'little Briton'). The novel is a product of the reflective mood that succeeded Wells's early optimism, when it became apparent that the war was certain to be prolonged and the toll of casualties grew continually higher. Much of the novel is no more than a vehicle for Wells's own reflections, but, as its huge success indicated, these were very much in tune with public feeling at the end of 1916, when the Somme disaster had had a chastening effect on even the most ebullient patriots. Wells, in the person of Mr Britling, whilst still accepting the rightness of the Allied cause and insisting on the guilt of Germany both in starting the war and in perpetrating the Belgian atrocities, tries to get beyond narrow patriotism, to form a vision of a post-war world when war itself shall be abolished, and when a purged Germany, professing the traditional German virtues, is once more a member of the family of nations. In fact, there is a certain conflict in the book, which Wells exemplifies in the tormented puzzling of Mr Britling, between the aspirations of the patriot and those of the visionary internationalist: whilst sternly denouncing German war crimes, he recalls that comparable offences have been committed by the British and French in the establishing of their colonial empires. He even insists that the Germans did not have a monopoly of cruelty in the conduct of the war – a remarkably frank admission for 1916.

In the final chapters Wells succumbed to the curious spirit of religious sentiment that temporarily possessed him during the war years; he imagines the fallen as somehow caught up by God, though a Finite God who is very unlike the Almighty of Christian orthodoxy. (Wells adumbrated this notion further in such wartime works as *God the Invisible King* and *The Soul of a Bishop*, though he soon abandoned it, and in later years regarded this 'religious' phase with some embarrassment.) *Mr Britling Sees it Through* had an intense but transient vogue – comparable in some ways to Robert Nichols' *Ardours and Endurances* – but it is still a work of lively interest. Douglas Goldring described it as 'a brilliant exposition of that first awakening from intellectual numbness which took place in England after the first year of the War. The book did not bring about this awakening, it recorded it. It was published at precisely the right moment and was an immense success.'[1]

Wells's friend Arnold Bennett was another literary propagandist, active as an administrator as well as a writer; at the end of the war he was briefly in charge of the whole British propaganda programme. Like Wells, he took physical and psychological time off from this work to write a novel. This was *The Pretty Lady*, published in the spring of 1918, when it was read with enjoyment by Wilfred Owen. It is a study of life in smart wartime London; the 'pretty lady' of the title is Christine, a French prostitute – though of so elevated a kind that she never thinks of herself as such – who is kept by G.J. Hoape, a cold, wealthy bachelor. As Buitenhuis remarks, he bears some

---

[1] *Reputations*, p.92.

similarity to Bennett: 'in the nature of their war work, their sybaritic tastes, their emotional coldness, their love of music, fluent French, and their age; but G.J. is by no means a self-portrait'. Christine loves G.J. passionately, but he ruthlessly ditches her when he thinks, wrongly, that she has betrayed him. It is a sombre story, and very effective in the manner of the French naturalists whom Bennett had long admired. Much of the interest comes from its atmosphere and incidental details rather than its plot. There is an account of a Zeppelin raid, which leaves bomb damage and casualties (melodramatically including a child's severed arm found in the street). Shell-shocked soldiers on leave come to the West End in search of sex and excitement. Rich men like Hoape attend committees and observe with satisfaction how the war is increasing their wealth. Bennett is satirical about the pseudo-charitable activities of Society ladies, and looks with a cold but fascinated eye at the hedonistic goings on in a fashionable night club. In Buitenhuis's words, 'In this scene and others, Bennett begins to chart the vast changes in sexual and social mores that later became the territory of Huxley, Waugh and other satirists of the 1920s.'

Some years after the war Bennett looked back on it in *Lord Raingo* (1926), which recapitulates elements from *The Pretty Lady* and draws heavily on his own wartime experiences in the Ministry of Information, and those of his friend and boss, Lord Beaverbrook. The eponymous Raingo is an immensely able and energetic self-made businessman who is brought into the government to be in charge of propaganda. Like Hoape, he is a rather cold personality with an adoring mistress, but he also has a wife, whom he does not love, and a son who is a prisoner of war in Germany. *Lord Raingo* reflects the cynicism and disillusionment about the war that were common in the twenties. It is nearly a major novel; those chapters where the confident but unskilled Raingo gets involved in the intricacies of government, enjoys the feeling of power, and then encounters the inescapable betrayals of politics are first-class political fiction, of a kind that is rare in English, apart from Trollope's Palliser series. Winston Churchill, who appears as the fire-eating minister Tom Hogarth, confirmed Bennett's remarkable accuracy in showing Lloyd George's War Cabinet in action (Beaverbook had provided him with the necessary details). But Bennett seems to have had considerable difficulty in developing Raingo's personal life, perhaps because he was such a hollow man. In the end, he is killed off – he takes an unconscionably long time dying of pneumonia – and so are his wife and mistress. But all is not lost. At the end of the

novel, in a gesture which echoes the movement towards a better
future enacted by the survivors in a Shakespeare tragedy, Raingo's
son, who has escaped from captivity, cynical but not without hope,
is to marry the younger sister of Raingo's mistress. He is the new
Lord Raingo.

Another eminent writer whom the war provoked into a charac-
teristic literary response was Rudyard Kipling: the conflict came as
no surprise to him, for he had long foreseen it, but it brought him
personal tragedy with the death of his only son, and much of his war-
time writing is correspondingly bitter. From the publication of 'For
All We Have and Are' Kipling continued to address exhortatory
poems to the nation (in May 1918 a bogus Kipling poem called 'The
Old Volunteer' appeared in *The Times*, the work of an unknown
hoaxer). And under the stress of war Kipling also produced some
savage short stories, of which the most famous is 'Mary Postgate',
written, as it happens, some time before his son's death. In literary
terms, it is one of Kipling's most brilliant compositions. In this story,
the faded spinster Mary Postgate hears of the death in the Flying
Corps of the boy Wynn she had helped to bring up; a little later a
child is killed nearby by a bomb from a German plane. Soon after-
wards when she is burning Wynn's toys and books in an incinerator,
she discovers a German airman lying wounded in a nearby shrub-
bery; she refuses to help him and threatens him with a pistol, repeat-
ing: '*Ich haben der todt Kinder gesehn.*' She waits for his death, in
fact urging him to die, and when the end comes she experiences a
clearly orgiastic satisfaction. In a perceptive analysis of this story,[2]
W.W. Robson has shown that it is far more than a crude anti-German
tract, being, in essentials, a study in the warped psychology of Mary
Postgate. Whilst accepting the point of this interpretation, one
doubts if the story was read with such sensitive understanding when
it first appeared in 1915: for many readers, in the pressures of a war-
time context, the story must have seemed an object-lesson in hating
the child-killing Hun. And 'Mary Postgate' was published together
with a poem called 'The Beginnings':

> It was not part of their blood,
> It came to them very late
> With long arrears to make good,
> When the English began to hate.

One of the things that had disturbed Mr Britling was the anti-English

---

[2] *Kipling's Mind and Art*, ed. A. Rutherford (Edinburgh, 1964), pp.271-4.

'Hymn of Hate', sung by the Germans with such enthusiasm: it seemed to him the product of a pathological state of mind. But 'The Beginnings', though possibly more controlled in its sentiments, is a similar phenomenon.

Bernard Shaw was one of that small radical minority who adopted a less partisan and more openly sceptical attitude to the war. He saw with greater clarity than the assertive patriots just how far the war was causing the break-up of the pattern of civilization that had seemed so inviolable in 1914, and he embodied something of this vision in a play, *Heartbreak House* (1919), which he subtitled 'A Fantasia in the Russian manner on English themes'. In his preface Shaw wrote: 'HEARTBREAK HOUSE is not merely the name of the play which follows this preface. It is cultured, leisured Europe before the war.' The play offers a microcosm of cultivated English society, futile, elegant, mildly eccentric, which is shattered at the end by bombs from a Zeppelin.

There were two other civilian writers who registered with great clarity their conviction that a phase of British civilization was in dissolution. They are both now seen as major innovators in twentieth-century literature, and they shared with the Georgian soldier-poets a feeling for traditional England, an England which they doubted could survive the war. I am referring to Ezra Pound and D.H. Lawrence. Both were in different ways somewhat detached spectators of the national effort: Pound because he was an American citizen (though he had lived in London since 1908), and Lawrence because of the working-class origins which made him feel an alien in Establishment circles. By the outbreak of war he had become déclassé, and his pacifist convictions, together with the influence of a German wife, meant that he spent the war years as what would now be termed an 'internal emigré', regarded with suspicion and harrassed by the authorities.

Pound crystallized his response to the war in two of his major poems: *Homage to Sextus Propertius* (1917) and *Hugh Selwyn Mauberley* (1920). In the first he deals with the contemporary situation by indirection. The crisis of the British Empire is described in terms of Propertius' Rome: like London, a great metropolis and the centre of a great Empire. In 1931 Pound wrote of this poem: 'it presents certain emotions as vital to me in 1917, faced with the infinite and ineffable imbecility of the British Empire, as they were to Propertius some centuries earlier, when faced with the infinite and ineffable imbecility of the Roman Empire.'[3] But it was in sections

---

[3] Quoted by Noel Stock in *Poet in Exile: Ezra Pound* (Manchester, 1964), p.96.

IV and V of *Mauberley* that Pound, who had once delighted in the
theatrical belligerence of 'Altaforte', directly confronted the war and
wrote some of his finest poetry about it:

> There died a myriad,
> And of the best, among them,
> For an old bitch gone in the teeth,
> For a botched civilization,
>
> Charm, smiling at the good mouth,
> Quick eyes gone under earth's lid,
>
> For two gross of broken statues,
> For a few thousand battered books.

The high civilization for which men had died, and which should have
been a constant living source of value, has been contemptuously
reduced to a heap of disparate objects, broken statues and battered
books. In the very beautiful 'Envoi' of the sequence, Pound seems to
be addressing himself, as Donald Davie has suggested,[4] to the Eng-
land he had come to know and love, and which seemed increasingly
indifferent to her cultural riches. When the war ended, he found that
the quality of English life had deteriorated so much that he could no
longer bear to live in London, the city that had once seemed to him
the supreme literary and intellectual metropolis. He departed for
the Continent, living first in France and then in Italy, until he was
returned to the United States by the American army in 1945, charged
with treason following his collaboration with the Italian Fascist
regime. Yet, twenty-five years after his departure, picking over his
memories of the pre-1914 world in the prison camp at Pisa, he was
able to look back at the old, vanished England with a nostalgic
concern (and something of a Yeatsian feeling for the passing of
aristocratic tradition):

> Tudor indeed is gone and every rose,
> Blood-red, blanch-white that in the sunset glows
> Cries: 'Blood, Blood, Blood!' against the gothic stone
> Of England, as the Howard or Boleyn knows.
>
>   (*Canto* LXXX)

As an American, and one who thought instinctively in literary and
aesthetic categories, Pound had a somewhat external concept of

---

[4] *The Modern Age*, p.326.

English tradition. D.H. Lawrence, who was inalienably English by
birth and upbringing, had similar but more intimate feelings. As his
letters record, the war was an unbroken torment for him, and he was
quite specific in saying that he considered a German victory a lesser
evil than a continuation of the war. His pacifism was of the uncom-
promising kind that would face a foreign occupation with equanimity:

> I know that, for me, the war is wrong. I know that if the Germans
> wanted my little house, I would rather give it them than fight
> for it: because my little house is not important enough to me. If
> another man must fight for his house, the more's the pity. But it is
> his affair. To fight for possessions, goods, is what my soul will *not*
> *do*. Therefore it will not fight for the neighbour who fights for his
> own goods.[5]

Lawrence's conviction that the war was destroying traditional
England was expressed in some superbly poignant passages in his
wartime letters, as in the following paragraph from a letter to Lady
Cynthia Asquith written in November 1915:

> When I drive across this country, with autumn falling and rustling
> to pieces, I am so sad, for my country, for this great wave of civili-
> sation, 2000 years, which is now collapsing, that it is hard to live.
> So much beauty and pathos of old things passing away and no
> new things coming: this house of the Ottoline's – it is England –
> my God, it breaks my soul – their England, these shafted windows,
> the elm-trees, the blue distance – the past, the great past, crumbling
> down, breaking down, not under the force of the coming birds,
> but under the weight of many exhausted lovely yellow leaves, that
> drift over the lawn, and over the pond, like the soldiers, passing
> away, into winter and the darkness of winter – no, I can't bear it.
> For the winter stretches ahead, where all vision is lost and all
> memory dies out.

Lawrence conveyed a similar, though even more intense, epiphany
in a letter to Lady Ottoline Morrell, dated 1 December 1915, in
which he described his vision as being like that of a drowning man in
which he sees 'all his past crystallised into one jewel of recollection':

> The window-shafts, like pillars, like bars, the shallow Tudor arch
> looping over between them, looping the darkness in a pure edge,
> in front of the far-off reluctance of the dawn. Shafted, looped

---

[5] *Collected Letters of D.H. Lawrence*, ed. H.T. Moore (London, 1962), I, p.460.

windows between the without and the within, the old house, the perfect old intervention of fitted stone, fitted perfectly about a silent soul, the soul that in drowning under this last wave of time looks out clear through the shafted windows to see the dawn of all dawns taking place, the England of all recollection rousing into being. The wet lawn drizzled with brown, sodden leaves; the feathery heap of the ilex tree; the garden-seat all wet and reminiscent. Between the ilex tree and the bare, purplish elms, a gleaming segment of all England, the dark plough-land and wan grass, and the blue, hazy heap of the distance, under the accomplished morning.

Lawrence's vision of England, of a traditional, rural-centred order, had affinities with the nostalgia for England of the poets in uniform, though it was far more intense than theirs, and was made tragic by the conviction that this order was collapsing.

He expressed this sense in one of his most powerful short stories, 'England, My England'. It dominates his greatest novel, *Women in Love* (1921), which was written during the latter part of the war, and which Paul Delany, in his book about Lawrence's wartime life, calls a remarkable war novel which doesn't mention the war (apart from a fleeting reference to the Kaiser). Delany observes that Lawrence already had a tendency to see the world in terms of sharp oppositions, but the war strongly reinforced it, as is apparent in *Women in Love*:

> the war moved him further and faster in this direction by imposing on the entire European consciousness just such a system of binary oppositions: for or against, friend or enemy, kill or be killed.'[6]

In December 1916 Lawrence wrote of the then Prime Minister, Asquith: 'He is too much the old, stable, measured, decent England. Alas and alack, that such an England must collapse and be trodden under the feet of swine and dogs.' And a few days later, when Lloyd George, whom Lawrence loathed, had taken over the premiership, he commented with the savagery that became increasingly marked as the war continued: 'It is what the countryful of swine wanted, now let them have it. All we have to do is to wait for the debauch.'

Like Pound, Lawrence found England insupportable when the war ended, and in 1919 he left the country for good and embarked on the years of restless wandering that ended with his death in 1930.

---

[6] Paul Delany, *D.H. Lawrence's Nightmare* (Hassocks, 1979), p.211.

He returned to his wartime experiences in his Australian novel, *Kangaroo* (1923), in which he devotes a fifty-page chapter called 'The Nightmare' to an avowedly autobiographical recapitulation of his life in wartime England. It is a pure digression in the otherwise tedious narrative of *Kangaroo*, and it has the almost hallucinatory power and intensity of those passages in Lawrence's writing in which he describes his most searing personal experiences (the account of Ursula's first day as a schoolteacher in *The Rainbow* is a comparable example). 'From 1916 to 1919,' he wrote, 'a wave of criminal lust rose and possessed England, there was a reign of terror, under a set of indecent bullies like Bottomley of *John Bull* and other bottom-dog members of the House of Commons.' Lawrence's account of the tribulations he endured during the war frequently rises to the level of hysteria, but even after discounting the excesses of his tone, one is left with a vivid impression of the coarsening and corrupting effect that the war had in its later years on English life. Ford Madox Ford, in *Parade's End*, was to make, from another point of view, a comparable analysis and indictment.

At the end of the chapter Lawrence describes his final departure from what he had now come to see as a corpse-like England:

> There was snow on the Downs like a shroud. And as he looked back from the boat, when they had left Folkestone behind and only England was there, England looked like a grey, dreary-grey coffin sinking in the sea behind, with her dead grey cliffs and the white, wornout cloth of snow above.

(Lawrence was attached to the image of England as a coffin; he had already used it in *The Lost Girl*: 'England, like a long, ash-grey coffin slowly submerging'.)

For Pound and for Lawrence, and other postwar English expatriates, such as Ford and Aldington, the England they had known may well have seemed dead. But the life of a community continues in one form or another, no matter how radical the transmutations it has undergone. The literature of the early 1920s offers various reflections of the efforts to continue living made by those on whom the memories of the war weighed most painfully: the characters of *The Waste Land* (1922), for instance; or the exquisite Mrs Viveash in Aldous Huxley's *Antic Hay* (1923), incapable of feeling but still obsessed with the memory of her lover, Tony Lamb, killed in 1917; or, in Virginia Woolf's *Mrs Dalloway* (1925), the shell-shocked Septimus Warren Smith. If the war could not be forgotten, the refurbished postwar London, whose superficially relaxed atmosphere is evoked by the descriptions of Huxley and Virginia Woolf and by such works as Galsworthy's *A Modern Comedy* (1929), offered a variety of competing distractions. For a few years, there was to be no great public demand for books about the war.

9: Retrospect I
Autobiography

For those actively involved in the struggle, the immediate literary response to war had been necessarily confined to such compact forms as the private letter or diary entry, and, above all, to brief lyric poems. But several of the poets who survived returned to their experiences in longer, retrospective prose works written ten or more years after the Armistice. The years 1928-30 witnessed a remarkable return to public favour of books about the war, which coincided with the further stage of war literature represented by autobiographical works such as Blunden's *Undertones of War*, Sassoon's *Memoirs of a Fox-Hunting Man* and *Memoirs of an Infantry Officer*, and Graves's *Goodbye to All That*; and by novels like Aldington's *Death of a Hero* and Manning's *Her Privates We*. The success of Hemingway's *A Farewell to Arms* in America, and E.M. Remarque's *All Quiet on the Western Front* in Germany, showed the international nature of this interest.

Yet there had been a steady trickle of war books appearing from 1919 onwards, ranging from artless personal narratives to official histories of regiments or campaigns, which had attracted dedicated readers. One of the best of these earlier books is C.E. Montague's *Disenchantment*, published in 1922, which anticipates the temper of the retrospective studies of the end of the decade. It is a highly personal work, which offers, not sustained description or narrative, but a loosely linked series of studies, essayistic in manner and occasionally rising to stylistic distinction, of the changes in front-line morale during the course of the war. Montague writes as an ardent over-age volunteeer for the New Army of 1915, filled, like so many others, with idealism, zeal and high spirits: his sense of dedication was sorely tried by the corruption and minor stupidities of the military bureaucracy, and by the graver incompetences of the Staff. He expressed the common sentiment that the New Army consisted of 'lions led by donkeys'. In some respects an idealism as fine as Montague's was bound to be badly bruised in any form of organized military life; parts of his book do no more than express the perennial human resentment at 'The insolence of office, and the spurns/That patient merit of the unworthy takes'. Yet in other ways Montague provides an index of the attitudes and concerns that were manifested by all the writers who experienced the life of the trenches: in a positive sense, the camaraderie of active service and the almost cosy domesticity of the quieter sections of the Front; and, on the negative side, the increasing alienation of the troops from the empty jingoism of the Home Front, and, something which Montague passionately deplored, the loss of traditional standards of chivalry in the conduct of the war: he shows that the hate-mongering of the civilians affected some of the Staff, but the front-line soldiers largely rejected it and continued to respect their German opponents. Above all, Montague conveys the sense of waste and futility produced by the seemingly endless prolongation of the war, which proved so demoralizing to those who had once shown such ardour. One of his most moving passages describes his feelings on witnessing the final breakthrough of the British Army in August 1918: a sense of incredulity that this longed-for event was actually happening, combined with the sad realization that it was taking place *too late*: in 1916, even in 1917, it might have aroused the authentic exhilaration of victory, but it had been too long deferred and too much had been lost in the intervening years.

Prose accounts of the war can be divided between those which were avowedly subjective in their approach, like Montague's, offering the author's own reflections and showing the war as it affected his own development; and those which concentrated on objective narrative, suppressing the author's direct feelings and allowing emotion to be expressed only by implication in the descriptive process. A magnificent example of the latter mode is Herbert Read's brief study, *In Retreat*; this was first published in 1925, but was written as early as 1919, with all the detachment and objectivity of the narratives of ten years later, and is a classic of modern English prose. It deals with a few days in the retreat of the British Army following the German breakthrough in March 1918. Read divides his narrative into tiny units of experience, expressed by terse, compact sentences, and provides a sense of the rapid passage of time by frequently stating the time of day at which a particular event took place. The opening paragraphs show the narrative method in action; after the briefly informative opening sentences, the focus narrows to

provide a succession of isolated sense data (recalling Read's appren-
ticeship as an Imagist poet):

> We received the warning order just before dinner, and for a while
> talked excitedly round the mess fire, some scoffing at the idea of
> an imminent battle, others gravely saying that this time at any rate
> the warning was justified. Two deserters, with tales of massing
> guns and the night-movements of innumerable troops, had
> reached our lines the previous day. Of course, deserters usually
> had some such tale designed to tempt a captor's leniency, but this
> time it was likely to be the truth. What else could the enemy's long
> silence mean? To that question we had no answer. We went early
> to bed, expecting an early awakening. The harnessed horses stood
> in lowered shafts.
>
> There was scarcely a wall standing in Fluquières: everywhere
> demolition and bombardment had reduced the village to irregular
> cairns of brick and plaster. Winding among these cairns were the
> cleared roadways. Men and horses rested in patched sheds and an
> occasional cellar. S— and I were in a small repaired stable, each
> with a bed-frame in a manger. I had livened the cleanly white-
> washed walls of the place with illustrations from a coloured
> magazine. That evening all save our trench-kit had been sent to
> the transport-wagons, and we were lying on the bare netting with
> only our trench coats thrown over us.

In the hands of a less accomplished writer such baldness of narrative
style could easily diminish into flatness and banality; and it is true
that much of *In Retreat* recalls the simple, unadorned manner of an
official report. But Read is always fully in control of his language,
consciously selecting and placing significant details, though the total
effect is one of transparency, as though we were actively sharing in
the author's experiences without the intervention of the verbal
medium. Read's ability to convey the tension and the sheer physical
effect of rapidly ensuing action is apparent in the following para-
graph, describing a later stage in the retreat:

> At 8 a.m. we began to observe troops retreating in front of us.
> They came in little groups down the road, or straggled singly over
> the landscape. The mist gradually lifted. We heard machine-gun
> fire fairly near, somewhere on the right. The stragglers informed
> us that the enemy had crossed the canal in the early dawn, and
> was advancing in considerable force. We waited patiently. At
> 9 a.m. the enemy came into touch with our fellows on the left, and

here we rebutted him successfully. At 9.30 the troops on our right were reported to be withdrawing. About ten o'clock, there happened one of those sudden episodes, which would be almost comic with their ludicrous *bouleversement* were they not so tragic in their results. Seemingly straight from the misty sky itself, but in reality from our own guns, descended round after round of shrapnel bursting terrifically just above our heads, and spraying leaden showers upon us. Simultaneously, from the woods on our right, there burst a fierce volley of machine-gun fire, hissing and spluttering among us. We just turned and fled into the shelter of the village buildings. I shouted to my men to make for the position of the quarry. We scuttled through gardens and over walls. By the time we reached the quarry we had recovered our nerve. We extended and faced the enemy, who were advancing skilfully over the plain on our left. We on our part were a scrap lot composed of various units. We hastily reorganized into Sections. Retreat was inevitable. Then followed a magnificent effort of discipline. A major took charge of the situation, and we began to retire with covering fire, section by section, in perfect alternation.

The narrative detachment stops short of the passive impersonality of the camera-eye: there is sufficient human involvement for the final 'magnificent effort of discipline', preserving both life and order, to be praised. Again, on a later page, Read makes evident the famished troops' pleasure in finding food and hot coffee. But in general, *In Retreat* conveys a sense of the war as a large machine that transcends the separate humanity of those caught up in it; Read's prose provides a track of its movements over a short stretch of time as recorded by one individual consciousness.

Whereas *In Retreat* is in a dominantly objective mode, another, shorter piece, 'The Raid', is closer to the subjective end of the spectrum: it describes a trench raid that Read led in the summer of 1917, and contains the reflections on cowardice and the account of capturing a German officer that had already provided material for some of his poems. It is a fine piece of writing, even though it falls short of the distinction of *In Retreat*. These studies are included in Read's volume of autobiography, *The Contrary Experience*, which also contains his war diary. His literary records of the war are not extensive: the poems of *Naked Warriors*, *The End of a War*, and these brief prose narratives. Yet together they form a response unsurpassed in sensitivity and penetration by his more prolific contemporaries.

Another consciously objective writer is Edmund Blunden, whose

Undertones of War caught the rising tide of popular interest in 1928 and went into several editions. Blunden, like the other retrospective writers of the late 1920s, whether in autobiography or fiction, was writing in an attempt to make sense of his own experiences, to trace a pattern in the scarifying events that had impinged on his formative years. To some extent, this endeavour is true of all writers of auto-biography, and still more of autobiographical fiction. But the sur-vivors of the Great War had more urgent motives: in making an extended confrontation of their wartime lives they were engaging in a therapeutic activity. Blunden and Graves confessed that they had made previous attempts at describing their wartime experiences but had failed: not until a decade had elapsed could they write about them as they wished.

Undertones of War is much less than a full autobiography: it is a severely selective account of Blunden's experiences as a very young subaltern, on the Somme and at the Third Battle of Ypres. In reading this book we recognize the same persona that speaks through Blun-den's poetry – he describes himself in the final sentence as 'a harmless young shepherd in a soldier's coat' – with a characteristic sweetness and gentleness of disposition, an intensely observant love of nature and a thorough immersion in the traditions of literary pastoral. And yet we are given very little of the substance of the young Blunden's personality, merely a pronounced flavour of his mind and sensibility: this flavour is imparted by the quality of his prose, with its carefully composed sentences, sometimes idiosyncratic in their structure and out-of-the-way in their choice of words, conveying a sense of mellow, almost middle-aged reminiscence (though Blunden was only in his early thirties when writing this book). Throughout *Undertones of War* the author subdues himself to the succession of events, arranged in chapters each grouped round a separate narrative focus, and doesn't intervene with his reflections and opinions; though here and there we find some uncharacteristically direct comments, as when Blunden refers to his sympathy for Siegfried Sassoon's anti-war stand, and speaks of his 'convictions that the war was useless and inhuman'. But for the most part he maintains a studied reticence.

There is a marked austerity in the design of *Undertones of War*, in so far as its scenes are confined to life at the Front: when the author goes home on leave we do not follow him. The world of the troops in France is seen as forming a self-contained though bizarre civiliza-tion, with its own values, and even its own peculiar time-scheme. In 1916 the remnants of the early campaigns of 1914 seemed immensely ancient, relics of a far-off world:

The joyful path away from the line, on that glittering summer
morning, was full of pictures for my infant war-mind. History
and nature were beginning to harmonize in the quiet of that
sector. In the orchard through which we passed immediately,
waggons had been dragged together once with casks and farm
gear to form barricades; I felt that they should never be disturbed
again, and the memorial raised near them to the dead of 1915
implied a closed chapter. The empty farm houses were not yet
effigies of agony or mounds of punished, atomized material; they
could still shelter, and they did. Their hearths could still boil the
pot. Acres of self-sown wheat glistened and sighed as we wound
our way between, where rough scattered pits recorded a hurried
firing-line of long ago. Life, life abundant sang here and smiled;
the lizard ran warless in the warm dust; and the ditches were
trembling quick with odd tiny fish, in worlds as remote as Saturn.

Blunden does not draw any sharp, sardonic contrast between the
Two Nations, though in Chapter XXII he allows himself a sad
comment on the universally attested decline in the quality of civilian
life that had come about by 1917: 'During my leave, I remember
principally observing the large decay of lively bright love of country,
the crystallization of dull civilian hatred on the basis of "the last drop
of blood".' The texture of his prose is, however, permeated by a
contrast between the brutal realities of war and the remembered or
imagined beauties and harmonies of nature and the rural order. As
we have seen, this contrast was a dominant element in Blunden's war
poems; but in his prose he manipulates it with particular delicacy.
The contrast is not bitter or ironical; rather it forms a balance of
opposites that go to make up a unified picture:

> Waiting there in the gashed hillsides for Lewis, who had gone
> below for instructions, we looked over the befouled fragments of
> Ypres, the solitary sheet of water, Zillebeke Lake, the completed
> hopelessness. The denuded scene had acquired a strange abrupt-
> ness of outline; the lake and the ashy city lay unprotected, isolated,
> dominated finally. But farther off against the sunset one saw the
> hills beyond Mount Kemmel, and the simple message of nature's
> health and human worthiness again beckoned in the windmills
> resting there. There – and here!

Even when he is describing scenes of destruction, Blunden's choice of
phrases and images is such that the sense of disorder is blended with
a feeling for the continuity of what has been, for the time being,
disturbed:

The heart of the village is masked with its hedges and orchards from almost all ground observation. That heart nevertheless bleeds. The old homes are razed to the ground: all but one or two, which play involuntary tricks upon probability, balancing themselves like mad acrobats. One has been knocked out in such a way that its thatched roof, almost uninjured, has dropped over its broken body like a tea-cosy. The church maintains a kind of conceptional shape, and has a cliff-like beauty in the sunlight; but as at this ecclesiastical corner visitors are sometimes killed we may, in general, allow distance to lend enchantment. Up that naked road is the stern eye of Beaumont Hamel – turn, Amarylis, turn – this way the tourist's privacy is preserved by ruins and fruitful branches.

Constantly Blunden displays a sharpness and exactness of observation, whether of natural objects or the phenomena of war, or both, that recalls the notes of Ruskin or Hopkins:

It is true that steel helmets now became the rule, their ugly useful discomfort supplanting our old friendly soft caps; and the parachute flares winding down from the cloud of night glistened here and there on those curious green mushrooms, or domes, where listening-posts perhaps listened, probably dozed among the weeds and rustlings of No Man's Land.

Blunden continues the description, somewhat changing its tone and allowing himself a moment of overt reflection: this, the end of Chapter VII, is one of the slight climaxes of the book:

The dethronment of the soft cap clearly symbolized the change that was coming over the war, the induration from a personal crusade into a vast machine of violence, that had come in the south, where vague victory seemed to be happening. The south! what use thinking about it? If we were doomed to go, we thought, we were, and we pressed no further. No one seemed to have any mental sight or smell of that vast battle.

Many other writers were aware of the change in the character of the war that occurred after the Somme battles (on the German side it was noticed by Ernst Jünger), the transformation of the conflict into a 'vast machine of violence'. But Blunden does not dwell on the point. *Undertones of War*, as its title implies, is an undramatic book. Although Blunden does not shirk from describing the violence of battle when he was directly involved (displaying on occasion great

courage and enterprise), and gives a faithful account of death and
mutilation and the physical horrors of the Passchendaele front, he
does so in a quiet, unemphatic fashion that is at the opposite extreme
from the methods of a writer like Barbusse. If one compares the
poem 'Third Ypres' with Blunden's later prose account of the same
events, one notices the greater detachment of the latter. *Undertones
of War* might, perhaps, be criticized, not for not telling the truth
about war, for its authenticity is patent, but for presenting only a
narrow segment of the truth. Unlike most of the other retrospective
works of 1928-30 it does not attempt either an implicit or an explicit
criticism of the war, or the manner of its conduct. Blunden's book is
marked by its quality of quiet acceptance of all experience, even the
most violent. As I have remarked in discussing his poetry, Blunden
was aware of his own intellectual and artistic limitations, and it was
this realization that led to the severe selectivity of *Undertones of
War*. Yet, within these deliberate limits, the book is a masterpiece.
And one can assume that for Blunden, and for many others of his
generation who had been haunted for a decade by the memories of
the trenches, it provided a means of living more readily with their
memories: its gentle, exact, observant prose preserved those experi-
ences and at the same time removed their cruelty.

Robert Graves's *Goodbye to All That*, published in 1929, is a
classic in the exacting art of autobiography. The differences between
Graves's and Blunden's books are instructive: the former is a full-
scale autobiography, moving from Graves's childhood and school-
days at Charterhouse through to his period as a professor in Egypt in
the mid-twenties. But the central chapters of the book are those in
which Graves describes his four years of wartime service in the Royal
Welch Fusiliers. Any autobiographical writer must project some
kind of persona whose experiences and attitudes he is attempting to
trace; the ultimate self may be an unknowable metaphysical abstrac-
tion, but the autobiographer must write about someone who remains
recognizable to the reader in different situations, even though he may
embody only a fraction of all the writer's possible attributes. Blun-
den's narrator was the reticent but observant 'harmless young
shepherd in a soldier's coat'. Graves, in contrast, appears in *Good-
bye to All That* as a vigorously eccentric personality, almost insuffer-
ably knowledgeable and opinionated, ironically self-possessed, and,
like Blunden, a keen observer, though of human foibles rather than
of natural phenomena. His prose is lucid, economical, and continu-
ally alive with anecdotes, which are always entertaining though, in
many cases, disconcertingly without feeling. Graves gives away far

more of his own personality than Blunden, but only, one feels, as much as he wishes to: the attitudes that governed his literary persona and which were expressed in his stylistic devices were undoubtedly part of a technique for psychological survival. He made a conscious effort to appear before the world as an embodiment of the 'stiff upper-lip' attitude without its customary inflexibility of mind, just as he learned whilst at Charterhouse to become an accomplished boxer as a defence against bullying. Graves describes very frankly the shattering effect that four years of war, combined with the repression of feeling, had upon him: the writing of *Goodbye to All That* was pre-eminently a means to the recovery of psychological stability and wholeness.

Graves was never an enthusiast for the war, although he regarded Sassoon's anti-war gesture as a mistake. For the most part, he felt that 'the only way out was the way through', and stoically resigned himself to being as good a soldier as possible: this was very much Sassoon's attitude when he returned to the Front for his final spell of duty in 1918. One of the unexpected things about Graves's attitude, as compared with other war poets, is his concern with regimental tradition and the minor rituals of service life. Although he had joined the Royal Welch Fusiliers quite by chance, he soon became intensely proud of the regiment and its history, and reflected sagely on the difference in morale between one battalion and another in the manner of a seasoned regular officer. Indeed, Graves sometimes gives the regular's impression of regarding the actual fighting as rather an interruption to the real business of soldiering. There was always an element in Graves's make-up that responds to ritual, and in his later years he came to see the poetic vocation as a ritual service of the White Goddess. During the Great War his devotion to regimental tradition may well have been a device for the preservation of psychic equilibrium, akin to Blunden's loving observation of nature.

The following extracts from Chapter XIV of *Goodbye to All That* give some idea of Graves's method and attitudes. The dry, detached tone, the mathematical precision, the calculated toughness, do not entirely conceal the hints of an underlying humanity, though they are an effective means of distancing and controlling experiences that might otherwise be overwhelmingly painful.

> Like everyone else, I had a carefully worked out formula for taking risks. In principle, we would all take any risk, even the certainty of death, to save life or maintain an important position. To take life we would run, say, a one-in-five risk, particularly if

there was some wider object than merely reducing the enemy's manpower; for instance, picking off a well-known sniper, or getting fire ascendancy in trenches where the lines came dangerously close. I only once refrained from shooting a German I saw, and that was at Cuinchy, some three weeks after this. While sniping from a knoll in the support line, where we had a concealed loophole, I saw a German, perhaps seven hundred yards away, through my telescopic sights. He was taking a bath in the German third line. I disliked the idea of shooting a naked man, so I handed the rifle to the sergeant with me. 'Here take this. You're a better shot than I am.' He got him; but I had not stayed to watch.

About saving the lives of enemy wounded there was disagreement; the convention varied with the division. Some divisions, like the Canadians and a division of Lowland territorials, who claimed that they had atrocities to avenge, would not only avoid taking risks to rescue enemy wounded but go out of their way to finish them off. The Royal Welch were gentlemanly: perhaps a one-in-twenty risk to get a wounded German to safety would be considered justifiable. An important factor in calculating risks was our own physical condition. When exhausted and wanting to get quickly from one point in the trenches to another without collapse, we would sometimes take a short cut over the top, if the enemy were not nearer than four or five hundred yards. In a hurry, we would take a one-in-two-hundred risk; when dead tired, a one-in-fifty risk. In battalions where morale was low, one-in-fifty risks were often taken in laziness or despair. The Munsters of the First Division were said by the Welsh to 'waste men wicked', by not keeping properly under cover while in the reserve lines. The Royal Welch never allowed wastage of this sort. At no time in the war did any of us believe that hostilities could possibly continue more than another nine months or a year, so it seemed almost worthwhile taking care; there might even be a chance of lasting until the end absolutely unhurt.

Such phrases as 'it seemed almost worthwhile taking care' and 'there might even be a chance' indicate the nonchalance that, on the surface at least, took the place of traditional heroics on the part of many front-line fighters.

Graves's autobiography contains a wealth of anecdote, of which a representative example is the one concerning the soldier charged with murdering a French civilian in an *estaminet*:

It seems that a good deal of cognac had been going round, and the

French civilian, who bore a grudge against the British because of his faithless wife, began to insult the private. He was reported, somewhat improbably, as having said: '*Anglais no bon, Allmand très bon. War fineesh, napoo les Anglais. Allmand win.*' The private had thereupon drawn his bayonet and run the man through. At the court-martial the private was exonerated; the French civil representative commending him for having 'energetically repressed local defeatism'.

But the most extraordinary of all Graves's anecdotes, which forms the imaginative centre of his wartime chapters, is the account of his own 'death' from wounds. During the Somme battle an eight-inch shell burst three paces behind him, severely wounding him; he lay unconscious in a dressing-station for more than twenty-four hours and was assumed to be dead; his commanding officer duly wrote a letter of condolence to Graves's mother. Then it was discovered that he was still alive and he was taken to hospital (he had in the meantime been included on an official casualty list as 'died of wounds').

> I was semi-conscious now, and aware of my lung-wound through a shortness of breath. It amused me to watch the little bubbles of blood, like scarlet soap-bubbles, which my breath made in escaping through the opening of the wound. The doctor came over to my bed. I felt sorry for him; he looked as though he had not slept for days.

He was sent back to a hospital in London where he made a good recovery: 'I heard here for the first time of my supposed death; the joke contributed greatly to my recovery. People with whom I had been on the worst terms in my life, wrote the most enthusiastic condolences to my mother.' Following such an experience, Graves felt more than usually isolated from the civilian population; he described his repulsion from the prevalent hysteria of the Home Front and commented, 'I found serious conversations with my parents all but impossible.'

Much of the hard brilliance in Graves's writing may be directly attributable to the effects of having lived through this Lazarus-like experience; one might expect it to make a permanent and incalculable change of sensibility. Graves's early poems show a clear division between harsh realism and the pursuit of bucolic fantasy; for several years after the war his verse was all in the latter mode. With the composition of *Goodbye to All That* he returned to a new and deeper realism: physical in the accounts of battle (partly based on a wartime diary) and psychological in the frank analysis of his own attitudes and motives. Above all, this is a magnificently inclusive book, comic as well as harrowing. Graves's reputation as a literary figure rests principally on his poems; but *Goodbye to All That* has played a prominent part in establishing it.

Blunden and Graves were both survivors of the Somme – the supreme crisis of British arms – and so, too, was Siegfried Sassoon, whose prose reminiscences of the war, as contained in the Sherston trilogy, deserve a place alongside *Undertones of War* and *Goodbye to All That*; though in a literary sense they are, it seems to me, a smaller achievement. In some respects the Sherston volumes fall rather unhappily between the separate forms of strict autobiography and the autobiographical novel. 'George Sherston' is not Siegfried Sassoon: it is evident that some of his personal and family circumstances are different. And yet the underlying assumption seems to be that the events of Sherston's wartime life can be identified with Sassoon's own experience (Sassoon states as much in his later and purely autobiographical volume, *Siegfried's Journey*). The major difference between Sassoon and Sherston is that the latter is not a poet: he is made to appear a simpler and somewhat less sophisticated figure than his creator. The account of his act of anti-war rebellion in *Memoirs of an Infantry Officer* may well have corresponded exactly to Sassoon's own behaviour in the summer of 1917, but it would have acquired greater resonance if we had been told that this was the action of the author of *The Old Huntsman* and *Counter-Attack*. In fact, Sassoon seems himself to have felt a certain unease on this point, for *Siegfried's Journey* overlaps untidily with *Memoirs of an Infantry Officer* and *Sherston's Progress*, published in 1936. Reading the trilogy in the light of *Siegfried's Journey* one has a sense of muffling and diminution: one's knowledge of what is left out prevents a straightforward response (and some of the devices seem merely irritating, such as the transparent disguises for characters who clearly stand for living people). But no doubt in 1928, when he embarked on the trilogy, Sassoon did not feel ready to present his experience to the world without some attempt at fictional concealment.

Despite its considerable length, the Sherston trilogy provides on an extended scale the basic paradigm on which so many wartime poems were based: a poignant contrast between rural England and the horrors of trench warfare; here exemplified in Sherston's pre-war life (which seems to have corresponded with Sassoon's very closely) as a country gentleman of leisure, devoting his time to hunting and cricket, and his subsequent transformation into an infantry officer at the Front.

For Sassoon in 1928 the greater part of *Memoirs of a Fox-Hunting Man* would have represented a deliberate thrusting-back of memory and imagination to the idyllic pursuits of pre-war days. The sense of innocence is well preserved: there is no feeling in these chapters that the carefree scene is already overshadowed by the prospect of war, although there is an odd proleptic hint in Chapter V when the local Master of Hounds asks the members of the Hunt 'to do everything in their power to eliminate the most dangerous enemy of the hunting man – he meant barbed wire'. Here and there we are aware of Sassoon's deliberate attempts, in an almost Proustian fashion, to recover the vanished past:

> Yet I find it easy enough to recover a few minutes of that grey south-westerly morning, with its horsemen hustling on in scattered groups, the December air alive with the excitement of the chase, and the dull green landscape seeming to respond to the rousing cheer of the huntsman's voice when the hounds hit off the line again after a brief check. Away they stream, throwing up little splashes of water as they race across a half-flooded meadow. Cockbird flies a fence with a watery ditch on the take-off side. 'How topping,' I think, 'to be alive and well up in the hunt'; and I spurt along the sound turf of a green park and past the front of a square pink Queen Anne house with blank windows and smokeless chimneys, and a formal garden with lawns and clipped yew hedges sloping to a sunk fence. A stone statue stares at me, and I wonder who lived there when the house was first built. 'I am riding past the past', I think, never dreaming that I shall one day write that moment down on paper; never dreaming that I shall be clarifying and condensing that chronicle of simple things through which I blundered so diffidently.

The scene is vividly evoked. The idea of being a living part of English rural tradition is familiar in writing about the war, as in the passages from D.H. Lawrence's letters already quoted. Yet the choice of words raises the problem of the relation between Sherston and the Sassoon of 1918: Sassoon has not merely clarified and condensed his memories, he has simplified them, and Sherston has been given a remarkably simple consciousness. The phrase 'through which I blundered so diffidently' is significant, for a diffident blundering describes very well one's impression of Sherston's progress through the world.

In August 1914 Sherston joins up, is commissioned, and goes to the Front. Home on leave in 1916 he reflects, 'Looking round the room at the enlarged photographs of my hunters, I began to realize that my past was wearing a bit thin. The War seemed to have made up its mind to obliterate all those early adventures of mine.' Sherston's army experiences are continued in *Memoirs of an Infantry Officer*; this book covers many of the same experiences as Sassoon's wartime poems, and sometimes describes the same events, but the mode of presentation is significantly different. Instead of the bitterness and hard outlines of the poems, the prose accounts are gently reflective and curiously undramatic. Sassoon is not coolly detached in the manner of Graves: he is constantly aware of his own involvement in the scenes around him, but manifests an attitude of uncertainty and diffidence: 'Anyhow, I hadn't expected the Battle of the Somme to be quite like this,' he reflects, on seeing the body of a young German soldier. His prose is always effective, and at its best has an excellent if rather casual lucidity. A good example is Sherston's account of capturing a trench single-handed:

> Just before I arrived at the top I slowed up and threw my two bombs. Then I rushed at the bank, vaguely expecting some sort of scuffle with my imagined enemy. I had lost my temper with the man who had shot Kendle; quite unexpectedly, I found myself looking down into a well-conducted trench with a great many Germans in it. Fortunately for me, they were already retreating. It had not occurred to them that they were being attacked by a single fool; and Fernby, with presence of mind which probably saved me, had covered my advance by traversing the top of the trench with his Lewis gun. I slung a few more bombs, but they fell short of the clumsy field-grey figures, some of whom half turned to fire their rifles over the left shoulder as they ran across the open toward the wood, while a crowd of jostling helmets vanished along the trench. Idiotically elated, I stood there with my finger in my right ear and emitted a series of 'view-holloas' (a gesture which ought to win the approval of people who still regard war as a form of outdoor sport). Having thus failed to commit suicide, I proceeded to occupy the trench – that is to say, I sat down on the fire-step, very much out of breath, and hoped to God the Germans wouldn't come back again.

One accepts the authenticity of this incident as part of Sassoon's own experience – Graves has attested to his recklessness as a front-line fighter – but there is a strangely artless manner in the description, almost as if Sassoon wants us to see Sherston as something of a Wodehousian silly ass, blundering blindly about the battle-field. It is, perhaps, as good a way as any of suppressing the embarrassment that must inevitably attend a first-person account of heroic behaviour. Graves would have treated the incident with greater sardonic emphasis, bringing out the anecdotal possibilities.

Some of Sassoon's best prose is to be found in the later chapters that describe the fighting before the Hindenburg Line in April 1917, when Sherston is wounded. The narrator's sense of humour is evident when, lying in a London hospital, he reflects on the various types of visitor he gets and his differing approaches to them:

Some Senior Officer under whom I'd served: Modest, politely subordinate, strongly imbued with the 'spirit of the Regiment' and quite ready to go out again. 'Awfully nice of you to come and see me, sir.' Feeling that I ought to jump out of bed and salute, and that it would be appropriate and pleasant to introduce him to 'some of my people' (preferably of impeccable social status). Willingness to discuss active service technicalities and revive memories of shared front-line experience.

Middle-aged or elderly Male Civilian: Tendency (in response to sympathetic gratitude for services rendered to King and Country) to assume haggard facial aspect of one who had 'been through hell'. Inclination to wish that my wound was a bit worse than it actually was, and have nurses hovering round with discreet reminders that my strength mustn't be overtaxed. Inability to reveal anything crudely horrifying to civilian sensibilities. 'Oh yes, I'll be out there again by the autumn.' (Grimly wan reply to suggestions that I was now honourably qualified for a home service job.) Secret antagonism to all uncomplimentary references to the German Army.

Charming Sister of Brother Officer: Jocular, talkative, debonair, and diffidently heroic. Wishful to be wearing all possible medal-ribbons on pyjama jacket. Able to furnish a bright account of her brother (if still at the front) and suppressing all unpalatable facts about the War. 'Jolly decent of you to blow in and see me.'

Hunting Friend (a few years above Military Service Age): Deprecatory about sufferings endured at the front. Tersely desirous of hearing all about last season's sport. 'By Jingo, that must have been a nailing good gallop!' Jokes about the Germans, as if throwing bombs at them was a tolerable substitute for fox-hunting. A good deal of guffawing (mitigated by remembrance that I'd got

a bullet hole through my lung). Optimistic anticipations of next
season's Opening Meet and an early termination of hostilities on
all fronts.

It was during the subsequent period of convalescence that Sherston-
Sassoon decided to make his gesture of protest against the continua-
tion of the war. The remainder of *Memoirs of an Infantry Officer*
describes his ensuing experiences, and ends with his arrival at Craig-
lockhart Hospital, here called 'Slateford'. In the final volume of the
trilogy, *Sherston's Progress* we hear about Sherston's period at
'Slateford', his admiring acquaintance with the neurologist, W.H.R.
Rivers (though there is nothing about Wilfred Owen); his subsequent
service in Ireland and Palestine, and his final return to the Western
Front in the spring of 1918. He is again wounded, and the book ends
with Sherston once more in a London hospital, being visited by
Rivers. This volume is the least satisfactory of the three; it attempts
to compress too large and varied a range of experiences in a small
compass, and lacks unity of feeling, having neither the poignancy of
the remembered rural pleasures of the *Fox-Hunting Man* or the con-
centration of the battle scenes in the *Infantry Officer*.

The trilogy is an incomplete success: Sassoon fails to achieve the
limited but intense clarity of observation of Blunden's memoirs, or
Graves's sharp, highly controlled focus. In his use of a quasi-fictional
persona he has avoided rather than solved some of the pressing
problems of writing autobiography. Nevertheless, the first two
volumes, at least, deserve a significant place in the literature of the
Great War, though a lower one than that occupied by Sassoon's war-
time poems. *Siegfried's Journey* deserves a place, too; it is a work of
some stylistic distinction, and usefully supplements the Sherston
trilogy, not always to the advantage of the latter. A further dimension
to Sassoon's autobiographical writing emerged when his *Diaries
1915-1918* appeared in 1983. This work describes experiences that
were later to appear in his poems and in the Sherston books and in
Siegfried's Journey. It shows how self-conscious a writer Sassoon
was in his retrospective mode, and how he was prepared to reshuffle
his material. Part III of *Sherston's Progress* is supposed to be made
up entirely of diary entries; that is true in a way, but Sassoon sub-
stantially rewrote the diary entries before they appeared in the latter
work, even while keeping the original dates of the entries. At times
he appears in the diaries in a vigorously self-critical mode. After
some studied passages of descriptive writing he adds, 'This is rather
portentous stuff. I have obviously been rereading *Lord Jim*; and the

mixture of *War and Peace* and *Howards End* contributes to the mental hotchpotch.' The diary includes Sassoon's poem, 'Return', written on 11 March 1916; an entry dated 29 March remarks, 'An example of entirely artificial emotionalism; the dead are underground all right, but they don't care whether I come back or not. This is the sort of poetry I'm always trying to avoid writing.'

Read and Blunden, Graves and Sassoon, were all infantry officers: most of the literary records of the war, whether in prose or verse, were written from that point of view. But one celebrated English writer has left a vigorous account of the artilleryman's experience. Wyndham Lewis, founder of the Vorticist movement and subsequently well known as a painter, novelist and amateur of politics and philosophy, joined up in 1916 and after some delay was commissioned in the Royal Garrison Artillery. He describes his wartime experiences in his entertaining autobiography, *Blasting and Bombardiering* (1937). It was, perhaps, appropriate that Lewis, the belligerent propagator of the geometrical, anti-humanistic aesthetics of Vorticism should have found his place in the artillery; as, too, did his former associate, T.E. Hulme, who was serving at a battery about a quarter of a mile away from Lewis when he was killed. (The two men had become estranged, and Lewis regretted that he had not made an attempt at reconciliation before Hulme's death.) In *Blasting and Bombardiering* Lewis wryly commented about his choice of the artillery: 'I could not have been in the infantry: I am not nearly blood-thirsty enough.' In this book Lewis expressed anti-war sentiments almost as strong as those of avowedly pacifist writers like Aldington or Remarque, though his tone is dryly contemptuous rather than angry or hysterical: he frequently speaks of the stupidity of the operations he observed. His remarks are very much conditioned by the period at which he was writing. Lewis adopted a right-wing stance in the 1930s, when he was aware that a new war was in preparation, and he wished to emphasize that he had had quite enough of the first one.

At his best, Lewis is one of the finest of modern prose writers, as is evident from the war chapters in his autobiography. The writing, though angular and even clumsy, is full of compelling visual detail, recalling Lewis's quality as a painter:

> I can only remember that in the air full of violent sound, very suddenly there was a flash near at hand, followed by further flashes, and I could see the gunners moving about as they loaded again. They appeared to be 11-inch guns – very big. Out of their throats had sprung a dramatic flame, they had roared, they had

moved back. You could see them, lighted from their mouths, as
they hurled into the air their great projectile, and sank back as
they did it. In the middle of the monotonous percussion, which
had never slackened for a moment, the tom-toming of intermin-
able artillery, for miles round, going on in the darkness, it was as
if someone had exclaimed in your ear, or something you had
supposed inanimate had come to life, when the battery whose
presence we had not suspected went into action.

Later, Lewis became an official war artist and gave expression to
similar scenes in the medium of painting. His grimly sardonic sense
of humour pervades *Blasting and Bombardiering*, which contains
some splendid anecdotes. There is an example in Chapter IX, called
'Hunted with Howitzers': Lewis and a small party of men are
attempting to reach an observation-post in an unspeakably muddy
section of the Passchendaele front. He notices that this post is in turn
observed by another observer, situated in a German balloon not far
above their heads; before they can reach the post they are subjected
to the fire of a German howitzer battery, expertly directed by the
aerial observer. It is particularly aimed at Lewis and a corporal, who
are taking refuge in a very inadequate shell-hole, already bracketed
by the enemy guns:

> I should think that you could count on the fingers of your hands
> the soldiers who have been fired at in this *personal* way by weapons
> of such dimensions – and a whole battery of them if it was the
> whole battery that was after us. For obviously for that to happen
> you have to have all the various factors that made it possible.
> First, a sausage-balloon sitting with impunity up in the air above
> you, upon a nice clear day: secondly the Observer in the balloon
> with plenty of time on his hands, and in the mood for a little sport:
> and thirdly, two men practically underneath it, in an empty land-
> scape. Again, were it a larger collection of people, then it would
> no longer be *personal*.

This jaunty detachment was characteristic of Lewis's temperament,
which liked to give the impression of being a keen but contemptuous
observer of the follies of humanity (not excluding himself), though it
may have been helped by writing at twenty years' distance from the
events he describes.[1]

---

[1] There are more immediate and equally vigorous accounts of Lewis's wartime experi-
ence in his letters to Ezra Pound in *Pound/Lewis* ed. T. Materer (New York, 1985).

In 1933 there appeared a unique memoir of the war, written by one who had served with Graves and Sassoon in the Second Battalion of the Royal Welch Fusiliers. *Old Soldiers Never Die* by Frank Richards is a remarkable book for a number of reasons: its author was neither an officer nor an idealistic volunteer; he served as a private from August 1914 to November 1918, most of that time at the Front, and survived without a scratch, although he was saved from death by what seems a whole succession of incredibly happy accidents. Richards had been a ranker in the old Regular Army, passing many years in India, and when the war broke he was in one of the first detachments of the British Expeditionary Force to see action in France. Although not a formally educated man, he was a natural writer, and *Old Soldiers Never Die* is a brilliant narrative. Richards's colloquial, salty, sardonic manner is far removed from the other retrospective accounts; he is not reflective, always keeps close to particular facets of the private soldier's experience, whether he is describing heroism under fire or some behind-the-lines episode of womanizing or scrounging, and yet frequently transcends his immediate context. Much of Richards's tough and comic narrative recalls the long-suffering humour of Shakespeare's humble soldiers; David Jones also caught this note in several passages of *In Parenthesis*, but Richards sustains it for a whole book. Some of its flavour can be seen in these remarks about a royal inspection, late in 1914: 'No king in the history of England ever reviewed more loyal or lousier troops than what His Majesty did that day. To look at us we were as clean as new pins, but in our shirts, pants and trousers were whole platoons of crawlers.'

Another fine autobiography published in 1933 is Guy Chapman's *A Passionate Prodigality*, which has never had as much recognition as it deserves, perhaps because it appeared when the vogue for war-narratives was already declining. Against all the odds, Chapman survived for three years as a young officer in France. His recollections are extraordinarily detailed, set down in plain but careful prose, and in places are very harrowing, particularly when he describes the horror of the waterlogged battlefields around Ypres in 1917. His tone is disillusioned, as in most English war writing of the late 1920s and early 1930s, but it is never shrill or sensational. Chapman acknowledges what he calls the 'compelling fascination' of war: 'no wine gives fiercer intoxication, no drug more vivid exaltation. Every writer of imagination who has set down in honesty his experience has confessed it. Even those who hate her most are prisoners to her spell...' *A Passionate Prodigality* is a work of pondered maturity, which well illustrates Paul Fussell's account of the intensely literary way in which so many educated young Englishmen reacted to the war. The title comes from Sir Thomas Browne, and the sections and chapters are prefaced with quotations from many different authors, from Skelton and Shakespeare and Dryden to Verlaine and Arnold Bennett and Ezra Pound.

It is instructive to compare the English war memoirs with a German work that I have already mentioned, Ernst Jünger's *The Storm of Steel*, of which the English translation appeared in 1929, with the subtitle, 'From the Diary of a German Storm-Troop Officer on the Western Front'. Jünger went through much the same experiences as his English counterparts, including the Somme fighting, but his attitude is remarkably different from theirs. He, too, records violent death, mutilation, and every kind of physical squalor and privation; yet at no point does his enthusiasm for the war falter; his patriotic fervour and idealism are unimpaired until the very end of the war – and subsequently. For Jünger, despite all he had seen and undergone – and he almost died of a lung wound – continued to exalt war as a great and ennobling experience. It is as though the subject-matter of Owen and Sassoon had been combined with the sentiments of Brooke and Grenfell. If one compares the following passage with the extract from Edmund Blunden's *Undertones of War* quoted on p.144, the contrast is brought into sharp emphasis. They are dealing with a similar topic, the fact that about the time of the Somme battle both armies adopted the steel helmet, and thereafter the character of the war changed:

> The spirit and the tempo of the fighting altered, and after the battle of the Somme the war had its own peculiar impress that distinguished it from all other wars. After this battle the German soldier wore the steel helmet, and in his features there were chiselled the lines of an energy stretched to the utmost pitch, lines that future generations will perhaps find as fascinating and imposing as those of many heads of classical or Renaissance times.

Whereas Blunden speaks ruefully of the helmet's 'ugly useful discomfort' and looks back nostalgically at the soldiers' soft caps and the primitive stage of the war associated with them, Jünger sees the helmeted German soldier as a classical figure of heroic energy. Whatever the English writers felt, for him the heroic mode of perception had not been superseded. Eric Maria Remarque's celebrated *All Quiet on the Western Front* (1929) represents another German picture of the war, and one much closer to that of the English writers.

Jünger's final words form a nationalistic outburst that anticipates the Nazi spirit (though he was to become a conservative anti-Nazi after Hitler took power): 'Though force without and barbarity within conglomerate in sombre clouds, yet so long as the blade of a sword will strike a spark in the night may it be said: Germany lives and Germany shall never go under!'

There were other kinds of war in 1914-18 from that of the trench-fighters, even though their experience was predominant. One of them, C.E. Montague, deploring the decline of chivalry during the struggle, had wistfully reflected that only amongst the airmen had the traditional habits of chivalry remained possible. This theme was enlarged on in *Sagittarius Rising* (1936), the autobiography of Cecil Lewis, who had served throughout the war as a pilot in the Royal Flying Corps. Lewis is an uneven writer, excellent in his descriptions of flying and aerial combat, but much less satisfactory in the purple passages that embody his reflections about life in general. His book gives a vivid picture of the aviator's life in the Great War, with its continual contrast between the luxury of life on the ground, many miles behind the lines, and the daily confrontation with death in the air, where the airmen were menaced not only by the Germans but by the instability of the rickety aircraft of the time. Lewis describes the joys of single-handed aerial combat, as against the impersonal slaughter of the trenches:

> It was like the lists of the Middle Ages, the only sphere in modern warfare where a man saw his enemy and faced him in mortal combat, the only sphere where there was still chivalry and honour. If you won, it was your own bravery and skill; if you lost, it was because you had met a better man.
>
> You did not sit in a muddy trench while someone who had no personal enmity against you loosed off a gun, five miles away, and blew you to smithereens – and did not know he had done it! That was not fighting; it was murder. Senseless, brutal, ignoble. We were spared that.

In his feelings about the romanticism of flying, Lewis has affinities with Antoine de Saint-Exupéry.

Other theatres of war also produced their literary memorials. Of these the most famous is T.E. Lawrence's *Seven Pillars of Wisdom*, first published in full in 1935 (a shorter version, *Revolt in the Desert* appeared in 1927). This book, which describes Lawrence's part in organizing the revolt of the Arabs against the Turks and their German allies, has long been regarded as a classic of autobiography. As a writer of narrative Lawrence had great gifts, and the scenes of action in his book are superb; but he was excessively given to reflections of a pretentious kind, which had an undermining effect on the quality of his prose. Lawrence is loth to let events speak for themselves; one is uncomfortably aware of his domineering personality, with its scarcely concealed pressures towards self-advertisement.

By contrast, another narrative from one of the minor side-shows of the war has had rather less than its share of recognition. Francis Brett Young's *Marching on Tanga*, a work of brilliant reportage rather than retrospective recollection, was published in 1917; it describes the campaign against the retreating German colonial army in German East Arica in 1916, carried out by Rhodesian and South African troops under the command of General Smuts. Young, one of the more interesting of the Georgian poets and a doctor by profession, was attached to the column as a medical officer. His simple, straightforward account describes an extraordinarily gruelling campaign: a rapid pace had to be kept up whilst contending with tropical heat, unexplored terrain, mosquitoes, fever, wild animals, as well as intermittent battles with the retreating enemy. Nothing could have been more remote from the characteristic experience of the troops bogged down in France, and no doubt many of them would have considered it a welcome change. Like them, Young brooded nostalgically about an ideal England that seemed all the more desirable in such exotic surroundings. In addition to the *Oxford Book of English Verse* he carried with him a Bartholomew map of England, 'and there I would travel magical roads, crossing the Pennines or lazing through the blossomy vale of Evesham, or facing the salt breeze on the flat top of Mendip at will'. But the real war was being won or lost in the trenches of France and Flanders. It was here that the major crisis of English civilization was centred, and where most of the writers who responded to it underwent the experiences that were subsequently matured into autobiography or fiction.

I conclude this chapter with a work that is a classic of modern autobiography, by a writer who though not a combatant was as physically and morally close to the war as many of the fighting men. This is Vera Brittain's *Testament of Youth*, first published in 1933. When the war started she was twenty-one, the daughter of a prosperous Derbyshire businessman, and had overcome much parental opposition, and many other difficulties, to leave a stifling, late-Victorian provincial milieu and get herself admitted to Oxford. Vera Brittain portrays her young self as ardent and idealistic and passionate for learning and ideas, like a George Eliot heroine. But once the

war started she found undergraduate life insupportable and after
a year she left Somerville, despite the disapproval of the college
authorities, to train as a volunteer nurse. She had a very hard war for
the next three years. Despite her sheltered upbringing and sensitive
temperament she became inured to treating soldiers whose wounds
were sometimes so bad they could not bear to look at them them-
selves. She was also in physical danger, from being nearly torpedoed
when on a troopship, and from being bombed in a military hospital
behind the lines in France. She was often in conflict with the stupid
and repressive exercise of authority (frequently but not invariably
male authority; among other things, *Testament of Youth* is a seminal
feminist text).

Vera Brittain had to endure physical privations sometimes not far
short of those of the soldiers: bad living conditions, poor food, lack
of sleep, as well as the harrowing daily experience of nursing the
wounded. After an attack they would be brought in in large numbers,
and given the fairly primitive surgery of the time and the non-existence
of antibiotics many of them died of gangrene. More than this, Vera
Brittain faced repeated tragedy in her private life; the brilliant young
man she was engaged to was killed in France at the end of 1915. His
death was followed by that of her two closest male friends, and of
her beloved brother on the Italian Front in 1918. Even when the war
had ended, fate could not leave her alone; after she had returned to
her studies in an Oxford that she found peculiarly unsympathetic,
the one female friend she made suddenly died of pneumonia; no
novelist would try to get away with anything so crude. Some of her
responses corresponded with those of male writers; when the Armis-
tice was declared in November 1918 Vera Brittain could feel no
excitement; like C.E. Montague, she found it had come too late.

Testament of Youth is not a work of obvious literary distinction.
The prose is pedestrian, occasionally banal, but the narrative is
vigorous and compelling. And now and then it achieves a memorable
exactness:

> Whenever I think of the War today, it is not as summer but always
> as winter; always as cold and darkness and discomfort, and an
> intermittent warmth of exhilarating excitement which made us
> irrationally exult in all three. Its permanent symbol, for me, is a
> candle stuck in the neck of a bottle, the tiny flame flickering in an
> ice-cold draught, yet creating a miniature illusion of light against
> an opaque infinity of blackness.

One of the most intense and poignant parts of the book is Vera

Brittain's description of nursing German prisoners at a military hospital in France in 1918, most them severely wounded and probably destined to die. It was here that she acquired a particularly strong conviction of the futility of war, which led to her later career as an internationalist, a pacifist and a crusader for the League of Nations. *Testament of Youth* is a work of retrospective insight and to some extent of retrospective wisdom, written up from the immediate responses in the author's wartime diary (which was published in 1981).

10: Retrospect II
Fiction

The difference between avowed autobiography and fiction with a strongly autobiographical flavour is often one of degree rather than of kind. Autobiography must, if it is to make any claims to literary attention, involve a good deal of selectivity and discrimination in ordering the writer's past experience; the novelist does much the same thing, but has more freedom in selecting and rearranging. The heavily autobiographical origin of some of the war novels of 1928-30 is unmistakable, and one or two books of the period could be placed in either category. This is particularly true of Sassoon's Sherston trilogy: it is usually regarded as a work of slightly disguised auto-biography, but its fictional elements are sufficiently evident for a literal-minded librarian to consider classifying all three books as novels. Some writers treated their experience both directly and fictionally. Thus, C.E. Montague followed up *Disenchantment* with a collection of stories, *Fiery Particles* (1923), several of which gave a fictional embodiment to ideas and observations included in the earlier book. One of the most entertaining of them describes the war-time careers of two privileged young officers, both safely ensconced in staff jobs, who go through the war collecting a variety of medals for their administrative services and without ever going anywhere near the Front. The interest of the story lies in the contrast between their respective characters: one of them is clever, cynical and quite without self-respect; the other is stupid, complacent, and genuinely believes – unlike his rival – that he *deserves* the numerous decora-tions he is accumulating.

One of the principal differences between the autobiography and the novel is that the latter offers a wider angle of vision: the auto-biographer is limited to the single thread of personal experience, while the novelist can supplement or enlarge on this by an imagina-tive penetration into the experience of others. Among war novels the

ultimate ideal, of course, remains *War and Peace*, with its vast move-
ments along the spectrum ranging from the utterly intimate to the
cosmic impersonality of history. No English writer approached this
scale, but one or two made attempts to render the war on a broad
canvas: notably R.H. Mottram in *The Spanish Farm Trilogy 1914-
1918*, and Ford Madox Ford in *Parade's End*. Both works appeared
between 1924 and 1928; Mottram's received an immediate though
rather short-lived fame, whereas Ford's – a far more distinguished
work of literary art – has never been able to attract a wide reader-
ship.

Mottram's three volumes, *The Spanish Farm*, *Sixty-Four, Ninety-
Four!* and *The Crime at Vanderlynden's*, were published separately,
and then brought together as a trilogy, together with some related
short stories, in 1927. Mottram did not attempt to provide a narra-
tive of front-line life: his battle-scenes are infrequent and lack convic-
tion. His principal characteristic is that he is imaginatively interested
in the enormous effort and organization that goes to keep a great
modern army in being. He saw the British Army in France as a self-
contained civilization, with all its complex hierarchies and social
codes. The three volumes are only loosely linked together, but each
of them is centred round the Vanderlyndens' 'Spanish Farm', a relic
of the seventeenth-century Spanish occupation of Flanders, and now
not far behind a sector of the British line. The book's dominating
character is Madeleine Vanderlynden, daughter of the house and its
effective manager, who is an attractive but shrewd young French-
woman; Mottram makes her not only a representative of her class,
nation and sex, but also something of an embodiment of the *Ewig-
Weibliche*, who symbolizes the continuity of essential human con-
cerns and remains indifferent to the ebb and flow of such trivialities
as wars. The other principal figure of the two first volumes is Geof-
frey Skene, a young English officer of the New Army, with whom
Madeleine has a brief and tenderly described affair (though she
remains in love with a local aristocrat, long since vanished in the
French army). Skene is carefully characterized, but remains a some-
what shadowy figure.

As a literary artist, Mottram has affinities with his friend John
Galsworthy, who contributed a preface to the trilogy. That is to say,
he is – in a not wholly pejorative sense – a superficial writer, who is
most at home in rendering the characteristics of the social surface,
rather than in plunging to moral or psychological depths. Like
Galsworthy, his basic criteria are social. His presentation of Madeleine
is convincing, but she remains a figure who has been very skilfully

assembled from a number of constituent attributes; although a certain imaginative fusion has taken place, she lacks the totally autonomous quality of the great characters of fiction. Mottram remains at his best when he is writing about the army as a social organism, in respect of which the individuality of his characters is necessarily subordinated. His prose is unsubtle, even coarse-grained, but always clear, and moves forward with a steady narrative thrust – for all its length, the trilogy is remarkably readable. Many passages reveal the presence in Mottram of an essayist rather akin to C.E. Montague. The following extract, from near the end of *Sixty-Four, Ninety-Four!* describes Skene's response to the news of the Armistice; it shows Mottram's painstaking but somewhat unselective notation of physical detail, and it exactly echoes Montague's feeling that victory had come too late for anyone to feel much satisfaction in it:

> Rounds! He went outside into the chill and darkness of that November night. At the small factory where his men were billeted, he found his sentry; in the little pay-office, his superior New Army Corporal, reading a paper-covered novel over a brazier; – beyond, in the low sheds where his men were sleeping, his mules tied up and his carts stacked, all was in darkness and silence. 'Celebrations!' he thought. Emerging again into the little paved street, he met what to him was typical of war as he had waged it. In the lampless glimmer of the night, a string of square boxes on wheels, known as limbers, was being drawn with a springless rattle over the pavé, by weary mules, beside whom were men just sufficiently awake to guide them. At the head a muffled figure, for all the world like the leader of some North Pole Expedition, was plodding beside a somnambulistic horse.
>
> Abreast of Skene he muttered:
> 'This'll get me to Werlies, I s'pose! Is it true they've chucked it?'
> Skene nodded. 'I believe the Bosche are going to sign the Armistice terms in the morning!'
> 'Good job. We should have chucked it, if they hadn't!'
> And he stumped on.
> Skene pulled off his boots and got into his blankets. 'Too long,' he thought. 'Who cares now?'
> He had forgotten that this was Victory.

The third volume of the trilogy, *The Crime at Vanderlynden's*, is lighter in tone. It describes the efforts of a junior staff officer called Dormer to discover the perpetrators of a minor piece of damage at the Vanderlynden farm, for which a British soldier is allegedly responsible. The narrative forms, in effect, a humorous detective story, as Dormer travels the length and breadth of the British forces in France in vain pursuit of the criminal (or even of anyone who knows anything at all about the incident), himself chased by urgent directives from higher military authority, for by now the initially trifling incident has snowballed into a major issue affecting relations between the British army and the French civilian population. It affords Mottram the opportunity for some mild satire on the extra-military preoccupations of the Base that were such a vexation to the front-line troops; it also enables him to paint a large-scale picture, as we follow Dormer in his investigations, of the numerous ramifications of the army establishment behind the lines.

Henry Williamson, in an essay called 'Reality in War Literature' published in 1934, left a harsh judgement on *The Spanish Farm Trilogy*. Whilst admitting that it gives a fairly representative picture of the English soldier in France, he complains that 'the battle scenes are deficient and unsatisfying: they no more recreate actuality than a picture of paper and orange peel on Hampstead Heath or Coney Island beach after an August week-end recreates the life and turmoil of the happy masses'.[1] Undoubtedly, Mottram is at his weakest in such scenes, and one assumes that his original experience was much less extensive than Williamson's. But his trilogy, though constantly faltering before the depths of experience, does convey an effective picture of the quality of life behind the lines, and indicates something of the relations between the British soldiers and the French population. He is skilful, too, in showing us his representative Englishman, Skene, through the eyes of the archetypal Frenchwoman, Madeleine. He is, at the very least, a good story-teller.

Parade's End is a trilogy or a tetralogy, depending on whether one accepts the final volume, *Last Post*, as an integral part of the total design. The first section, *Some Do Not*, came out in 1924, *No More Parades* in 1925, and *A Man Could Stand Up* in 1926. *Last Post* appeared in 1928; it seems that Ford wrote it because of the importunate desire of a woman friend to know what happened to his characters, and a few years later he virtually disowned it, saying that if the work was ever to appear in a single volume he would like it to be as a trilogy. *Last Post* is, indisputably, very different in tone and technique from the first three volumes: it represents a certain desire on Ford's part to tie up loose ends, and at the same time to adopt a

---

[1] *Linhay on the Downs*, (London, 1934), pp.224-62.

radically different mode of narration. Ford's critics are at variance about the place of *Last Post* in the sequence: Robie Macauley and Richard Cassell believe that it is essential to round off the work; whereas John Meixner has argued vehemently against this opinion, claiming that *Parade's End* forms an artistic whole only as a trilogy, and he is supported in this by Graham Greene in his introduction to the Bodley Head edition.[2] I incline towards the latter opinion; *Last Post* seems to be so loosely connected as to form a detached sequel rather than an integral part of the novel. As Meixner says, the trilogy, beginning with Ford's hero, Christopher Tietjens, travelling in a luxuriously appointed railway compartment, and ending, in the last paragraph of *A Man Could Stand Up*, with Tietjens celebrating Armistice Day in the empty flat from which his vindictive wife has stripped all the furniture, does have a distinct unity and symmetry.

Parade's End deals with the long martyrdom of Christopher Tietjens, officer and gentleman, who is subject to constant persecution; from his wife, the beautiful sexual terrorist Sylvia, and, during the war, from his military superiors and from powerful civilians at home. *Parade's End* is the finest novel by an Englishman to have been produced by the Great War; but at the same time, it can hardly be regarded simply as a 'war novel', as can some of the other books discussed in this chapter. Indeed, the whole of the magnificent opening section of *Some Do Not* takes place some years before the outbreak of war. Nevertheless, *Parade's End* offers a profound imaginative analysis of the effect of the war on the traditional patterns of English life. We see a bringing together of the several dominant themes which, I have tried to suggest, characterized the literature of the Great War: the supersession of the Hero as a tangible ideal; a nostalgic love of rural England, combined with an anguished sense that centuries of English tradition were being overthrown; the alienation of the soldier from the civilians. Ford embodies all these themes in Christopher Tietjens, whose presence provides the necessary unity of the first three volumes (he is largely absent from the scene in *Last Post*), and who is at the same time made to bear an unusually wide range of significance: he is the last true Tory, the final anachronistic embodiment of the virtues of the eighteenth-century English gentleman, an Anglican saint, even something of a

---

[2] See Robie Macauley, 'Parade's End', in *Modern British Fiction*, ed. M. Schorer (New York, 1962); Richard A. Cassell, *Ford Madox Ford: A Study of His Novels*, (Baltimore, 1961); and John A. Meixner, *Ford Madox Ford's Novels*, (Minneapolis, 1962).

Christ-figure, turning the other cheek to his persecutors. And yet Tietjens is always recognizable as a living human being: fair, red-faced, large, slow-moving.

In the opening paragraph of *Some Do Not*, Ford brilliantly places Tietjens and his friend Macmaster in their appropriate context in the pre-war ruling class:

> The two young men – they were of the English public official class – sat in the perfectly appointed railway carriage. The leather straps to the windows were of virgin newness; the mirrors beneath the new luggage racks immaculate as if they had reflected very little; the bulging upholstery in its luxuriant, regulated curves was scarlet and yellow in an intricate, minute dragon pattern, the design of a geometrician in Cologne. The compartment smelt faintly, hygienically of admirable varnish; the train ran as smoothly – Tietjens remembered thinking – as British gilt-edged securities. It travelled fast; yet had it swayed or jolted over the rail joints, except at the curve before Tonbridge or over the points at Ashford where these eccentricities are expected and allowed for, Macmaster, Tietjens felt certain, would have written to the company. Perhaps he would even have written to *The Times*.

They live in a world which is ordered, controlled, predictable (even the railway upholstery's curves are both luxuriant and regulated); a world, too, of security and conspicuous consumption. And yet it is not entirely Tietjens's world, as the clear note of distancing irony in this description suggests; the succeeding paragraphs show that it is the young Scottish arriviste, Macmaster, who is the conscious upholder of Edwardian ruling-class attitudes. Tietjens, on the other hand, moves through this world with considerable indifference to the refinement of its *moeurs*. He is in but not of it – an outstandingly able mathematician working in the Imperial Department of Statistics – and his real allegiances are rooted in an older England, symbolized by the family home, Groby, in the North Riding.

Tietjens and what he stands for are heavily romanticized by Ford. Half-German by birth, and the precocious child of a cosmopolitan, artistic household, Ford had had little opportunity to make extensive observations of the English gentry. There is both a simplicity and a glamour in his picture of Tietjens's Tory ideals that suggests a foreigner's romantic image of England; hence, perhaps, the higher reputation of *Parade's End* in America (William Carlos Williams claimed that the four novels 'constitute the English prose master-piece of their time'). Yet Ford's image is exaggerated rather than false: he shows us a familiar subject in an unfamiliar light, which may distort but also illuminates. Tietjens, the Yorkshire squire, stands for a more remote England than the Liberal England, centred on the weekend cottage in the Home Counties, of Forster and the Georgian poets; he preserves something of the feudal manner. In *A Man Could Stand Up*, Tietjens reflects in the trenches: 'The Feudal Spirit was broken. Perhaps it would therefore be harmful to Trench Warfare. It used to be comfortable and cosy. You fought beside men from your own hamlet under the leadership of the parson's son.'

One finds, too, an almost Gothic romanticism in Tietjens's conviction that there is a curse on Groby because the house was once dispossessed from its Catholic owners (the Tietjens family came over from Holland with William and Mary), and that the curse will not be lifted until Groby is once more in Catholic hands (as will happen when it is inherited by Tietjens's son, whom Sylvia is having brought up as a Catholic). Yet his visions of England have affinities with those entertained during the war years by writers of quite different temperament. The following extract from one of Tietjens's reveries in the front line, evoked by hearing a cornet player practising an air by Purcell, recalls the passages from Lawrence's wartime letters quoted in a previous chapter:

> The only satisfactory age in England!...Yet what chance had it today? Or, still more, tomorrow? In the sense that the age of, say, Shakespeare had a chance. Or Pericles! or Augustus!
>
> Heaven knew, we did not want a preposterous drum-beating such as the Elizabethans produced – and received. Like lions at a fair...But what chance had quiet fields, Anglican sainthood, accuracy of thought, heavy-leaved, timbered hedgerows, slowly creeping plough-lands moving up the slopes?...Still, the land remains...
>
> The land remains...It remains!...At that same moment the dawn was wetly revealing; over there in George Herbert's parish ...What was it called?...What the devil was its name? Oh, Hell! ...Between Salisbury and Wilton...The tiny church...But he refused to consider the ploughlands, the heavy groves, the slow high-road above the church that the dawn was at that moment wetly revealing – until he could remember that name...He refused to consider that, probably even today, that land ran to... produced the stock of...Anglican sainthood. The quiet thing!

In part, the random, fragmentary quality of the writing here can be regarded as expressing Tietjens's disordered consciousness, still not properly recovered from shell-shock and amnesia. But these stylistic devices occur with uncomfortable frequency in the later parts of *Parade's End*; compared with the masterly writing of *Some Do Not*, their prose is apt to be uncontrolled and fluid, and the use of dots as punctuation becomes obsessive.

Like Lawrence, Ford was very conscious of living in a doomed society, though some of the reflections by which Tietjens expresses this conviction read a little oddly. As when, in *Some Do Not*, Tietjens is in earnest conversation with his brother Mark, and glances at the fountain of the Inner Temple by which they are standing: 'He considered the base of the fountain that was half full of leaves. This civilization had contrived a state of things in which leaves rotted by August.' Unlike Lawrence, Ford dramatizes rather than describes his conviction of social decay; there is nothing equivalent to the retrospective diatribes of *Kangaroo*. Tietjens is constantly shown as the honourable man harried by the low, unworthy forces that manifest themselves when the opulent Edwardian upper-class world, so vividly evoked in the novel's opening paragraphs, becomes corrupt in the atmosphere of war. Macmaster, the energetic social climber whom Tietjens has befriended and helped, picks his friend's brains and rises to a pinnacle of bureaucratic eminence, whilst Tietjens remains an obscure infantry officer. Tietjens is disgraced when his bank unjustly refuses to meet his cheques. We learn that the banker responsible is one of Sylvia's admirers. She explains to Tietjens:

> 'But of course he hates you for being in the army. All the men who aren't hate all the men that are. And, of course, when there's a woman between them, the men who aren't do all they can to do the others in. When they're bankers they have a pretty good pull...'

And from Sylvia Tietjens suffers many humiliations; in his study of their relationship Ford shows great psychological insight. For several years they have sustained a marriage without mutual love; indeed, Sylvia has actively despised Tietjens. But when he falls in love with the young suffragette Valentine Wannop, Sylvia's jealousy turns into a violent sexual passion for her husband, and when he fails to respond she turns to extremes of cruelty. Sylvia, though a monster, never entirely alienates the reader's sympathy. As V.S. Pritchett has shrewdly commented: 'One has a sneaking sympathy for his wife who at one moment complains that her husband is trying to be Jesus

Christ as well as the misunderstood son of a great landowner. Her cruelties are an attempt to turn a martyr into a man'.[3]

The word 'martyr' is indeed significant. Ford is trying to write a novel about a particular kind of hero; not the towering martial heroes of the Renaissance whose insufficiencies for the life of the Western Front had been sardonically glanced at by Barbusse; nor the ardent young votaries of the early months of the war, whose spirit was summed up in Julian Grenfell's 'Into Battle'. In so far as Tietjens is intended by his creator to be more than a private man, to embody certain national traditions and habits of mind, he has remote affinities with the heroes of epic, though he reflects Virgilian *pietas* rather than Homeric *virtù*. More specifically, Tietjens is a passive and suffering hero, whose triumphs arise, not from violent action, but from patience (derived from *patior*, to suffer). The great example in English of this kind of hero is the Christ of *Paradise Regained*. Yet Ford, working without Milton's theological frame of reference, is less able to convince us of Tietjens's ultimate triumph. The novel (as opposed to such sharply generic forms as the thriller and the western) is not an easy form in which to accommodate heroic figures; its natural bias is so much to the realistic, the typical, the ordinary, that the presence of any figure of conspicuous stature and virtue is liable to set up ironic tensions. The drama remains, still, a more convincing vehicle for such types. In our final glimpse of Tietjens in *Last Post*, he has retired into quiet country life with Valentine, as a small-holder and antique-dealer; Sylvia has at least abated her hostility, and this perhaps represents a triumph for Tietjens, but he is now purely a private man and not a representative figure. His ancestral home, Groby, is leased to a crazy and destructive American woman; the symbolism is unmistakable.

In those scenes of *Parade's End* that deal specifically with the war in France, Tietjens's role as a suffering figure is underlined. In the opening chapter of *No More Parades*, Tietjens refuses – for very good reason – to give compassionate leave to a Welsh private called O Nine Morgan. A few minutes later the man is killed by a shell splinter. Tietjens bends over the body:

> The heat from the brazier was overpowering on his bent face. He hoped he would not get his hands all over blood, because blood is very sticky. It makes your fingers stick together impotently. But there might not be any blood in the darkness under the fellow's

---

3 'Talented Agrarians', *New Statesman*, 2 August 1963.

back where he was putting his hand. There was, however: it was very wet.

Tietjens associates Morgan's death with his refusal of leave, and assumes a corresponding burden of guilt. Again, in the sustained section set in the trenches in *A Man Could Stand Up,* Tietjens rescues the young subaltern, Aranjuez, after he had been partly buried by a falling shell; he is carrying Aranjuez to safety when the boy suddenly runs off screaming, with his hands to his face. Tietjens thinks, disapprovingly, that Aranjuez has lost his nerve. Only later does he hear that he had been hit by a sniper and has lost an eye. Tietjens, already tormented beyond endurance by his private life, has to bear the infantry officer's common load of compassion and guilt for the sufferings of his men. He is also subjected to the animus of his new commanding officer, General Campion, a friend of Sylvia's, who transfers Tietjens to the ignominious task of guarding prisoners of war.

These trench scenes frequently manifest the excessive fluidity of writing that is one of the faults of the later sections of *Parade's End.* And Henry Williamson attacked them in his essay, 'Reality in War Literature', for inaccuracy of military detail and a general air of inauthenticity. Nevertheless, to an uninitiated reader, and despite their stylistic weaknesses, they convey a compelling impression of front-line life; more vividly, in fact, than many exact documentary descriptions. Ford was invariably an impressionistic artist rather than a reporter.

This discussion of *Parade's End* has looked at only a few of its salient features, and has not done justice to its outstanding literary qualities. A full analysis, for instance, would trace Ford's virtuoso use of time shifts in the first part of *Some Do Not* and would examine in detail the superbly sensitive effects he could achieve in his impressionistic prose, and the richness of character portrayal. Tietjens himself, Sylvia, Valentine, General Campion, Edith Ethel Duchemin, all have an instinctive vitality. At the same time, one admits the work's unevenness: effects which were triumphant in the early parts become weakly repetitive in later ones. In particular, some of Ford's uses of time-shift seem like devices for evading a possibly tricky narrative climax. The great expanse of the three – or four – volumes makes it clear that Ford was weak at sustaining the architectonics of a large fictional structure; his numerous successes are all local rather than large-scale, and *Parade's End* is, *in toto,* rather less than the sum of its distinguished parts.

Yet the work's traditional novelistic virtues do, in my view undoubtedly transcend its failures of technique. In contrast to other prose works produced by the Great War, *Parade's End* offers little concrete documentation but much briliant insight into the effects of that war. Tietjens's romantic Tory England was an extravagant concept; but its affinities with the more modest visions of the poets in uniform are sufficient to produce a recognizable picture. As I have suggested, *Parade's End*, more than any other work, succeeds in combining the dominant literary preoccupations of the war.

In his discussion of *Parade's End*, V.S. Pritchett remarked, 'As a character Tietjens escapes from the cliché of almost all the war novels of that time in which the hero conveys that the whole war has been declared against him personally.' This remark leads us to a very different novel, written by one who had been a young acquaintance of Ford's in pre-war literary circles: Richard Aldington's *Death of a Hero*, published in 1929. If *Parade's End* is an attempt to delineate a hero of a rare and particular kind, then *Death of a Hero*, which is a very much cruder work, undertakes a savage debunking of the whole concept of heroism. As a very young man, before 1914, Aldington had been an Imagist poet of rather fragile delicacy; he was deeply embittered by the war, and his later literary personality became increasingly rancorous and disagreeable, though his autobiography, *Life for Life's Sake*, contains some vigorous anecdotes and an absorbing account of Pound's early London circle.

On the face of it, *Death of a Hero* tells the life-story of George Winterbourne, a young painter, who grows up in and escapes from an atmosphere of stifling Victorian respectability, enjoys a brief taste of moral and cultural freedom in pre-war London bohemia, joins the army, and is killed a few days before the Armistice. It is a wilfully formless book, which Aldington unashamedly used as a vehicle for his own lengthy first-person reflections on life and ideas. Indeed, a sizeable portion of the novel is taken up by these interpolated essays. Even in the dramatic and narrative portions, the pressure of the author's presence is always felt, and the book might be described as a massive ejaculation of pent-up venom. Seldom can a work of fiction have been written in such a consistently sour and hectoring tone: Aldington hammers away with coarse sarcasm and derision at a large number of predictable targets: the Victorians, the Edwardians, the upper-classes and Establishment generally, civilians in the Great War, the higher command in the British Army. In one or two places, the author's intensity of feeling raises these interludes to a higher plane than nagging:

'You have a vendetta of the dead against the living.' Yes, it is true,
I have a vendetta, an unappeased longing for vengeance. Yes, a
vendetta. Not a personal vendetta. What am I? O God, nothing,
less than nothing, a husk, a leaving, a half-chewed morsel on the
plate, a reject. But an impersonal vendetta, an unappeased con-
science crying in the wilderness, a river of tears in the desert. What
right have I to live? Is it five million, is it ten million, is it twenty
million?...

On Sundays the Union Jack flies over the cemetery at Etaples.
It's not so big as it was in the old wooden-cross days, but it's still
quite large. Acres and acres. Yes, acres and acres. And it's too late
to get one's little lot in the acres. Too late, too late...

In the face of such heavy authorial intervention, George Winter-
bourne is not much more than a briskly manipulated puppet. Never-
theless, his adventures in the pre-1914 literary and artistic avant-
garde are entertaining and illuminate the period: among various
other lampoons, Aldington offers a vindictive portrait of Ford as Mr
Shobbe. Yet Aldington's own animus is always evident, giving an
excessively personal flavour to the satirical observation. Winter-
bourne becomes heavily entangled with two beautiful girls, Elizabeth
– whom he marries – and Fanny, and his attempts to maintain a
ménage à trois fail miserably, despite their theoretical moral emanci-
pation. He tries to keep up an uneasy triangular relationship with
Fanny and Elizabeth when he is on leave, but they get bored when
he talks about his experiences. They think his abstracted, half-lost
manner – common among soldiers returning from the trenches – is
rather absurd, and the dirt engrained in his hands positively distaste-
ful. George, they conclude, is not the man he once was, while he
comes to feel betrayed by them.

The situation is drawn directly from Aldington's own circum-
stances. Elizabeth is a portrait of H.D. – Hilda Doolittle – whom he
married in 1913: 'A slender figure in red silk; black, glossy hair
drawn back from a high intellectual forehead; large, very intelligent
dark eyes; a rather pale, rather Egyptian-looking face with promi-
nent cheek-bones, slightly sunken cheeks and full red lips; a nervous
manner'. Fanny is drawn from Dorothy (otherwise Arabella) Yorke,
who became Aldington's lover, and who was an expatriate Ameri-
can, like H.D.

After George has joined the army he looks admiringly at a group
of seasoned front-line troops returning from leave; he is seized by an
exalted sense of masculine exclusiveness and contempt for women,

such as we have already observed in Sassoon and Owen (though unlike them, Aldington was vehemently heterosexual):

> 'By God!' he said to himself, 'you're men, not boudoir rabbits and lounge lizards. I don't care a damn what your cause is – it's almost certainly a foully rotten one. But I do know you're the first real men I've looked upon. I swear you're better than the women and the half-men, and by God! I swear I'll die with you rather than live in a world without you.'

Here Aldington recognizes, in almost traditionally romantic terms, the heroic stature of the soldiers. But his main concern in the battle sections of *Death of a Hero* (which take up less than half the total length of the novel) is to show how their heroism is consistently wasted and betrayed by the 'foully rotten' cause for which they are fighting. These chapters contain by far the best writing in *Death of a Hero*; less digressive and strident than the pre-war sections, conveying the nature of front-line experience, including such horrors as gas-attacks, with a fierce direct realism, relieved at times by passages of striking metaphor: 'From about half a mile to the north, southwards as far as he could see, the whole front was a dazzling flicker of gun-flashes. It was if giant hands covered with huge rings set with searchlights were being shaken in the darkness, as if innumerable brilliant diamonds were flashing great rays of light'. Many of the descriptive passages in Aldington's novel are not much inferior to the other prose accounts that I have discussed. Yet to compare them with Blunden or Graves is to become aware of his limitations: he is concerned to impose, not merely to trace, a pattern of experience. He lacks the patient exactness and detachment of the finest autobiographical writers. *Death of a Hero* is written to advance a thesis; in this case, that the war was wholly pointless and fraudulent, and those who took part in it were wantonly robbed of life and its possibilities. The danger with didactic fiction is that one's attention is deflected from its quality as literary art to the nature of the argument. In Aldingon's novel, the approach is so crude, so oversimplifying, that the argument loses conviction by excess of emphasis. An attitude that seems altogether convincing when expressed in the brief compass of one of Sassoon's savage wartime lyrics seems merely rhetorical when blown up into a novel of over 400 pages. *Death of a Hero* does not, in short, make effective propaganda for the pacifist case.

One obvious reason lies in Aldington's use of a single vehicle of consciousness, and one very close to his own state of mind: inevitably one feels, in Pritchett's words, 'that the whole war has been declared against him personally'. Barbusse, an earlier anti-war novelist, avoided this in *Under Fire*, subtitled 'the story of a squad', by describing the effects of war on a group of comrades, rather than a single exacerbated sensibility. For George Winterbourne, the war seems merely the culininating element in a whole series of burdens that he has had to bear from childhood: his parents, his stultifying bourgeois background, the trying entanglement with the two girls he loves. Admittedly the war kills him, and Aldington turns him into a figure of significant pathos by suggesting that, in effect, Winterbourne virtually committed suicide when under fire, and by placing his death only a few days before the Armistice; thereby giving him some of the terrible poignancy that in real life was acquired by Wilfred Owen.

In *Death of a Hero* we are aware of several successive stages in the development of Aldington's own attitudes: we have the young rebel who was one of the signatories of the *Blast* manifesto of 1914, eager to blow up the remains of Victorian respectability; the disillusioned soldier, turning to a Sassoon-like bitterness; the iconoclast of the 1920s, taking part in the fashionable debunking of former idols, and with a strong flavour, too, of D.H. Lawrence's tirades against English hypocrisy and spiritual deadness. It was too strong a mixture for the artistic coherence of the novel.

It is interesting to compare *Death of a Hero* with H.D.'s auto-biographical novel about her life during the war, *Bid Me to Live*, which was first drafted in 1927 but not published until 1960. This, too, is something of a *roman à clef*, in which Hilda is 'Julia' married to 'Rafe Ashton' (who has Aldington's initials), who is having an affair with her friend 'Bella'. The novels are of very different kinds; Aldington's is long, explicit and argumentative, reducing situations to a poster-like boldness and simplicity; H.D.'s is very short, elusive, poetic, with a modernist fluidity in the treatment of time. Yet there are recognizable common elements, like the description of the Aldingtons' flat in Mecklenburgh Square, and references to Herrick's poem, 'To Anthea', from which H.D. takes her title. And Julia's remarks about how her husband has been sadly transformed by the war seem to support George's complaints in *Death of a Hero*:

> His moods were more violent. He was not really the young officer on leave; that was not Rafe, well, let it be not-Rafe; the disin-tegrating factor was the glance, the look, the throwing aside of the uniform and the turn of the head, a stranger standing over by the

book-shelf *was* Rafe Ashton. That is my husband, that is the man I married...Julia Ashton is the last person in the world to minimise the thing he goes through. Back and forth from France – now he is actually enjoying it. Now he likes it. But I cannot serve God and Mammon, not serve poet and hearty over-sexed ('we have them on the run') young officer on leave. I love you Rafe, but stay away, don't come back...

Julia comes across as intensely self-absorbed, and no doubt H.D. was too. Rafe appears in a better light in her novel than Elizabeth does in Aldington's, though in neither of them is there much sense of the sadness and human cost of such estrangement, aggravated if not wholly caused by the war.

Like other survivors, Aldington wished to show the contrast between the glittering but fragile pre-war order and its violent destruction, or its corruption from within, during the war years. He had this much in common with Ford, but, unlike Ford, was not able to focus his perceptions in a truly representative central character; Tietjens represents a class, a society, a tradition, without losing his humanity; Winterbourne is no more than an isolated agonized consciousness. Yet both writers present the pre-war order on the eve of its destruction: Aldington by his rambling excursion back into Victorian times, Ford by the packed microcosm of Tietjens's weekend at Rye in the first part of *Some Do Not*.

A similar intention is evident in H.M. Tomlinson's novel of 1930, *All Our Yesterdays*. Tomlinson was not, it seems to me, a novelist by conviction, but a distinguished journalist who used the novel as a vehicle for reflections and observations, without a firmly established structure of plot, action and characterization. Yet his book, though imperfect as fiction, is extremely interesting and contains some fine prose. It is narrated by a shadowy unnamed figure who combines his personal narrative with the prerogatives of the omniscient author. The story opens in the East End of London at the turn of the century, when we are introduced to a family called the Bolts, followed by a spirited description of Mafeking night. Later, there is a lengthy Conradian interlude about the adventures of Jim Maynard, a journalist friend of the narrator's, in Darkest Africa. We learn, too, of the activities of Charley, the Bolts' eldest son, who has given up schoolteaching for journalism. But Tomlinson seems to have not much more than a perfunctory interest in these characters, and his notion of constructing a novel was artless in the extreme. These opening chapters, meant to give an impression of the multifariousness of the

Edwardian world, are thin and slow-moving. They also show Tom-
linson's less impressive attributes as a stylist: reared in the traditions
of 'fine writing', he was liable to engage in the bellettristic embellish-
ment of trivialities.

In the wartime section, however, the book comes properly alive,
and the writing, though always careful, even elegant, gains a new
force and conviction. The plot still remains secondary – we are
shown something of the everyday tragedy that befalls the Bolt family
– but much of the narrative description is superb, and derived, no
doubt, from Tomlinson's own experiences as a war correspondent.
Particularly memorable is the account of a journey by train across
the sunlit fields of Northern France in August 1914, just ahead of the
advancing German army, culminating in a deserted, apprehensive
Paris, which, before the Battle of the Marne, was hourly expecting
the entry of the enemy. Tomlinson had a subtle, reflective mind,
which was well able to grasp the complexities of experience. If,
ultimately, *All Our Yesterdays* can be classed as an anti-war book it
is in a very different vein from *Death of a Hero*. Thus, in the passages
to which I have just referred, Tomlinson vividly renders the excite-
ment and confusion of war, as well as the fear of the advancing
Germans. At the same time, he sets against this the calm unconcern
of the peasants in the countryside through which the train is passing
with such trifling irritations as war:

> If they were not undismayed, they baffled the prompting to panic.
> Tough stuff, common men and women! An enemy, with terrors
> which could only be hinted, was at their doors. Yet it is hard to
> forsake one's door. There are the cows to be fed, and the legumes
> for the winter to be tended, the sick child, the gates to be watched
> at the road crossing, the lock at the canal, the barn to be roofed,
> the railway trucks to be shunted; therefore the unimportant ones
> continue to revolve this earth, without knowing why. Wheat must
> grow. The earth should not cease to turn from morning to night,
> and back to morning again, until a veritable comet smite it finally
> from the blue. They paused, these folk, and looked severely to the
> distance when we heard thunder begin on the skyline. The guns!
> They did not pretend that thunder was any better than it sounded;
> then they turned patiently to whatever belonged to the hour, they
> went about the next job.

This is a fine statement of the attitude of those who live closer to
the rhythms of nature than to the changing movement of political
organisms; it had been earlier expressed in the lines Yeats gave to his

Irish airman: 'No likely end could bring them loss/Or leave them happier than before.' Although he was lacking in a dramatic sense, Tomlinson had the gift of giving his perceptions a concrete imaginative embodiment, and his language was often genuinely poetic. One can, for instance, compare his account of the massive preparations for the Battle of the Somme with Mottram's description in *Sixty-Four, Ninety-Four!*: Mottram is lucid, detailed, but pedestrian; whereas Tomlinson's prose is metaphorically vivid:

> The broad valley crawled with humans, cattle, and machinery, and distance merged horses, men and engines into a ceaseless stirring on the hairless hide of the planet. The interest of man had settled on the valley, and had worn it as dead as an ash-pit. From a distance, it was not an army of men you saw there, but merely an eddying of clusters and streams of loose stuff. It was not men, but man-power, which moved into that valley without ceasing, and the power was pumped into it from the reservoirs of distant cities to keep revolving the machinery of war. If life clotted, it was deflected into those hospital tents.

Here, Tomlinson's choice of words is instrumental in establishing the dehumanizing effect of the war, and prepares for the mass slaughter on the Somme and the subsequent concept of the 'war of attrition'. Or again, one may consider the bizarre but compelling juxtapositions in the following extract, which recalls Owen's 'Spring Offensive':

> With the hawthorn buds, we knew, must come the new crops of emplacements for guns and gas cylinders. Here again there appeared to be signs of it, though Easter was far away. Those signs were becoming familiar to us. The 'Spring Offensive' was our name for the new interest of the vernal season; it was the advental efflorescence, for us, of surgical saws, bandages, and suppuration, as natural as the wind-flowers and little blue eggs in the shrubbery.

When he describes the fighting, or its effects, in terms of human destruction and mutilation, Tomlinson does so with a quiet exactness that, again, reminds one of Owen. He describes revolting episodes in a calm, unemphatic prose that makes their horror all the more striking, and is far more effective than Aldington's stridency. The total effect of Tomlinson's book is elegiac, for it culminates in an extended 'anthem for doomed youth':

Maynard spied, lonely in a corner of a field, a gathering of wooden crosses. All young men, all young men! There must be something more important than life, thought Maynard, or else why are these boys there?

There must be? Well, there ought to be; and if there ought to be something more...

He was stopped, for a moment, by the appeal of that congregation of outstretched wooden arms. All young men, all reluctant, and all lost! There must be something more important than life, or else the sun, moon and stars were nothing but an unintended joke, with nobody even to grin at it.

This was, indeed, the central dilemma that the war forced upon so many acute sensibilities: the conviction that life was the supreme value, in opposition to the traditional patriotic ethos that is eager to sacrifice it in a supposedly higher cause, was the driving motive behind much anti-war poetry and prose. In another passage, Tomlinson underlines the change in attitude that the mechanization of war had brought about: ' "As things are," an officer explained, "a consumptive machine gunner, too scared in an attack to bolt, can sit in a lucky hole in the ground and scupper a company of the best as they advance. Courage isn't what it used to be. The machine runs over us and we can't stop it." '

An outstanding novel by a survivor is Frederic Manning's *Her Privates We*, which was a great success when it was published in 1930. His realistic representation of soldiers' speech had to be bowdlerized to fit the publishing conventions of the time (a necessity which had inserted many rows of asterisks in *Death of a Hero*); in later years an unexpurgated edition was published under the title of *The Middle Parts of Fortune*, but as the book is best known under its original title I shall refer to it by that. There was nothing about the elegant aestheticism of Manning's earlier career as man of letters and poet to prepare one for the unrestrained realism of this, his single novel. Arnold Bennett wrote, 'it depends for its moral magic on a continuous veracity, consistent, comprehending, merciful and lovely'.

Her Privates We has a timeless quality, in contrast with the period flavour that now characterizes many books about the Great War; for all its concentration on detail and its narrow scope, it rises in places to the universality of major literature. Unlike most other literary records of the war, Manning's novel is written from the point of view of the ordinary private soldier; it is centred on a small group of infantrymen serving on the Somme during the late summer and autumn of 1916. The most usual kind of war writing was the work of young infantry officers, and reflected the anguished isolation and self-awareness of such a position; they shared and were yet separated from the experiences of their men, occupying an uneasy place between the mass of the other ranks and the higher military command. Such a viewpoint offered unique opportunities for observation and understanding. Nevertheless, the infantryman's was the truly common experience of the war, though it was rarely given articulate expression. When it was, as in *Her Privates We*, one has a momentary insight into a massive universal process, as opposed to the necessarily particularized and individual quality of the junior officer's response. Everything, in the end, rested on the private soldier; as Manning sardonically remarks at one point: 'That is what is called, in the British Army, the chain of responsibility, which means that all responsibility, for the errors of their superior officers, is borne eventually by private soldiers in the ranks.'

Her Privates We is marked by its austere concentration on the soldiers' existence at or near the Front, to the exclusion of any other kind of life; in this respect, it resembles *Undertones of War*. Unlike most writers who wrote retrospective accounts, Manning does not establish any kind of contrast between the realities of battle and a nostalgically recalled England. Apart from one or two unflattering remarks about the home front, he does not even dwell on the alienation of soldiers from civilians. He shows the men as immersed in a totally self-contained world with its own laws and values, in which civilian attitudes are best forgotten, and in which the only reminder that there is another kind of life comes with letters and food-parcels from home. Having established this world, Manning shows its workings with a wealth of convincing detail; in particular, he possessed a keen ear for dialogue, and a sensitive awareness of the various unexpected ways in which human qualities can appear in conditions of stress. At the same time, his use of Shakespearian chapter-headings indicates his desire to place the story on a universal plane, to underline the continuity of experience between the British troops on the Somme in 1916 and Henry V's battered army at Agincourt. *Her Privates We* is not an anti-war book; Manning does not flinch from rendering the brutality and bloody waste of battle, but he accepts the war as a total and inescapable experience and does not speculate about the possibility of things being otherwise. In his reflective passages, he has something of the tragic vision of some existentialist philosophers:

It was not much use telling them that war was only the ultimate problem of all human life stated barely, and pressing for an immediate solution. When each individual conscience cried out for its freedom, that implacable thing said: 'Peace, peace; your freedom is only in me!' Men recognised the truth intuitively, even with their reason checking at a fault. There was no man of them unaware of the mystery which encompassed him, for he was a part of it; he could neither separate hinself entirely from it, nor identify himself with it completely. A man might rave against war; but war, from among its myriad faces, could always turn towards him one, which was his own.

In his preface, Manning wrote: 'War is waged by men; not by beasts, or by gods. It is a peculary human activity. To call it a crime against mankind is to miss at least half its significance; it is also the punishment of a crime.'

Manning uses as his centre of consciousness a private called Bourne; we know nothing of his antecedents, nor even his Christian name, but he is obviously an educated man, a lover of good food and, particularly, of wine, and he seems to be fairly well off. At the same time, he is a good mixer and is thoroughly at home in the ranks; he is very popular with his comrades and the NCOs, though rather less so with some of the officers, who resent the fact that a man of their own class and education should be serving as a private. He is urged to apply for a commission, but he is reluctant to leave the ranks, and only towards the end of the novel does he agree. Bourne is an interestingly complicated figure: an intellectual of a philosophical turn of mind, he is also, in the way of private soldiers, an expert scrounger, and possesses an Odysseus-like cunning; above all, he manages to be totally detached from his surroundings. *Her Privates We* describes the adventures, in the trenches or in billets, of Bourne and his two comrades, Shem and Martlow; in essentials, Manning's novel is an exploration of comradeship, which, as so many writers testified, emerged as the supreme value amongst fighting men. As Manning insists, it was not the same as friendship; Bourne, Shem, and Martlow were very different types who would have had little in common in peace-time; but the shared experiences of war form a close union between them, which endures until it is bloodily broken.

Comradeship as an existentially lived value was meaningful to the men, whereas they were indifferent to all forms of patriotic and idealistic exhortation:

When at last Mr Rhys left them, they relaxed into ease with a sigh.

Major Shadwell and Captain Malet they could understand, because each was what every private soldier is, a man in arms against the world, a man fighting desperately for himself, and conscious that, in the last resort, he stood alone; for such self-reliance lies at the very heart of comradeship. In so far as Mr Rhys had something of the same character, they respected him; but when he spoke to them of patriotism, sacrifice, and duty, he merely clouded and confused their vision.

Manning reveals another of war's 'myriad faces' in his portrayal of Weeper Smart, a finely realized character: Smart is a lugubrious and shambling soldier who is an embodiment of envy, discontent, and defeatism. His attitude to fighting is an exact anticipation of Joseph Heller's Captain Yossarian: ' "All that a says is, if a man's dead it don't matter no more to 'im 'oo wins the bloody war," said Weeper.' On the face of it, Weeper is a thorough coward, and yet Bourne feels 'that in any emergency he would not let one down, that he had in him, curiously enough, an heroic strain'. And in the event, Weeper does prove himself capable of heroic behaviour. He is contrasted with the deserter, Miller (though even he has the energy and ingenuity to escape several times from captivity).

Her Privates We concentrates firmly on a small, clearly defined area of front-line life, and is saturated in that life: it avoids the significant contrasts posited by other novelists, and does not attempt to illustrate the decline in English civilization as a whole. And yet it treats of war with a Shakespearean inclusiveness, concretely presenting the humour as well as the horror and the pathos. Manning's close-textured prose maintains an effective balance between the salty vigour of the colloquial exchanges of the soldiers and Bourne's probing, existential reflections; his philosophical concern provides an additional dimension and unifies the novel's disparate realistic observations. This blend of the particular and the universal gives the book, at times, a certain epic flavour. Only in David Jones's *In Parenthesis* do we find anything approaching this particular quality.

One of the most original and savagely satirical of the retrospective war novels is Henry Williamson's *The Patriot's Progress* (1930). Williamson was born in 1895, commissioned in 1915, served on the Western Front and survived the war to embark on a literary career; his most celebrated work, *Tarka the Otter*, appeared in 1927. *The Patriot's Progress* was written as a text accompanying a series of wood-engravings by the Australian artist William Kermode, rather than a separately planned novel. It does not attempt to convey character in depth; the hero, John Bullock, is a flat Everyman figure, whom we follow from his enlistment as a patriotic young volunteer in 1914, through four years in the trenches, to his discharge minus a leg after the Armistice. *The Patriot's Progress* is fast-moving, narrow in focus, and sour in tone. Within its limitations, it is a considerable literary achievement. At Christmas 1914 Williamson had partici- pated in the truce when British and German soldiers in many parts of the Front came out of their trenches and fraternized. This behaviour was strongly disapproved of by the military authorities and it was never allowed to happen again. For Williamson, it was one of the key experiences of his life, leaving him with a strong conviction that ordinary Englishmen and Germans had everything in common and should never go to war again. In the 1930s this basically admirable conviction led him to a disastrously pro-fascist stance, in which he saw Hitler as a simple ex-soldier who was redeeming his country and with whom Britain should cultivate friendship. Williamson was an admirer of Sir Oswald Mosley and his fascist leanings caused him to be interned for a while early in the Second World War.

In the 1950s Williamson embarked on the task of recreating his whole life in a long autobiographical novel in many volumes, *A Chronicle of Ancient Sunlight*. Five of the volumes look back at his experience of the Great War: *How Dear is Life* (1954), *A Fox Under My Cloak* (1955), *The Golden Virgin* (1957), *Love and the Loveless* (1958), and *A Test to Destruction* (1960). Williamson's persona is Phillip Madison. Three previous volumes, beginning with the marriage of his parents, have shown the boy growing up during the Edwardian years in a south-east suburb of London; in *How Dear is Life* he is in his late teens, working in a City insurance office, and is a Territorial: on the outbreak of war he is called up, and volunteers for overseas service. Phillip's character, as Williamson draws it, is complex: he is inconsequential and often light-hearted; at the same time, he is remarkably lacking in self-confidence and plagued by anxieties; and is liable, for the best of motives, to act in a foolishly rash or blundering manner. The principal key to his character is his unhappy relationship with his father, which recalls similar relation- ships in several early twentieth-century novels and autobiographies. In Williamson's *Chronicle* the antipathy between Phillip and his father gives added and poignant emphasis to the customary aliena- tion between front-line troops and the Home Front. As the war develops, we see Phillip maturing, though his character does not fundamentally change: he is transformed from the naive young Territorial private of August 1914 to a seasoned soldier who, by the summer of 1918, has reached the exalted height of acting lieutenant-colonel, has been temporarily blinded in a gas attack, and awarded the DSO.

Phillip's career takes him through nearly all the principal campaigns of the British Army in France during the Great War. He gets to Flanders in November 1914, just in time to take part in the bloody First Battle of Ypres, and to participate in the Christmas Truce. He is at the Battle of Loos in 1915; he is wounded in the Somme offensive in 1916. In 1917 he takes part in the assault on the Hindenburg Line and is in the muddy stalemate at Passchendaele; in 1918 he is in the British retreat before St Quentin. Although Phillip endures the horrors of battle, Williamson's *Chronicle* lacks the bitterness and animus of *The Patriot's Progress*; in a note in the 1968 reprint of the latter he remarked of his later work, 'I wanted to write balanced novels; the Staff also had their problems.'

Even though Williamson waited so many years before embarking on a fictional treatment of his life in the Great War, his memories lost none of their vividness. In fact, his narrative resembles an act of total recall by a patient undergoing analysis. The reader is all but swamped in a flood of indiscriminate detail, with the important and the trivial thoroughly mixed together. Nor is there much sense of fictional structure, for the constituent volumes seem merely to mark convenient intervals in the narrative flow, rather than to form separate artistic unities in themselves. The climaxes in Williamson's story are dictated by facts external to it – usually in the actions in which Phillip is involved – not by the necessities of the narrative. And in the unbroken outpouring of remembered material, considerations of style tend to become forgotten: throughout the wartime volumes, Williamson's prose is at best undistinguishedly adequate for his purposes, and at worst very slipshod.

Yet despite its marked inadequacies, Williamson's novel has impressive and memorable features. Its unremitting saturation in the atmosphere and material details of life both in the Army and on the Home Front gives an accumulative sense of 'felt life', prodigally unselective though it may be. And the amiable vagaries of Phillip's consciousness relieve the deadening effect of prolonged stretches of rigorously naturalistic fiction. The five volumes are in fact given a certain moral unity by two linked themes. One of them lies in Phillip's attitude to his father, and the other stems from his experience of the Christmas Truce. Phillip is deeply moved by his discovery that the ordinary German soldier is very like his British opposite number in attitudes and aspirations; and he concludes that the war is a wanton folly dividing two sets of brothers, though he never goes so far as an anti-war revolt in the manner of Sassoon. But whenever possible Phillip challenges the anti-Hun hysteria of the civilians, and particularly of his father, paying tribute to the qualities of the German Army and pointing out unpalatable facts: for instance, at Christmas 1915, when some German soldiers attempted to repeat the truce of the previous year, gathering in their front line with carols and lanterns, they were shelled out of existence by British artillery. Williamson unites the two themes in Chapter 21 of *A Test to Destruction*, with the blazing row that Phillip has with his father in November 1919, on the first anniversary of the Armistice, a magnificently sustained piece of mutual haranguing; it ends with Phillip stalking out of the house with disastrous results.

There is one other work of that period which needs to be mentioned, if only briefly, in this section, and that is R.C. Sherriff's famous play, *Journey's End*, first performed in December 1928 – with Laurence Olivier in the role of Stanhope – and thereafter assured of a permanent place in the hearts of the public. Sherriff's play is a glib but competent piece of theatre, sentimental, and full of characters and situations which are none the less artificial for being found in a British dugout on the eve of the German offensive in March 1918. At the same time, it faces the issues that more genuinely imaginative writers were concerned with: in confronting the starry-eyed young subaltern, Raleigh, with the hard-drinking, nerve-shattered company commander, Stanhope, whom the boy had idealized when they were at school together, Sherriff is exhibiting the collapse of the public-school ethos under the pressure of war, and suggesting the breakdown of the traditional English values that had been sustained by this ethos. And in Stanhope's relation with Hibbert, Sherriff first acknowledges, then evades, the whole difficult question of cowardice which writers such as Herbert Read had more deeply examined. On the whole, Sherriff was giving theatre audiences what they wanted: they were prepared, after ten years, to take a fresh interest in the war, and his play provided a degree of realism and affecting sentiment without making excessively uncomfortable demands.

The British writers of those years who returned to their wartime experiences were only one element in a large international wave of interest in the subject. This lies beyond the confines of this study, but one can note that those writers who are most accessible to English readers, the Americans, exhibited a degree of protest and disillusion that was more extreme than the attitudes of most British writers. As Frederick J. Hoffman comments in the excellent discussion of

American war books in his *The Twenties* (1962): 'That sense of violation is present in each of the principal works of American war literature. (English writers were "disenchanted", disabused of their sacrifices *pro patria*, but in only a few cases had a comparable feeling of outrage.)' John Dos Passos's *Three Soldiers* had appeared in 1921 and E.E. Cummings's *The Enormous Room* in 1922. Hemingway published *A Farewell to Arms* in 1929, and this was to prove one of the most celebrated of all war – or anti-war – novels. After the retreat from Caporetto Hemingway's hero abandons any vestige of attachment to a scheme of public values that had become meaningless to him, and is impelled only by the motive of self-preservation. He retreats to a small world of personal values, but even this fails when Catherine Barkley dies in childbirth. In *A Farewell to Arms* Hemingway registers the collapse of the heroic ideal; though in his later fiction we see him attempting to restore it, very much on his own terms.

Not all the international war books of 1928-30 were pacifist in their orientation – I have discussed Jünger's *Storm of Steel* – but many of them were. Some notion of their general character can be gained from the attack on them contained in *The Lie About the War* (1930), a pamphlet by Douglas Jerrold, a right-wing journalist of romantic inclinations who had fought throughout the war and who took a very different view of it from most of the writers he discusses. Jerrold's vigorous essay is a reminder that no matter how exigent the *Zeitgeist* may seem to be, one can always find people who resist its pressures. Jerrold did not disapprove of all the writers he mentioned: he admired *Undertones of War*, and, with reservations, *Goodbye to All That*. Otherwise, he was concerned to denounce a wide range of distinguished writers, including Hemingway, Remarque, Aldington, Barbusse, and Arnold Zweig. Jerrold claimed that they gave a false picture of war; or even when they presented a fairly accurate picture, they distorted the underlying motives of the conflict:

> It is this obsession of futility, not any special depth of sympathy or humanitarianism which accounts for the piling up of the individual agony to so many poignant climaxes remote from the necessities or even from the normal incidental happenings of war.

It is undoubtedly true that the demands of dramatic intensity made many imaginative writers convey the certainly false impression that life in the line consisted of unbroken periods of bloody and destructive action, whereas for a great deal of the time it was fairly quiet. Jerrold complains that the 'frank' war books leave out the inactivity and boredom that made up nine-tenths of the life of the infantry soldier.

He also argues that, considered from the standpoint of the individual private or junior officer, the war must inevitably seem a meaningless muddle; only when regarded from the exalted position of the corps, or even army, commander, could its movements make any sense at all. He complains that nearly all the war books he discusses generalize from purely personal experience, without taking the broad view:

> These writers know as well as I do that the only possible tragedy of the war, *considered as war*, lay in its inevitability, that to deny the element of fatality must be to deny that it was a tragedy at all. Yet to accept the element of fatality would be to invest the war with a grandeur which these novelists are determined to deny it. Hence the frantic attempt to get the dramatic quality out of every kind of struggle except the struggle of one army against another and so to get a significant novel without having to admit that it was a significant war.

Jerrold seems to discuss the war with the detached tones of a critic describing the tragic grandeur of a play by Racine; but presumably his own wartime experiences were no less authentic than those of the writers he is attacking. The ultimate difference between them is that Jerrold remains secure in traditional habits of mind, which the others have abandoned. He regarded the conflict as both necessary and significant; they saw it as meaningless and so without significance. The concrete historical question of whether the war was unnecessarily prolonged, and might have been settled sooner by negotiation, is one which Jerrold avoids discussing in detail. He would certainly have claimed that the necessity and justice of the Allied cause meant that one *had* to accept all the slaughter and mutilation involved to achieve victory; his opponents would have claimed that no cause that involved such bloody destruction of life could be just or necessary. Between two such radically opposed points of view, rooted in such different ethical attitudes, there could be no common ground and so no argument.

Some of Jerrold's contributory points now seem unfortunate. In an attempt to show that the war, terrible though it was, had good results, he points to the elimination of militarism and the establishment of parliamentary democracy in Germany. Three years later, the Nazis, deriving much of their appeal from opposition to the Treaty of Versailles, came to power and begin preparing for another war.

Some of his other comments retain a certain validity. It is undoubtedly a limitation of many war novels that they could present only the responses of a single, usually isolated consciousness, and made no attempt at a Tolstoyan largeness, though the reasons for this limitation were as much philosophical as literary.

11: Remythologizing
David Jones's *In Parenthesis*

The dominant movement in the literature of the Great War was, to adopt the terminology of some modern theologians, from a myth-dominated to a demythologized world. Violent action could be regarded as meaningful, even sacred, when it was sanctified by the traditional canons of heroic behaviour; when these canons came to seem no longer acceptable, then killing or being killed in war appeared meaningless and horrible. This, in essentials, is the difference between Brooke or Grenfell, and Sassoon or Owen; or, to take another contrast, between *The Storm of Steel* and *Death of a Hero*. Throughout the nineteenth century poets had lamented the advance of scientific and positivistic modes of thought, which had stripped nature of her mysteries and her abiding myths. And yet the traditional pastoral mode obstinately endured, at least until the Georgians, when it gave a final flicker of life. Compared to the Georgians, the Imagists were the first poets of a demythologized world, concerned to make poetry from the naked, isolated object, stripped of all outworn mythical accretions. This, at least, was their theory; in practice, Imagist poets such as Pound, Aldington, and H.D., were heavily literary, drawing much of their inspiration from classical motifs. But we can see the logical working-out of the Imagist tenets in the poetry of William Carlos Williams, and his followers, the Objectivists, who concentrated on the naked object as it presented itself to the senses. Williams's slogan was 'No ideas but in things'; he was living and working in an America that, he felt, owed nothing to the myths and literary conventions of Europe (though in his later years he very beautifully translated an idyll of Theocritus, first of Western pastoral poets).

Similarly, the myths that had given value and significance to war were to be stripped away by the poets of 1914-18. As I have suggested, the process owed a great deal to the mass use of such unchivalrous and anti-heroic weapons as the machine-gun and heavy artillery. But this was certainly not the whole of the story: the bayonet was a fairly traditional weapon, and yet Herbert Read in his poem, 'The Happy Warrior', dwells on the gruesome business of stabbing a fallen enemy with a bayonet, whilst deliberately alluding to Wordsworth's poem, which complacently expounds the virtues of the soldierly life. Read describes the physical fact, whereas Wordsworth describes the attitudes that should, ideally, surround the fact. If one juxtaposes the two poems one can see clearly enough what the demythologization of war meant.

For a time this process seemed to have been brought to finality with the poetry of 1916-18 and those later prose works which aimed, misleadingly, to 'tell the truth about war', as if there could be any such single entity. And this has proved a permanent shift of sensibility: the mood and the rhetoric of 1914-15 now seem irrecoverably lost. But at the same time, war, as a subject, could not remain wholly stark and impoverished of all mythical accretions. Although the nineteenth-century rationalists and their literary opponents had both felt that the mythic mode of consciousness would be shrivelled up by the fierce light of science and positivistic thought, and might well disappear altogether, the twentieth century has seen events turn out rather differently. The philosophers of symbolic forms and the archetypal psychologists have shown that the mythopoeic faculty is deep-rooted in humanity, and is not likely to be weakened, even in a scientific and technological age; new myths arise, or old ones appear in new forms, as we see in such literary manifestations as science fiction. And in a more deliberate way, the most significant literature of our age is marked by its use of legendary and mythological material, often with an anthropological backing: one need only mention *The Waste Land* and *Ulysses*. Taken far enough, the demythologizing tendencies in movements like Imagism can transform themselves into new forms of mythic creation, as Northrop Frye has indicated. The literary use of myth by twentieth-century writers is, however, very conscious: instead of myth, as in other ages, being rooted in a system of public and shared beliefs, and so acting as a focus for the consciousness and aspirations of a community, it is used by the modern writer as a means of restoring contact with the past, of temporarily living and feeling in terms of vanished systems of value. Its use is therefore necessarily individualistic and fragmentary. Nevertheless, it serves as a means of escaping from the positivistic concentration on the thing-in-itself. It is in this context that one can, I think, profitably study the achievement of David Jones in *In*

Parenthesis, which is an attempt to place the experience of war in a fresh mythic perspective.

David Jones, who was born in 1895, was known as a visual artist – principally an engraver and water-colourist – long before he emerged as a writer. *In Parenthesis* was his first literary work, and took many years to complete, for it was started in 1928 but did not achieve publication until 1937. It is one of the few works of literature by a native Englishman (or Anglo-Welshman) to contribute importantly to modernist literature. It owes an evident debt to *The Waste Land*, and has some affinities with the later work of Pound and Joyce, and it wholeheartedly follows Pound's injunction to 'make it new'.[1] Jones uses a combination of prose and free verse, and forms which can be regarded as either, though the difference is not deeply significant, for the prose resembles Joyce's in being so carefully wrought, with such care for the placing, resonance and interrelations of his words, that in everything except external form it is poetry. Jones exploits all the possible resources of language in order to convey his meanings, in a way that ignores conventional expectations about literary forms. At the same time, despite its complexity, *In Parenthesis* has a sharp simplicity of narrative line. Its substance was well described by one of Jones's commentators, René Hague:

> The basic theme of *In Parenthesis*...is simple enough, treated with a classical plunge into action, and in each section, a classical respect for the unities: the story of how John Ball, a private in a new-army battalion of a Welsh Regiment (the choice of name, that of the priest executed for his share in the peasant rising of 1381, stresses the continuity of Welsh and British tradition), parades with his battalion for overseas embarkation, of the journey to Flanders, the march up the line, the first day in the strange trench world, their assimilation to the alien rhythm, their march to the assembly point for the Somme offensive, and the final attack on Mametz wood, in which John Ball is wounded and many of his comrades are killed.[2]

Jones is faithful throughout to the material circumstances of an infantryman's life, for he has an imagistic accuracy of response to the data of the physical world. But at the same time, John Ball's progress as a soldier is placed against a richly-textured background of multiple literary allusion; in Hague's words: 'There is a close and natural

---

[1] Jones had not yet read Pound at the time he wrote *In Parenthesis*.
[2] 'David Jones: A Reconnaissance', *Twentieth Century*, July 1960, pp.27-45.

association with Shakespeare (in particular with *Henry V*), with Welsh epic, with Malory, with biblical imagery, with the liturgy – a favourite metaphor is the hieratic order of soldierly manoeuvre.'

In the preface of a later work, *The Anathemata* (1952), Jones described himself as 'a Londoner, of Welsh and English parentage, of Protestant upbringing, of Catholic subscription'. This rather unusual grouping of attributes underlies *In Parenthesis*, starting with the realistic observation that Ball's battalion is made up of a mixture of cockneys and Welshmen. Like Pound and Eliot and Joyce, Jones is an eclectic writer, who deals with disparate fragments of cultural deposits, working them into a closely woven tapestry. But he is a far more rooted writer than they are; certainly when compared with the expatriate Americans, Pound and Eliot, and even with Joyce, whose entire theme was Dublin but who could only cope with it in exile. Jones's interest in Celtic and early English literature, and in Catholic liturgy, is more than just 'a heap of broken images', because it springs directly from his origins and commitments as a man. Furthermore, Jones sees these interests as having their own interrelations and points of contact; as Hague puts it: 'the Welsh element is presented not as something on the periphery of, or even extraneous to, England, but as the core of the Romano-British-Angle tradition, so that London, with the sister figures of Troy and Rome, is above all the city.' This, then, is a very limited degree of eclecticism, when compared with the shifts in Pound's *Cantos* from China to medieval Siena to Jefferson's America to Ancient Egypt. Nevertheless, few readers are likely to possess quite the same range of interests and knowledge as David Jones, so he has provided *In Parenthesis* with copious notes, which are more genuinely enlightening than those attached to *The Waste Land*. Ideally, no doubt, a work should be self-contained but in an era of cultural fragmentation this is not always easily achieved. The best approach is to regard the notes to *In Parenthesis* as an integral part of the author's composition, rather like Pope's notes to *The Dunciad*.

What, in particular, Jones does have in common with the great practitioners of literary modernism is his use of the ideogrammatic method, the suppression of conventional narrative links in favour of the juxtaposition of two disparate images or phrases. Thus Jones points to a constant relation between Private Ball and his comrades and various soldiers of the past, such as Henry V's troops and, above all, the doomed warriors fighting a desperate foray described in *Y Gododdin*, a sixth-century Welsh heroic poem, which provides Jones with the epigraphs for each section of *In Parenthesis*. Jones was doubtless influenced here by the interpenetration of past and present in *The Waste Land*, and perhaps also by Eliot's stress, in 'Tradition and the Individual Talent', on the contemporaneity of significant literary experience. Jones does not make his juxtapositions with ironical effect; there is no question of contrasting the sordid present with the beauties of a more or less legendary past: if anything, the humble infantrymen, enduring the misery of the trenches and then slaughtered in the attack on Mametz wood, are in some measure transfigured by the light of the earlier heroes.

In fact, Jones is concerned to restore the mythology of heroism, but with crucial differences. Whereas earlier literary representations of the hero, from Renaissance drama to the poetry of the early days of the Great War, had been rooted in an implicit but assured complex of assumptions and attitudes that were shared by the writer and his readers, Jones, writing in a post-heroic phase, has laboriously to construct an *ad hoc* frame of reference from his acquaintance with literature, showing the continuity of human attitudes in the conditions of battle. And this demonstration, this concrete embodiment of experience, is in no way rhetorical or assertive; thus, it is at the opposite pole from the expressions of the heroic mode that we find in the speeches of Tamburlaine or Hotspur, or, for that matter, in the sonnets of Rupert Brooke. It is unique and personal, valid only for Jones's particular purposes in writing *In Parenthesis*.

This uniqueness means that the quality of epic that some critics have discovered in *In Parenthesis*, notably John H. Johnston in *English Poetry of the First World War* (1964), needs to be discussed with some qualifications. As I have already remarked about Manning's *Her Privates We*, the private soldier's experience of total immersion in a vast inhuman process gave more scope for epic understanding than the officers' narratives; and this is true, also, of *In Parenthesis*; indeed, both Manning and Jones have a common element in their use of Shakespeare's picture of the soldier's life as a strand in their narratives. Jones undoubtedly does move towards the level of epic, in that he reproduces a sense of shared experience and transcends the limitations of the purely individual standpoint. But true epic, I take it, reaches out beyond the personal to appeal to a system of public and communal values which are ultimately collective, national, and even cosmic. And this Jones does not do; he may feel that Celtic myth is central and not peripheral to his understanding of British tradition, and he may have some success in persuading a discerning reader that this is so. Nevertheless, such knowledge will not already be there to provide a ready response in the consciousness of most of his readers. Quite apart from an author's subject-matter and treatment, the question of epic involves the author's relation with his audience. Jones, in this respect, was no differently placed from other twentieth-century avant-garde artists with a strictly minority appeal. Although he aspires towards the impersonality of epic, his perceptions remain individual, rooted in the accidents of his own experience and reading. One can reasonably doubt whether the conditions for epic – the existence of a shared scheme of communal values and assumptions – are ever likely to be fulfilled in modern society.

In Parenthesis remains, however, the nearest equivalent to an epic that the Great War produced in English. It is far more objective than the wartime poetry or the post-war novels and memoirs. Jones employs Private Ball simply as a focus for typical experience and not as a dominating vehicle of consciousness. In the first section the battalion is assembled and marches through the wet streets to embark for France – 'The people of that town did not acclaim them, nor stop about their business – for it was late in the second year'; they reach France and journey on to a base behind the lines. This opening section employs Jones's stylistic narrative norm, a flowing descriptive prose largely derived from Malory, interspersed with the cockney that serves as the lingua franca of army life. In the later sections, the texture is less even, more broken up into verse and less regular forms, conveying disparate moments of violent experience.

In Part 2 the troops continue their training in France:

> They were given lectures on very wet days in the barn, with its great roof, sprung, upreaching, humane, and redolent of a vanished order. Lectures on military tactics that would be more or less commonly understood. Lectures on hygiene by the medical officer, who was popular, who glossed his technical discourses with every lewdness, whose heroism and humanity reached towards sanctity.

The image of the barn is significant: the great vaulted roof reminds us of the roof of a Gothic church, and both typify the pieties of an agrarian order. Jones's Catholicism is an important element in his work, though he is not a conventionally religious writer. But he is deeply involved with the cultural forms that have grown up around Western Catholicism, and, in particular, the liturgy. Like his friend and co-religionist, Eric Gill, Jones sees man as *homo faber*, who is closest to God when he is making order out of chaos, whether in building barns or cathedrals, or devising ecclesiastical ritual or military manoeuvres. The artefact is always a sign of something beyond itself – pointing to man's essential humanity as maker – and like Hopkins, whom he occasionally quotes in *In Parenthesis*, Jones sees the natural world as continually signifying its creator. As against the bleakness of the positivist *Weltanschauung* Jones posits not merely a mythic but a sacramentalist view of the world.

Thoughout *In Parenthesis*, the ritual element in military orders and words of command is stressed, as in this extract from Part 3, where the troops are marching up to the line, having to avoid shell-holes and the trailing field-telephone wire. The repeated injunctions soon acquire a ritual quality:

> The repeated passing back of aidful messages assumes a
> cadency.
> Mind the hole
> mind the hole
> mind the hole to left
> hole right
> step over
> keep left, left.
>   One grovelling, precipitated, with his gear tangled,
> struggles to feet again:
> Left be buggered.
>   Sorry mate – you all right china? – lift us yer rifle –
> an' don't take on so Honey – but rather, mind
> the wire here
> mind the wire
> mind the wire
> mind the wire
> Extricate with some care that taut strand – it may
> well be you'll sweat on its unbrokenness.

Part 4 presents Ball and his comrades fully absorbed into the life of the trenches. The section opens with an evocation of a December daybreak in the front line, which combines descriptive precision with verbal richness (the opening words are from Malory):

> So thus he sorrowed till it was day and heard the foules
> sing, then somewhat he was comforted.
>
>   Stand-to.
>   Stand-to-arms.
> Stealthly, imperceptibly stript back, thinning
> night wraps

unshrouding, unsheafing –
and insubstantial barriers dissolve.
This blind night-negative yields uncertain flux.
At your wrist the phosphorescent dial describes the
equal seconds.
    The flux yields up a measurable body; bleached forms
emerge and stand.

Much of the distinctive quality of Jones's poetic writing lies in the
often strange combination of a sharp registration of sense impres-
sions and a mannered diction and syntax. Another aspect of it is seen
in the lyrical compression of his account of Christmas morning ('his
morning parapets', etc., are the Germans', always referred to by the
collective 'he'):

It was yet quite early in the morning, at the time of
Saturnalia when men properly are in winter quarters,
lighting His birthday candles –
all a green-o.
When children look with serious eyes on brand-new miracles,
and red berry sheen makes a Moses-bush, to mirror in
multiplicity the hearth-stones creature of fire.
    But John Ball, posted as 1st Day Sentry, sat on the fire-
step; and looking upward, sees in a cunning glass the image
of: his morning parapets, his breakfast-fire smoke, the
twisted wood beyond.

Such passages show much more clearly than any attempt at para-
phrase the nature of Jones's concern with myth and ritual.
    At the same time he is capable of a novelistic realism in rendering
some of the stranger manifestations of the civilization of the trenches:

A man, seemingly native to the place, a little thick man, swathed
with sacking, a limp, saturated bandolier thrown over one shoulder
and with no other accoutrements, gorgeted in woollen Balaclava,
groped out from between two tottering corrugated uprights, his
great moustaches beaded with condensation under his nose.
Thickly greaved with mud so that his boots and puttees and
sandbag tie-ons were become one whole of trickling ochre. His
minute pipe had its smoking bowl turned inversely. He spoke
slowly. He told the corporal that this was where shovels were
usually drawn for any fatigue in the supports. He slipped back
quickly, with a certain animal caution, into his hole; to almost
immediately poke out his wool-work head, to ask if anyone had

the time of day or could spare him some dark shag or a picture-paper. Further, should they meet a white dog in the trench her name was Belle, and he would like to catch any bastard giving this Belle the boot.

> John Ball told him the time of day.
> No one had any dark shag.
> No one had a picture-paper.
> They certainly would be kind to the bitch, Belle.

They'd give her half their iron rations – Jesus – they'd let her bite their backsides without a murmur. He draws-to the sacking curtain over his lair.

This has a Dickensian vigour; whilst words like 'gorgeted' and 'greaved' place this apparition in a perspective stretching back to Malory and beyond.

The earlier parts of *In Parenthesis* lead on to the Somme offensive and the unit's part in the assault on Mametz wood. Jones described the preparations without bitterness, but with the front-line soldier's customary sardonic intonation:

>   And for the born leaders
> the top boys
> the hero's grave squad
> the Elect
> the wooden-cross Dicks
> – for the White-men with Emergency Archie: all these types
> are catered for, but they must know exactly how to behave.

The book reaches a superb climax with the assault in Part 7. The state of mind of the men waiting to go over the top is rendered with acute sensitivity:

> Racked out to another turn of the screw
> the acceleration heightens;
> the sensibility of these instruments to register,
> fails;
> needle dithers disorientate.

As the attack proceeds Ball sees his comrades shot down on either side of him, but he is so far unscathed. Jones can describe death in battle with the directness of a Sassoon – 'Wastebottom married a wife on his Draft-leave but the whinnying splinter razored diagonal and mess-tin fragments drove inwards and toxined underwear' – but his lengthier accounts of it have a stylized, ritual quality which makes

them, if anything, more moving – as with the death of the young
subaltern, Mr Jenkins:

> He sinks on one knee
> and now on the other,
> his upper body tilts in rigid inclination
> this way and back;
> weighted lanyard runs out to full tether,
>> swings like a pendulum
>> and the clock run down.
> Lurched over, jerked iron saucer over tilted brow,
> clampt unkindly over lip and chin
> nor no ventaille to this darkening
>> and masked face lifts to grope the air
> and so disconsolate;
> enfeebled fingering at a paltry strap –
> buckle holds,
> holds him blind against the morning.

The last line catches the note of the early heroic poetry that was such
an inspiration to Jones.

The detailed description of the savage fighting in the wood con-
tains scenes unsurpassed for energy and exactitude anywhere in the
literature of the war. At the same time, Jones, although unfaltering
in his realism, also stresses the mythic dimension. The wood, now
the scene of carnage, is also, like all woods, a traditional focus for the
numinous, and we have been reminded of this by earlier references in
the book – 'To groves always men come both to their joys and their
undoing'. Eventually Ball is wounded in the legs and tries to crawl to
safety, but he finds his rifle an encumbrance:

> It's difficult with the weight of the rifle.
> Leave it – under the oak.
> Leave it for a salvage-bloke
> let it lie bruised for a monument
> dispense the authenticated fragments to the faithful.

He is reluctant to abandon the rifle, the well-loved artefact that has
shared his battle-experiences and which, as his instructors have so
often told him, is the soldier's best friend: 'You know her by her bias,
and by her exact error at 300, and by the deep scar at the small, by the
fair flaw in the grain, above the lower sling-swivel –' but he must leave
it. As Ball crawls away among the British and German dead he
imagines the fallen in some way commemorated by a local deity – 'The

Queen of the Woods has cut bright boughs of various flowering.' We are not told that Ball survives, but we must suppose he does and is responsible for the narrative we have just read. At the last, Ball and the author seem to become one. In the final words of *In Parenthesis*, Jones quotes from the *Song of Roland*, indicating for the last time that the struggle we have just witnessed must be regarded in the heroic perspectives of the past, and simultaneously emphasizing the front-line soldier's feeling of having participated in a unique and noncommunicable experience, which sets him apart from other men: 'The geste says this and the man who was on the field...and who wrote the book...the man who does not know this has not understood anything.'

Jones is distinguished from the poets who wrote during the course of the war both by his impersonality and by the far wider emotional range of his work. As Johnston has observed, 'Unlike Owen, Jones found little poetry in pity; pity was an emotion that might be aroused under certain circumstances, but the full reality of war was much too complex to be viewed through the eyes of pity alone.' Jones was, however, very aware of the sacrificial elements in the soldiers' experience, which he understood in Christian terms. Johnston acutely remarks: 'Positive, aggressive heroism of the epic character is seldom possible in modern war; a man may perform valiantly in action, but for every valiant moment there are weeks of inactivity, boredom, suffering, and fear. Thus the virtues of the modern infantry-man are Christian virtues – patience, endurance, hope, love – rather than the naturalistic virtues of the epic hero.' As we have seen, this concept of the Christian hero had already been foreshadowed in Ford's Tietjens. Jones admits in his preface that the period of the war he was writing about – the early months of 1916 – was still amenable to such treatment: it had not become entirely mechanized and depersonalized. Whether he could have written similarly about the post-Somme phase, so much more massive in its brutality, which produced the other war poets, is open to doubt.

Again, Jones resembles his contemporaries in seeing the actualities of the war against a background of traditional values, but differs from them in his manner of doing so. He looks much farther back than the nostalgically recalled Home Counties pastoral scenes of the Georgians, or even than Ford's Yorkshire squirearchy. Jones feels that his roots are British rather than narrowly English, and emphasizes the Romano-British elements in the national character (surviving in mythology if not in continuing social forms) rather more strongly than the Anglo-Saxon and subsequent strains. Thus, Jones establishes a comprehensive though eclectic frame for his action, whose closest parallel is perhaps to be found in the vision of the British past in Kipling's *Puck of Pook's Hill* (1906). As I have suggested, the degree of Jones's cultural eclecticism may, for many readers unfamiliar with his material, tend to obscure his comprehensiveness, though this difficulty diminishes on successive readings of *In Parenthesis*. In one other important respect, Jones's method differs from that of other war poets and prose writers: whereas they establish contrasts, whether nostalgic or ironical, between the past and the realities of the Front, Jones is concerned always to find parallels, to emphasize the underlying unity rather than the discontinuity of experience. *In Parenthesis* has attracted criticism as well as admiration, but I believe it is the greatest work in English to have come out of the First World War, and a still slightly neglected masterpiece of modernist literature.[3]

---

[3] It is as well to remember that Jones regarded *In Parenthesis* as not just a book about war but as part of his idiosyncratic and wide-ranging reading of history. He writes in the Preface:

> I did not intend this as a 'War Book' – it happens to be concerned with war. I should prefer it to be about a good kind of peace – but as Mandeville says, 'Of Paradys ne can I not speken propurly I was not there; it is fer beyond and that for thinketh me. And also I was not worthi'. We find ourselves privates in foot regiments. We search how we may see formal goodness in a life singularly inimical, hateful, to us.

T.S. Eliot, who first published *In Parenthesis*, regarded it as a work of genius, but some good critics have found it hard to take; D.J. Enright sees the style as at odds with the subject-matter, and so does Paul Fussell, who in *The Great War and Modern Memory* struggles unsuccessfully to think well of Jones's text. There is an interesting account of *In Parenthesis* in Evelyn Copley, *Representing War: Form and Ideology in First World War Narratives* (Toronto, 1993). This is an intelligent but deeply perverse study in a latter-day mode of academic criticism, drawing on Marxism, psychoanalysis and poststructuralism; the author argues that many war narratives, even when they seem to register protest, are really complicit with the war, since they employ the literary devices – coherent narrative development, a sense of actual reality to be observed and registered, a consistent centre of observing consciousness – which are part of the ideological power structure which leads to and sustains war. The author sees *In Parenthesis* as a partial exception; she writes, 'Jones's modernist mode of representation stresses the inadequacy of Enlightenment meta-narratives whose ideological assumptions continue to dominate war accounts in the realistic tradition'. Her discussion of Jones is sometimes acute, though I am not sure how far she really understands *In Parenthesis*. Ultimately she finds it wanting, in terms rather similar to Fussell's: 'Jones's advocacy and practice of a highly self-conscious textuality stops short of a postmodern celebration of heterogeneity. The discontinuous narrative surface is recuperated by a unifying deep structure of intertextual allusions to a chivalric tradition'. But she does acknowledge that the earlier battles Jones invokes are defeats. There is a convincing rebuttal of Fussell on *In Parenthesis* in Elizabeth Ward, *David Jones: Mythmaker* (Manchester, 1983).

12: Myth and Memory

The First World War, and the Treaty of Versailles which officially concluded it, led in due course to the Second World War. That produced its own crop of poetry and fiction, which I have discussed elsewhere.[1] But it is still the Great War, shorter in duration though, for the British, more traumatic and destructive of life, that remains the archetypal conflict. Paul Fussell has remarked on the unexpected ways in which it survives in the casual clichés of our bureaucratic daily life, where one may be 'bombarded with forms' or 'face a barrage of complaints'; where negotiators adopt 'entrenched positions' but still look for a 'breakthrough'; and where once precise terms such as 'no man's land' or 'to go over the top' have largely lost their original meaning. Fussell has also shown how the myths and images of the First World War survive in American novels about the Second, by Norman Mailer and Joseph Heller and Thomas Pynchon.

In Britain the academic historiography of the war continues vigorously. The regularly revived stage musical *Oh What a Lovely War!* reduces historical complexities to Brechtian simplicities, but remains entertaining and moving, particularly in the songs. For poets and novelists born after the war ended it persists as a mixture of public myth and private memories; not direct memories, but those passed on by fathers or grandfathers. Anthony Burgess was born during the Great War; he would have been too young to remember it, but in his novel *The Wanting Seed* (1962) he makes a vivid, caricatural reproduction of it. This novel is a dystopian futurological fantasy, describing a world in which over-population has become such a problem that the authorities go to extreme lengths to overcome it, encouraging homosexuality, discouraging procreation and condoning infanticide. The narrative culminates with a large battle deliberately staged in the interests of population control, somewhere in the West of

---

[1] See Bergonzi, *Wartime and Aftermath* (Oxford, 1993).

Ireland. It is an exact replica of one of the big offensives on the Western Front, with every military detail in place and the background noise of an artillery bombardment relayed from loudspeakers:

> There were still distant crashes and bumps – a twenty-four hour performance, probably with three shifts of lance-corporal disc-jockeys – but no fire in the sky. At noon an ancient aircraft – strings, struts, an open cockpit and waving goggled aeronaut lurched over the camp and away again. 'One of ours,' Mr Dollimore told his platoon. 'The gallant RFC.'

A more personal and immediate response appears in Vernon Scannell's fine poem, 'The Great War':

> Whenever war is spoken of
> I find
> The war that was called Great invades the mind:
> The grey militia marches over land
> A darker mood of grey
> Where fractured tree-trunks stand
> And shells, exploding, open sudden fans
> Of smoke and earth.

The poem concludes with a beautiful confluence of images:

> And through the misty keening of a band
> Of Scottish pipes the proper names are heard
> Like fateful commentary of distant guns:
> Passchendaele, Bapaume, and Loos, and Mons.
> And now,
> Whenever the November sky
> Quivers with a bugle's hoarse, sweet cry,
> The reason darkens; in its evening gleam
> Crosses and flares, tormented wire, grey earth
> Splattered with crimson flowers,
> And I remember,
> Not the war I fought in
> But the one called Great
> Which ended in a sepia November
> Four years before my birth.

Peter Porter makes a similar evocation in 'Somme and Flanders':

> Who am I to speak up for the long dead?
> Three uncles I never knew say I'm right.

Their tongues are speaking in my head
I'm related to their flesh by fright.

Their world was made of nerves and mud.
Reading about it now shocks me – Haig
Gets transfusions of their blood,
Plum-and-apple feeds them for the plague.

Those Harmsworth books have sepia'd
Their peasants' fields sown with barbed-wire.
In Nineteen-Nineteen, crops of crosses appeared
Seeded by bodies ripened in shell-fire.

One image haunts us who have read of death
In Auschwitz in our time – it is just light,
Shivering men breathing rum crouch beneath
The sandbag parapet – left to right

The line goes up and over the top,
Serious in gas masks, bayonets fixed,
Slowly forward – the swearing shells have stopped –
Somewhere ahead of them death's stopwatch ticks.

Both Scannell and Porter use the word 'sepia', referring to the dark brown photographic illustrations in early twentieth-century magazines.

Philip Larkin's poem, 'MCMXIV' – the Roman numerals deftly evoke the remote era – is a poignant meditation on the beginning of the war, with queues of men waiting to volunteer:

Those long uneven lines
Standing as patiently
As if they were stretched outside
The Oval or Villa Park,
The crowns of hats, the sun
On moustached archaic faces
Grinning as if it were all
An August Bank Holiday lark.

But it is the present Poet Laureate, Ted Hughes, whose imagination has been most profoundly affected by the Great War, so much so that he has been described as 'the last of the War Poets'. The war is recalled in 'Bayonet Charge' and 'Six Young Men' among his early poems, and 'Mayday on Holderness' juxtaposes the remembered images of war with those evoking the violence of nature:

The North Sea lies soundless. Beneath it
Smoulder the wars: to heart-beats, bomb, bayonet.
'Mother, Mother!' cries the pierced helmet.
Cordite oozings of Gallipoli,

Curded to beastings, broached my palate,
The expressionless gaze of the leopard,
The coils of the sleeping anaconda,
The nightlong frenzy of shrews.

More recently Hughes has returned to the Great War, in 'For the Duration' and 'The Last of the 1st/5th Lancashire Fusiliers: A Souvenir of the Gallipoli Landings'. In the former, a hauntingly powerful poem, he tries to recreate his father's wartime experiences, which he would not speak about though they returned in night-mares:

I felt a strange fear when the war-talk
Like a creeping barrage approached you.
Jig and Jag I'd fitted much of it together.
Our treasure, your D.C.M. – again and again
Carrying in the wounded
Collapsing with exhaustion.

Novelists who recreate the Great War are writing historical fiction, and they are likely to have a bias either to actual history or to mythmaking (though at certain deep levels myth can affect history itself). One excellent novel that is in a sense 'about' the war though it does not mention it until the final pages is Isabel Colegate's *The Shooting Party* (1980). She evokes the final sunset of the long Edwardian afternoon in an aristocratic shooting party in the autumn of 1913, on the Oxfordshire estate of Sir Randolph Nettleby. The novel is a subtle, observant and witty essay in a central vein of English social comedy, and on that level it is a notable achievement. But Isabel Colegate's shooting party also points metaphorically towards the infinitely greater shooting match which breaks out a year later, and which removes one of the central characters at the Battle of Loos in 1915. At the end of her book we see that it is an anatomy of a society on the edge of dissolution, comparable to that of Ford Madox Ford in the first part of *Parade's End*. For most writers, as for most English people, the focus of the war and the source of its characteristic images was the Western Front. But there were other war zones, such as the bloody and futile Gallipoli campaign to which

Rupert Brooke was on his way when he died, and which Ted Hughes
has evoked. In *An Ice Cream War* (1982) William Boyd writes enter-
tainingly and informatively about one of the oddest and least-known
side-shows of the Great War, the campaign in German East Africa
which Francis Brett Young described from first-hand experience in
Marching on Tanga. In this novel Boyd uses and ironically trans-
forms the conventions of the popular novel of colonial adventure.

But it is the war in France and Flanders to which novelists, like
historians, have been most drawn, and above all the terrible slaughter
on the first day of the Somme campaign, 1 July 1916. This is the
subject of John Harris's *Covenant with Death* (1961), which was
written at a time when there were still many survivors whose memories
could be drawn on, as the author gratefully acknowledges in a note.
It is a work of solidly and traditionally realistic fiction, thoroughly
researched and congruent in tone with the records of those who had
fought in the war and survived to write about it. *Covenant with
Death* tells in the first person the experiences of Mark Fenner, a
young journalist in a Yorkshire city, from the moment he joins the
city's volunteer battalion of the New Army in August 1914 to the
point when he is one of a handful of survivors of the battalion's
desperate attack in the face of German machine-gun fire on the
morning of 1 July 1916. Almost all of his comrades are wiped out in
the effort to reach the German lines. The novel ends with the words,
'Two years in the making. Ten minutes in the destroying. That was
our history.' Harris's novel is limited by its conventional narrative
technique and characterization; but it tells its terrible story compel-
lingly. It deserves a place among the later literary annals of the war.

Both Susan Hill's *Strange Meeting* (1971) and Sebastian Faulks'
Birdsong (1993) indicate a debt to Wilfred Owen; the former by its
title, taken from one of Owen's best known poems, and perhaps also
in its sensitive study of the homoerotic attraction between two young
officers. The latter novel contains an epigraph from Tagore – 'When
I go from hence, let this be my parting word, that what I have seen is
unsurpassable' – that was quoted by Owen in a letter to his mother
in 1918. Much of the action takes place in tunnels constructed by
military sappers under the front lines, which, again, recalls the
archetypal tunnel of 'Strange Meeting'. Both novels describe the
carnage of the first day of the Somme offensive.

Strange Meeting is a short, intense work, sharply and economi-
cally written. It focuses on two central characters, but it is well
informed about the routines and privations of life in the trenches,
about the nature of battle and the kinds of death and wounding and

mutilation that it produces. The first of Susan Hill's characters is a
seasoned young officer, John Hilliard, still only in his early twenties
but already left empty and affectless by his experiences. He misses
the Somme campaign because in the summer of 1916 he is on leave
at home recovering from a minor wound; he is not happy there
because of his sense of alienation from his well-meaning but quite
incomprehending family; here Hill picks up a common motif in
soldiers' records. John returns to his battalion as soon as he can, only
to find it decimated by the fighting on the Somme, of which he hears
harrowing accounts, and generally shattered in morale. A new
young subaltern arrives, David Barton. At first John resents him, but
David is a friendly, good-hearted youth, who becomes generally
popular. He embodies the literariness to which Fussell has referred,
in being a dedicated reader of an edition of the works of Sir Thomas
Browne. John feels increasingly drawn to him, and eventually has to
admit that he is in love with David, though there is no overtly sexual
dimension to the story. He dreads David's death more than any-
thing, but he is not spared this loss. David is reported missing, pre-
sumed killed, and John is badly wounded. He has a leg amputated
and is discharged from the army. At the end of the novel he is about
to visit David's family, with whom he has been corresponding and
who seem more human and approachable than his own. As he draws
near their house, deep in rural seclusion, he has a curious pastoral
epiphany, reminiscent of the loving evocations of England in the
poems of Edward Thomas or Ivor Gurney. *Strange Meeting* is as
much a tragic love story as a 'war novel'; either way, it is haunting
and memorable.

Sebastian Faulks' *Birdsong* is much longer, and much more com-
plex and ambitious. But it has something in common with Hill's
novel, beyond the wartime settings. Faulks's central figure, Stephen
Wraysford, is like John Hilliard, an existentially empty person, whose
experiences at the Front have deprived him of feeling or the capacity
to feel. Before the war when we first meet him, he had been capable
of passion, but even then, as Faulks describes him, he seems a chilly
and remote figure. The novel begins in 1910, when Stephen, a young
executive in the textile trade who has already lived for several years
in France, is spending a few weeks in Amiens on a business assign-
ment. During that time he has a tempestuous affair with his French
employer's young wife and, unknown to him at the time, conceives
a child. The greater part of the novel is about Stephen's experiences
as a junior officer at the Front between 1916 and 1918, when although
he is an infantry officer he works closely with the sappers who are

digging tunnels under the enemy lines. Towards the end of the novel he almost dies – indeed, on any rational probability he *should* have died – when the tunnel he is in is blown up. He survives the war, but we are told that he did not speak for two years, rather like Mark Tietjens in Ford's *Last Post*. There is a further dimension to the book set in the future, in the London of 1978, in which Stephen's granddaughter Elizabeth, a woman in her late thirties who was born after he died, becomes interested in him and starts to study the coded diaries of his wartime life that she discovers.

Birdsong is an impressive novel and is extraordinarily powerful in places, in its accounts of trench warfare and of the tense, desperate business of tunnelling. And the descriptions of the emotional resonses of the ordinary soldiers to loss and tragedy can be deeply moving. At its best the novel recalls Manning's *Her Privates We*. But I think it has more power than art, and does not properly fulfil its formal ambitions. The relation between the wartime scenes and those set sixty years later is arbitrary and unworked out. Faulks makes gestures towards symbolic links; Elizabeth travels to work through the tunnels of the London Underground, which one of the military sappers had helped to construct before the war. But he does much less with Elizabeth than he might, though she has a baby in the final pages of the novel, which ends with a pastoral epiphany somewhat reminiscent of Susan Hill's. It would have been artistically more resonant and unifying, for instance, if we learnt that the wartime narrative had been written up from Stephen's diaries. The novel suffers from its slackness in construction, and from the remarkable unevenness of its style. Faulks is able to write really well, but only, it seems, when he is describing episodes of physical and moral extremity; in the peacetime episodes, whether in France in 1910 or in London in 1978, his prose lapses into banality. *Birdsong* is a strong but flawed novel, perhaps the most thorough and ambitious recreation of the Great War so far made in latter-day English fiction.

Birdsong was a bestseller, which is a sign of the fascination that the war continues to evoke. It is by now a permanent fact of historical consciousness, that writers and other kinds of artists are likely to return to. The memory of that excitement and waste and dumb heroism seems ineradicable. It started as a war to end wars, but instead it pointed forward to totalitarianism, to an even greater war and a concept of unlimited conflict in which not merely uniformed armies but whole populations, down to the smallest child, are regarded as appropriate victims for destruction on a scale that makes the slaughter on the Somme appear ordinary. The poets sensed some of this, though, in Owen's phrase, all they could do was warn. If we now regard war as, on occasion, still necessary, in the way that abattoirs and operating-theatres are necessary, we do not feel the need to adorn it with the tinsel of a factitious glory. This much we have learnt from the writers of the Great War, who absorbed its shock and employed their art to change a generation's modes of feeling. In the course of doing so, they undermined a whole range of traditional responses: heroism, as a kind of behaviour, might still be possible, but not the rhetoric and gestures of heroism. The response of the English writers was perhaps more intense than that of other nations. John Terraine has suggested that for centuries the English were in the habit of letting other people do their fighting for them, and the initial exposure of the civilian volunteer soldiers to large-scale technological war was correspondingly more painful. But the best of them did more than register a hopeless trauma. In their writing they communicated new, extreme and sometimes unimaginable experiences by turning them into art, and ultimately into the beguiling but dangerous order of myth.

Appendix
The Problem of War Poetry

War poetry is easier to talk about than to define; if it has claims to be a literary genre, then it is a very loose one. This much is apparent from the *Oxford Book of War Poetry*, edited by Jon Stallworthy, which came out in 1984. It ranges very widely, beginning with the Book of Exodus and the death of Hector in the *Iliad* and ending with Peter Porter's poem about the outbreak of nuclear war. The English poems written before the end of the eighteenth century have a decidedly marginal and miscellaneous aspect, as though the editor had been hard put to it to get a convincing number of them together. We have among other things, an extract from Chaucer's 'Knight's Tale', Michael Drayton's 'Ballad of Agincourt' Lovelace's 'To Lucasta, Going to the Wars', Marvell's 'Horatian Ode', and a disappointingly brief extract from the war in heaven in *Paradise Lost*. The eighteenth century provides 'Rule Britannia', and Johnson's powerful lines about Charles XII of Sweden from *The Vanity of Human Wishes*. But the next poem to Johnson's in the anthology is much closer to what we have come to think of as war poetry; providing not celebration or mere description but the note of angry rejection:

> I hate that drum's discordant sound.
> Parading round, and round, and round:
> To me it talks of ravaged plains,
> And burning towns, and ruined swains,
> And mangled limbs, and dying groans,
> And widow's tears, and orphans' moans;
> And all that Misery's hand bestows,
> To fill the catalogue of human woes.

That is from 'Ode' by John Scott, published in 1782; Scott is nowadays known only for this one poem. Early in the next century Byron writes scathingly about the human propensity to make war, in *Don Juan*:

> 'Let there be light!' said God, and there was light!
>   'Let there be blood!' says man, and there's a sea!
> The fiat of this spoiled child of the Night
>   (For Day ne'er saw his merits) could decree
> More evil in an hour, than thirty bright
>   Summers could renovate, though they should be
> Lovely as those which ripened Eden's fruit;
> For war cuts up not only branch, but root.

Nevertheless, at the end of his short life Byron was preparing to fight in the just cause of Greek independence and ready to lay down his life:

> If thou regret'st thy youth, *why live?*
>   The land of honourable death
> Is here: – up to the Field, and give
>   Away thy breath!
>
> Seek out – less often sought than found –
>   A soldier's grave, for thee the best;
> Then look around, and choose thy ground,
>   And take thy rest.

In those concluding stanzas from 'On This Day I Complete My Thirty-Sixth Year' one hears sentiments that nearly a century later were to reappear in the suspect rhetoric of Rupert Brooke. Byron is divided in his attitudes to war, and this division is, I believe, characteristic of much subsequent poetry.

In some ways the history of war poetry is the history of wars. The first truly modern war was the American Civil War, large-scale and mechanized, given mobility by the railway, and greatly increased fire-power by advances in weaponry. Melville and Whitman, then in their forties, wrote moving poems about the fraternal slaughter. Whitman's poetic sequence, *Drum-Taps*, arising from his experiences as a wound-dresser, unflinchingly conveys the horrors of mutilation and the waste of young lives, and seems directly to anticipate the poetry of the Great War. It was seen in this light by a poet of that war, Isaac Rosenberg, who wrote in a letter in 1917: ' "Drum Taps" stands unique as War Poetry in my mind. I have written a few war poems but when I think of "Drum Taps" mine are absurd.'[1] At the

---

[1] *The Collected Works of Isaac Rosenberg*, ed. Ian Parsons (London, 1979), p.267.

end of the nineteenth century Britain was involved in the Anglo-Boer
war, to give it its proper title, which persists in folk memory as a
combination of a colonial war and a rehearsal for the war which
broke out in 1914. It was marked in English poetry by Kipling and
Hardy and many lesser poets. Malvern Van Wyk Smith's book,
Drummer Hodge: the Poetry of the Anglo-Boer War (1978), gives a
valuable account of the poetry – or the verse – written on both sides
of the conflict, in English and Afrikaans, together with some curio-
sities, such as poems from the Boer side written in English. Stallworthy
prints a harshly realistic poem, called simply 'War', which describes
a wounded soldier brought into a field hospital; it recalls *Drum-
Taps*, and anticipates Sassoon or Owen. Here is the final stanza:

> The clink of a stopper and glass:
>   A sigh as the chloroform drips:
> A trickle of – what? on the grass,
>   And bluer and bluer the lips.
> The lashes have hidden the stare...
>   A rent, and the clothes fall away...
> A touch, and the wound is laid bare...
>   A cut, and the face has turned grey...
> And it's *War*! 'Orderly, take It out.
>   It's hard for his child, and it's rough on his wife,
> There might have been – sooner – a chance for his life.
>   But it's *War*! And – Orderly, clean this knife!'

Like many of the poems of that war this seems to owe quite a lot to
the popular recitations of the music-halls, in its combination of
jauntiness and sentimentality. But it may have a more literary model
in W.E. Henley's sequence of poems called 'In Hospital'. The author
was Edgar Wallace, who is now remembered as a prolific thriller
writer, but who served in South Africa as a war correspondent.

It is difficult to avoid the impression that all the poetry which
takes up the first half of Stallworthy's anthology is no more than an
extended prelude to the war poetry of 1914-18. Indeed, I believe that
the loose but potent concept of 'war poetry' is itself a product of the
Great War, so that we tend to interpret the earlier poetry in terms
of the attitudes of that conflict. Indeed, when schoolchildren or
students are studying the 'war poets' we can have a pretty good idea
of who they will be reading: Owen and Sassoon certainly, and possibly
selected works by Rupert Brooke, Charles Sorley, Robert Graves,
Isaac Rosenberg, Edmund Blunden, Ivor Gurney and Herbert Read.
They are unlikely to be reading poems published before 1914, and

not very likely to be reading the poets of the Second World War, such as Keith Douglas or Alun Lewis, or the Americans included in Stallworthy's anthology, such as Louis Simpson and Randall Jarrell.

The literature of the Great War first began to look like a recognizable entity in the early 1930s, after a wave of prose writing, in memoirs or autobiographical fiction, by the survivors of the Western Front: Blunden, Sassoon, Graves, Aldington, Manning, among others. In poetry, the appearance of Edmund Blunden's edition of Wilfred Owen in 1931 was a significant event. Owen became something of a cult figure to the young poets of the Auden generation, and he was rapidly incorporated into Auden's personal mythology. He wrote in a poem of 1933:

> 'The poetry is in the pity,' Wilfred said
> And Kathy in her journal, 'To be rooted in life,
> That's what I want'.

('Kathy' was Katherine Mansfield, another admired figure for the young Auden.) The prominence of Owen provoked a notorious reaction from W.B. Yeats, who, perhaps without realizing it, was one of the first people to make a theoretical statement about the nature of war poetry. It occurs in his preface to the *Oxford Book of Modern Verse*, that courageously eccentric compilation. Yeats writes 'I have a distaste for certain poems written in the midst of the great war', and justifies his reasons for omitting them from his anthology. He says of the officer poets:

> their letters are vivid and humorous, they were not without joy –
> for all skill is joyful – but felt bound, in the words of the best
> known, to plead the suffering of their men. In poems that had for
> a time considerable fame, written in the first person, they made
> that suffering their own. I have rejected these poems for the same
> reason that made Arnold withdraw his *Empedocles on Etna* from
> circulation; passive suffering is not a theme for poetry. In all the
> great tragedies tragedy is a joy to the man who dies; in Greece the
> tragic chorus danced.[2]

Yeats's words imply not just critical disagreement but a clash of what Wittgenstein called 'forms of life'. He regards tragedy in a religious or transcendental perspective, which was inaccessible to the trench poets, who were forced back on the basic emotions of

---

[2] W.B. Yeats, ed., *The Oxford Book of Modern Verse 1891-1935* (Oxford, 1936), p.xxxiv.

horror and pity and anger. Yeats amplified his remarks in a letter to
Dorothy Wellesley, in which he described Owen as 'unworthy of the
poets' corner of a country newspaper...He is all blood, dirt and
sucked sugar-stick...There is every excuse for him, but none for
those who like him.' Yeats was wrong, of course, but it is the kind of
provoking wrongness that can illuminate its subject better than
unthinking praise. What is particularly interesting is that sentiments
similar to Yeats's were expressed at about the same time by a writer
at the opposite end of the ideological spectrum, the Communist
critic, Christopher Caudwell. He wrote in *Illusion and Reality*: 'If
the tragedy did not make the Athenians feel better, in spite of its
tragedy, it was bad. The tragic poet who made them weep bitterly at
the fate of their fellow Hellenes in Persia was fined. A similar imposi-
tion suggests itself for our own purely sentimental war literature.'[3]
By the time *Illusion and Reality* appeared in 1937 Caudwell was
dead, fighting for the Spanish Republic.

Keith Douglas, whom I take to be the finest English poet of the
Second World War, served in the North African desert as a tank
commander and was killed in Normandy in 1944. In his poem,
'Desert Flowers', he wrote, 'Rosenberg, I only repeat what you were
saying', and in an essay, 'Poets in This War', he refers with admira-
tion to the soldier-poets of the earlier war, Owen, Sassoon, Sorley,
and Rosenberg. As far as Douglas is concerned, a genuine 'war poet'
is someone who, like them, had had experience of fighting:

> There is nothing new, from a soldier's point of view, about this
> war except its mobile character. There are two reasons: hell
> cannot be let loose twice: it was let loose in the Great War and it
> is the same old hell now. The hardships, pain and boredom; the
> behaviour of the living and the appearance of the dead, were so
> accurately described by the poets of the Great War that every day
> on the battlefields of the western desert – and no doubt on the
> Russian battlefields as well – their poems are illustrated. Almost
> all that a modern poet on active service is inspired to write would
> be tautological.[4]

Douglas thought that everything that could be said about war had
already been said about the Great War. Nevertheless, he was already
writing his own distinctive war poems, and I think he overestimated
the continuity of experience. There is little of what Yeats denounced

---

[3] Christopher Caudwell, *Illusion and Reality* (London, 1977), p.63.
[4] Keith Douglas, *A Prose Miscellany* (Manchester, 1985), pp.119-20.

as 'passive suffering' in Douglas's poetry. There was, after all, a great difference between the active, mobile warfare of the desert and the waterlogged stasis of the trenches, where men were likely to be passive victims of artillery bombardment or gas attacks. A tank commander in the hot, empty spaces of the desert, like Douglas, was a physically and perhaps morally freer being than the young infantry officers in the Great War; and the difference shows in the poetry. Nevertheless, there is a line of succession suggested by the fact that Douglas invoked Rosenberg, and Rosenberg praised Whitman.

Douglas, as a soldier and a poet, established his own relationship with his predecessors. Yet whatever individual readers made of it, the poetry of the Great War does not fully emerge as a coherent literary and academic subject until about 1960. In that year Dennis Welland published the first critical study of Wilfred Owen, and this was followed over the years by many studies of a few poets: works of criticism and biography, editions and anthologies, selected poems and case books. The 'war poets' have become an established subject for study in schools and universities, though likely to include fewer than a dozen of the more than 2,000 poets listed in Catherine Reilly's bibliography of Great War poetry. The subject has become academically respectable and institutionalized, in teaching and research. I see the culmination of the process in Stallworthy's splendid edition in two volumes of Owen's complete poems and fragments, where he receives more devoted scholarly attention than any other twentieth-century poet except Yeats. Academic practices have, in fact, become fused with the national myth-making that led to the unveiling in 1985 of a monument to the poets of the First World War in Westminster Abbey. Dominic Hibberd has commented, 'Imagine a monument there to the Metaphysical Poets or the Restoration Dramatists or the Victorian Industrial Novelists', adding that at least half of the sixteen poets commemorated are in his view distinctly second-rate.[5]

Critical studies and pedagogic discussions of the poetry of the Great War are likely to fit it into a pattern of illusion being replaced by disillusion and anger, in which the naive patriotism of Rupert Brooke and Julian Grenfell was superseded, once the war became literally bogged down in the trenches and intermittent mass slaughter of the Western Front, by the pity of Owen and the protest of Sassoon. This attitude is evident in *Heroes' Twilight*, but I now think it needs to be treated with caution. The movement from illusion to disillusion

[5] Dominic Hibberd, 'Who Were the War Poets, Anyway?', *English Literature of the Great War Revisited*, ed. Michel Roucoux (Amiens, 1989), p.109.

is certainly there, in a number of well-known poets, but one must beware of seeing it as representative of all literary responses to the war, and still less of the general attitudes of the soldiers. There is a danger when students, and indeed their teachers, take a handful of war poems, perhaps backed up by the spectacle of *Oh, What a Lovely War!*, and treat them as sufficient evidence of what the First World War was all about. Owen and Sassoon conveyed with memorable intensity the horror and the pity and the anger that the experience of war provoked in them; but they gave what could only be a close-up of a single aspect of its appalling complexity, which had so many dimensions, historical, military, diplomatic.

There is, in fact, an attractive mythic drama that underlines the study of these poets, which exists almost independently of their poetry. The particular protagonists are Owen, Sassoon and Graves. Sassoon, who had been a courageous and exemplary officer, decides in 1917 that the war is being unjustifiably prolonged, and that he will take no further part in it. He throws the ribbon of his Military Cross into the River Mersey; he attempts to make a public protest against war, hoping that he will be court-martialled, but the authorities decline. His younger but more worldly friend, Graves, was no more enthusiastic about the war than Sassoon, but was convinced that the public protest would be ineffective and that he had to be protected against himself. Following Graves's representations, Sassoon was deemed to be suffering from shell-shock and was sent to Craiglockhart Hospital near Edinburgh to recover. It was there that he had a crucial encounter with a fellow-patient, Wilfred Owen; he recognized and encouraged Owen's genius as a poet, and later introduced him to London literary circles. In 1918 both Sassoon and Owen voluntarily went back to the front; Sassoon was wounded and came home, while Owen was killed, poignantly, just one week before Armistice. It is a moving story, but it is liable to distort the reading of the poetry.

In 1973, when I was a visiting lecturer in a Polish university, I gave a talk to students of English on the poetry of the Great War, emphasizing, as one does, the element of protest in Owen and Sassoon. When it was over and questions were invited, a young man asked me in careful English, 'These poets you have been telling us about, were they patriots?' I did my best to explain that in their own terms the poets did regard themselves as patriots and lovers of their country, but they were not fighting on their own soil, and were protesting against a war which they did not believe to be justified. I could see that the Polish student was not satisfied with my reply, and this little encounter left me reflecting on a clash between attitudes and forms of life. The Poles, for much of their history, have had to fight for their independence and national identity against alien oppressors, and for them patriotism is an intense and positive value. Furthermore, the Poles, like other European nations, are accustomed to conscription, so that military service and citizenship go together. The English tradition is basically anti-military, as Kipling sardonically complained in his poems about army life, and the best-known poetry of the Great War was the work of civilians in uniform.

As critical and scholarly studies of the poetry of the war have multiplied two opposing views of it have emerged. The former continues to uphold the pattern of illusion turning to disillusion, affirming that the best poetry of the war – that is in the work of the poets who emerged after the patriotic hopes of 1914-15 were dashed – was poetry of outrage and protest, and that the principal value of 'war poetry' is that it is anti-war poetry. This broadly pacifist position has been argued for by Jon Silkin in *Out of Battle* (1972) and his influential *Penguin Book of First World War Poetry* (1979), and by Desmond Graham in *The Truth of War* (1984). Silkin, in the introduction to his anthology, sees the development of the subject in four phrases: first, unreflective patriotism; second, anger; third, compassion; fourth, anger and compassion merging in a desire for a new order of things. These stages are represented by, respectively, Brooke, Sassoon, Owen and Rosenberg. There is something unconvincing about a set of categories each of which contains only one representative, and Silkin's argument is, I think, an attempt to justify his conviction that Rosenberg was the greatest of the war poets. The opposing position might be called sceptical or revisionist, and it has been advanced by Andrew Rutherford in *The Literature of War* (1978), and by Dominic Hibberd in *Owen the Poet* (1986) and in the anthology *Poetry of the Great War* (1986), which he edited with John Onions. The interest of this debate, and perhaps its ultimate importance, is that it takes one beyond the particular problems of interpreting the poetry of the Great War and raises basic questions about the nature of literature and how we respond to it.

Dominic Hibberd, in the revisionist camp, yields to no one in his admiration for Owen and Sassoon, about whom he has written very well, but, like Andrew Rutherford, he is at pains to stress their unrepresentative quality; unrepresentative, that is, of most of the poetry, or perhaps one should say verse, written by soldiers in the Great War. Silkin's anthology is, as he explains in his introduction, indicative of his personal conviction that good war poetry is, in some

sense, protest or anti-war poetry. Even so, the need to be representa-
tive forces him to include a number of poems whose attitudes or
values he dissents from, but which are so well-known that they
would have been difficult to exclude, and which he marks with an
asterisk to indicate his dissent. They include Grenfell's 'Into Battle',
Alan Seegar's 'I Have a Rendezvous with Death' and John McCrae's
'In Flanders Fields', which were all very popular during the war; but
also, interestingly, Sorley's 'All the hills and vales along' and Owen's
'Anthem for Doomed Youth'. The Hibberd-Onions anthology has a
similar title to Silkin's, but it is informed by very different principles.
It aims, above all, to be broadly representative, of the kinds of poetry
written by both fighting men and civilians, during and after the war.
'Poetry' in the title means what was regarded as poetry at the time,
rather than what critical opinion now would necessarily regard as
such: it is equivalent, in effect, to the descriptive and non-evaluative
term, 'verse'. The interest of the material is as much historical as
literary, assuming that one can continue confidently to make that
traditional distinction which continues to inform my own thinking —
though the advent of the New Historicism, treating literary texts as
historical exhibits, may have somewhat blurred it for many readers.

   Hibberd and Onions do not claim poetic merit for much of their
material, but it is enlightening in its own way, and provides a context
for the canonical 'war poetry' that is now read and admired and
studied. It is worth recalling that two of the major war poets, Rosen-
berg and Owen, who were both killed in 1918, were virtually
unknown during the war and their reputations are entirely posthum-
ous. One gets an idea of the poets who *were* famous from a piece of
undistinguished verse that Hibberd and Onions include, 'The Soldier
Poets' by Wilfred Meynell. It was published in 1918, and commem-
orates various poets who had been victims of the war. Two of them,
Brooke, who died on his way to the Dardanelles campaign, and
Grenfell, who was killed in France, are still familiar names. The
others, E.A. Mackintosh, W.N. Hodgson, E.W.Tennant, and Gerald
Caldwell, are no longer so. Hibberd, in his note, describes them
as 'some of the most well-known soldier-poets of the "officer and
gentlemen" class'. All of them wrote patriotic poetry, of the kind
that Silkin places in his first category.

   It is a common assumption that once people discovered what war
is really like, no one could still write about it as Julian Grenfell did in
'Into Battle'. The reality is otherwise, as we see from a poem called
'War the Liberator' by E.A. Mackintosh, one of the most popular
war poets at the time. He had been awarded the Military Cross in

1916 and was wounded and gassed later in the same year. He returned
to the front in 1917 and was killed in November; 'War, the Libera-
tor' was written not long before. It is dedicated 'To the Authoress of
"Non-Combatants"' (this was the popular poet Jessie Pope). Here is
the opening:

> Surely War is vile to you, you who can but know of it,
> Broken men and broken hearts, and boys too young to die,
> You that never knew its joy, never felt the glow of it,
> Valour and the pride of men, soaring to the sky,
> Death's a fearful thing to you, terrible in suddenness,
> Lips that will not laugh again, tongues that will not sing,
> You that have not ever seen their sudden life of happiness,
> The moment they looked down on death, a cowed and beaten thing.

Mackintosh's experience of the horror and suffering of the war was
at least as great as that of Owen and Sassoon, and he was writing at
the same time, but his response was very different. The immediate
counter-argument is to say that they were better poets than Mackin-
tosh, or Grenfell, and one has to agree. But are they better poets
because they are anti-war poets? To see this as self-evidently true is
to fall into a circular argument: good war poetry is anti-war poetry,
and it is good because it is anti-war. Intelligent criticism has to do
better than this. The problem may be partly deconstructed by
suggesting that not all of the war poetry that we admire can be
simply regarded as 'protest' poetry. Indeed, the concept of 'protest'
poetry projected back on to the Great War from the 1960s and the
emotions aroused by Vietnam may be inappropriate. If we are to
apply it, then I believe that only Owen and Sassoon fall clearly into
that category. Other poets of the Great War described the misery
and the destruction and the waste of life; but such awareness is not,
in itself, anti-war. Again, to write satirically about the top brass and
the military high command may be a protest about the way the war
is being fought rather than against the war as such. Rosenberg offers
an interesting instance. Silkin has quoted a phrase from one of
Rosenberg's letters, 'Nothing can justify war', which looks like an
unambiguously pacifist statement. But it is immediately qualified by
the next sentence, which is not quoted by Silkin: 'I suppose we must
all fight to get the trouble over.'[6] Rosenberg's celebrated and terrify-
ing poem 'Dead Man's Dump' begins:

---

[6] Jon Silkin, 'Sassoon, Owen, Rosenberg', Roucoux, op. cit., p.107; Rosenberg, op.
cit. p.227.

> The plunging limbers over the shattered track
> Racketed with their rusty freight,
> Stuck out like many crowns of thorns,
> And the rusty stakes like sceptres old
> To stay the flood of brutish men
> Upon our brothers dear.

Hibberd has raised the question, who are the 'brutish men' if not the German enemy? I think they were, though to accept this reading is not to suggest that Rosenberg was a jingoistic or triumphalist poet. He clearly was not; but on the evidence of his writing, I do not think he was a wholly pacifist poet either. He seems to have found the experience of war appalling, but in a strange way magnificent too. His 'Break of Day in the Trenches', which, like Paul Fussell, I now regard as the greatest poem to come out of the Great War, offers a serene and ironic balance between opposed forces; the English soldier and the German are divided by war and united by the casual manifestations of nature; the rat which runs freely between the front lines, and the poppies, nourished by the dead, which grow in No Man's Land. Whitman's *Drum-Taps*, which Rosenberg so much admired, may be relevant. Whitman writes with immense compassion of the sufferings of the soldiers he tended in hospital, and in 'Reconciliation' he beautifully expresses that sense of the enemy's common humanity that we find in poems such as 'Break of Day in the Trenches' and Owen's 'Strange Meeting':

> For my enemy is dead, a man divine as myself is dead,
> I look where he lies white-faced and still in the coffin – I
>   draw near,
> Bend down and touch lightly with my lips the white face in
>   the coffin.

Yet Whitman was a committed supporter of the Northern cause, and elsewhere he expressed his appreciation of the traditional trappings of martial glory: 'The drum-corps' rattles ever to me sweet music, I love well the martial dirge/ With slow wail and convulsive throb leading the officer's funeral.'

Owen and Sassoon, we may agree, were 'anti-war' poets when they met in 1917, the year when Sassoon made his courageous but ineffectual protest. Yet they, like other young officer-poets, were caught up in a cruel conflict between protest and solidarity with their fellows, particularly the private soldiers for whom they felt such an agonizing sense of quasi-paternal responsibility. As Andrew Rutherford has put it, 'Their dilemma, basic, unresolvable, was that they subscribed to two conflicting ethics – one based on courage and comradeship and the other on compassion – so that the claims of duty co-existed for them with those of protest. The former predominated in their lives, the latter in their poetry.'[7] This division needs to be kept in mind to offset the too simple equation, war poetry = protest poetry. The divided consciousness of Owen and Sassoon runs like a thread through their writing and their lives, particularly after they returned to the Front in 1918. Hibberd believes that Sassoon was modifying his attitudes by the spring of that year, and he includes in his anthology a previously unpublished Sassoon poem from that time called 'Testament', which ends with the words 'O my heart/Be still; you have cried your cry; you have played your part', suggesting that he felt his protest was over and done with. In Sassoon's war diary we see evidence of his divided state of mind; he was happy to be back in France and seemingly eager to go into action. In an entry for 14 June 1918 he writes, ' "Damn it, I'm fed up with all this training!" I exclaimed in a loud voice, pushing back my chair on the brick floor and getting on my feet. "I want to go up to the Line and fight!" said I, with a reckless air.' In the next paragraph he adds, 'Thus had I boasted in a moment of folly catching my mood from the lads who look to me as their leader.'[8] His second-in-command, Vivian de Sola Pinto (who appears as 'Velmore' in *Sherston's Progress*), wrote of Sassoon's *Counter-Attack*, 'It seemed to me a strange paradox that the author of those poems full of burning indignation against war's hideous cruelty should also be a first-rate soldier and a most aggressive company commander.'[9]

Owen, too, was a divided man who found a curious serenity in division after his return to France in September 1918. On his previous period of service in 1917 he had described himself as 'a conscientious objector with a very seared conscience', and his fundamental convictions had not changed. Yet in the final weeks of the war and of his life Owen showed a new calm and maturity. After being in action in October 1918 he wrote to his mother, 'I lost all my earthly faculties, and fought like an angel...My nerves are in perfect order.'[10] That last phrase greatly appealed to the young Auden, who quoted it more than once. Owen may still have been a pacifist in uniform, but in

---

[7] Andrew Rutherford, *The Literature of War* (London, 1979), p.85.
[8] Siegfried Sassoon, *Diaries 1915-1918*, ed. Rupert Hart-Davis (London, 1983), p.269.
[9] Vivian de Sola Pinto, *The City That Shone* (London, 1969), p.226.
[10] Jon Stallworthy, *Wilfred Owen: A Biography* (Oxford, 1977), p.278.

those final weeks he fought with great courage and determination. Hibberd has suggested that he had become a figure rather like Conrad's Lord Jim, determined to live down what he felt was the disgrace of the previous year, when his nerves had collapsed, he was found unfit to command men and was invalided home. He was amply vindicated when he won the Military Cross: the citation read, 'He personally manipulated a captured enemy machine gun in an isolated position and inflicted considerable losses on the enemy. Throughout he behaved most gallantly.'[11] Just over a month later he was killed, having performed in his life what in his poetry he most deplored.

Owen was a more complex and contradictory figure than superficial impressions of him suggest. Indeed, the well-known words of the draft preface to his poems can themselves be misleading: 'Above all I am not concerned with Poetry. My subject is War, and the pity of War. The Poetry is in the Pity.' They might suggest that Owen was dismissing poetry as a formal art in the interests of raw emphatic statement, as was indeed done by some forms of protest writing later in the twentieth century. Owen was always concerned with poetry, as we see from the care with which he composed his drafts, and he took immense pride in being a poet, and indeed a poet in the late-Romantic, aesthetic tradition. The one book of poems that Owen had with him on his last period of service in France was Swinburne's *Poems and Ballads*. This aspect of Owen has been illuminatingly discussed in Dominic Hibberd's excellent book, which dismisses the conventional picture of the sensitive young poet tormented into protest by the horrors of war, who believed simply that 'the poetry is in the pity'. Owen's poetic art was brought to its extraordinary forced maturity in the trenches, but its origin lay in the French and English Decadence of the late nineteenth century. In Hibberd's reading, Owen's imagination was pervaded by the Romantic Agony well before he encountered the literal agonies of war. His early poems and drafts combine images of ideal beauty or ambiguous eroticism with those of death and destruction and mutilation. At the Front Owen's imaginative obsessions took on a terrible reality, but in a sense he was already prepared for it. As Hibberd puts it, 'Owen's war poems are not simply protests or statements of pity. They constantly return to certain obsessive images and to guilt, desire, darkness and blood. He might have gone mad as many of his fellow soldiers did but instead he got his imagination under control and wrote with an

---

[11] Ibid., p.279.

increasingly serene self-discipline.'[12] Hibberd's discussion of Owen is a particular instance of Fussell's general thesis about the British literature of the Great War: that it was intensely literary, using the themes and topics and devices of earlier literature, English and Classical, to respond to an unprecedented reality.

Much present-day discussion of the subject assumes that there were only two possible attitudes to the war, militarist or pacifist, Grenfell's or Owen's; and that the war itself was unjustified, and was only kept going, as Owen and Sassoon believed, by the bloody-mindedness of politicians and generals. In fact, the most common attitude among soldiers, whether poets or not, seems to have been neither militarist nor pacifist: patriotic heroics were derided, and war was seen as terrible, but there was a stoical belief that, as Rosenberg put it, 'we must fight to get the trouble over'. This was the view of the philosopher and imagist poet, T.E. Hulme, who saw active service in France, was wounded in 1916 and killed in 1917. He soon lost what little sense he had of the glory of war: 'it's the most miserable existence you can conceive of,' he wrote in his diary about life in the trenches. At the same time, Hulme was convinced that the war had to be fought. He wrote, 'These sacrifices are as negative, barren, and as *necessary* as the work of those who repair sea-walls. In this war, then, we are fighting for no great liberation of mankind, for no great jump upward but are merely accomplishing a work, which, if the nature of things was ultimately "good," would be useless, but which in this "vale of tears" becomes from time to time necessary, merely in order that bad may not get worse.'[13] These sentiments reflect Hulme's pessimistic and conservative view of history and human nature, and his conviction that German hegemony would be a disaster for Europe and had to be resisted.

The First World War, and British involvement in it in particular, was an enormous disaster. but it had the inescapability as well as the sense of loss of a great tragedy. Once the fragile international order collapsed in the summer of 1914, British involvement in the war would have been extremely difficult to avoid. And once the war started, the initial hopes of an early end were soon dashed, as developments in military technology gave a heavy advantage to the defence, resulting in the stalemate of trench warfare and continued futile attempts at a breakthrough by both sides – and when a break-

---

[12] Dominic Hibberd, *Owen the Poet* (London, 1986), p.83.
[13] T.E. Hulme, *Further Speculations*, ed. Samuel Hynes (Minneapolis, 1955), pp. 157, 184.

through finally came in the spring of 1918, it was the Germans who made it. The honourable hopes for a negotiated peace that were raised by the Pope and others in 1917, and were shared by Owen and Sassoon, seemed to have had little chance of success. The war machine was so vast and complex that there was no way of stopping it, apart from the collapse of one side or other. History suggests that Imperial Germany had no intention of abandoning its attempt at European hegemony whilst there was any chance of carrying it through: the brutally punitive and expansionist settlement that Germany imposed on Russia at the treaty of Brest-Litovsk is telling evidence. For the Western powers the fate of Belgium was a major sticking-point, even though that was derided in the inter-war years. Louis MacNeice wrote during the Munich Crisis of 1938:

> And we who have been brought up to think of 'Gallant Belgium'
>   As so much blague
> Are now preparing again to essay good through evil
>   For the sake of Prague;
> And must, we suppose, become uncritical, vindictive,
>   And must, in order to beat
> The enemy model ourselves upon the enemy,
>   A howling radio for our Paraclete[14]

Myth resists history, and in the late twenties and early thirties, when the moving and vivid records of the survivors began to appear, and Owen's poems to be read, the Great War was widely mythologized as the great unjust war: Weimar Germany was admired, and there was a passionate conviction that there must be No More War. Within a few years this pattern of feeling was replaced by another, as fascism became an increasing menace, particularly after the outbreak of the Spanish Civil War, which was soon seen as a shining instance of that impossibility, a just war, and a different powerful myth emerged. In Spain, as Auden put it, 'Our fever's menacing shapes are precise and alive'. Erstwhile pacifists volunteered for the International Brigades, in the spirit that had sent Byron to fight for Greece, and young left-wing intellectuals who had treated the Officers' Training Corps at their public schools with derision and satire strove to remember their military training. George Orwell mockingly wrote, in his essay 'Looking Back on the Spanish War', 'here were the very people who for twenty years had hooted and jeered at the "glory" of war, at atrocity stories, at patriotism, even at physical

---

courage, coming out with stuff that with the alteration of a few names would have fitted into the *Daily Mail* of 1918'.[15] Orwell exaggerated a little, as he was inclined to when he got carried away, but he had earned the right to comment by having himself fought in Spain and been severely wounded. One can see what he means from the final stanza of 'Full Moon at Tierz', by the young poet John Cornford who was killed fighting in 1936 at the age of twenty-one:

> Freedom is an easily spoken word
> But facts are stubborn things. Here, too, in Spain
> Our fight's not won till the workers of the world
> Stand by our guard on Huesca's plain,
> Swear that our dead fought not in vain,
> Raise the red flag triumphantly
> For Communism and for liberty.

Cornford provides a transposed version of the patriotic rhetoric of 1914.

In the Second World War, Keith Douglas, who acknowledged his allegiance to the poets of the earlier war, went on from them to write a different kind of poetry, though it learnt from their example; it showed no taste for glory or patriotic fervour, but accepted the war as both horrible and inescapable and in the end necessary, in T.E. Hulme's sense, given the need to resist Nazi Germany. Douglas's 'Vergissmeinnicht' is now a familiar anthology piece, a parallel to Owen's 'Futility'. The contrast between Owen's anguish at the sight of a young, dead English soldier and Douglas's seeming coolness at a dead and decaying German points beyond differences of temperament to a difference in ways of apprehending war. Reading Douglas, I think of Eliot's remark that we know more than the dead poets, and they are precisely what we know. In certain ways Douglas went further than his predecessors. It is one thing to write about a dead man, as Owen and Douglas did, and Graves did in 'Dead Boche'. It is something else again to write a poem about killing a man, as Douglas does in 'How to Kill', of which these are the middle stanzas:

> Now in my dial of glass appears
> the soldier who is going to die.
> He smiles and moves about in ways

[15] George Orwell, *Collected Essays, Letters and Journalism*, (Harmondsworth, 1970), Vol.2, p.288.

his mother knows, habits of his.
The wires touch his face: I cry
NOW. Death, like a familiar hears

and look, has made a man of dust
of a man of flesh. Being damned, I am amused
to see the centre of love diffused
and the waves of love travel into vacancy.
How easy it is to make a ghost.

In this discussion I have concentrated on the poetry of the Great
War, seeing earlier instances as anticipations of it, and the poetry
from later wars as footnotes to or developments of it. Ultimately the
problem of war poetry is the eternal problem of war itself. Does one
fight to defend what one believes to be good and to resist evil, even
though fighting is itself an evil and the cause of further evil? Orwell
wrote in his uncompromising way during the Spanish Civil War:

> the horror we feel of these things has led to the conclusion: if some
> one drops a bomb on your mother, go and drop two bombs on his
> mother. The only apparent alternatives are to smash dwelling
> houses to powder, blow out human entrails and burn holes in
> children with lumps of thermite, or to be enslaved by people who
> are more ready to do these things than you are yourself: as yet no
> one has suggested a practicable way out.[16]

It is this dilemma and the tensions it sets up that I believe inspire
the best war poetry, from whatever war, rather than any straight-
forward element of 'protest'.

Turning to smaller and more tractable topics, I suggest that one
particular problem concerning the poets of the Great War is that,
however they approached their subject, they were traditionalists
about poetic form. This was as true of Owen and Sassoon as it was
of Brooke and Grenfell; indeed, Owen, as we have seen, has his
poetic roots in late-Romantic aestheticism. One of the things Yeats
objected to in Owen was his unreconstructed poetic diction, com-
plaining, 'he calls poets "bards", a girl a "maid", and talks about
"Titanic wars"'. In rather different terms, the war poets were at
the heart of a major crisis in civilization, but had nothing to do with
the literary and artistic transformations of modernism, though I
would make a tentative exception for Rosenberg. The point was put

---

[16] Ibid., Vol.1, pp.329-30.

succinctly by Michael Alexander in his book on Ezra Pound, where he remarks that what Pound saw as the essential insularity of English literary culture is 'evidenced by the current offering of the English poets of the Great War not as witnesses to a great national tragedy, but as modern poets of real stature'.[17] Alexander's point is well taken, but I am not sure if he has the emphasis right. It might be truer to say that there is a significant dichotomy in the way twentieth-century poetry is taught and studied: Owen and Sassoon are read as witnesses to a great national tragedy, and poets of direct human impact, despite their traditional form; while Eliot and Pound are read as the modernist masters who remade twentieth-century poetry.

There is perhaps a further dimension to the question. The study of vernacular literature, in England and elsewhere, has always been inspired by the great myths of national identity; as Hopkins put it in a letter, a great work by an Englishman was like a great battle won by England. On the other hand, the study of the Classics, which the study of the vernacular partly replaced, was a European and inter-national concern. And this concern was reintroduced into English, in a new accent, by Eliot and Pound, the poets of Franco-American modernism, both with strong Classical interests. In pragmatic terms, it is curiously difficult to consider war poetry and modernism in the same focus. If *The Waste Land* is a great poem, then how valuable are Owen and Sassoon? Alternatively, if after three-quarters of a century those poets can speak to young readers today with such force and immediacy, then isn't *The Waste Land* what literary conserva-tives have always thought it was, an exercise in sterile cosmopolitan academicism?

For some concluding thoughts on the subject I will turn to a non-English source, the French poet and scholar, Jacques Darras. In 1989 he delivered the Reith Lectures for the BBC – he is a great anglophile and a fluent English speaker – and in the fourth of them he reflected on the Great War.[18] He pointed out that although the French suffered much greater loss of life, and huge devastation of their territory, they do not dwell on that war in the nostalgic, mythopoeic spirit of the English. For us the 'Somme' is a battle, of terrible suggestive power, whereas for the French it is merely an unimportant river in the north of their country. Nor were there any French equivalents to the English war poets, with the possible exception of Apollinaire, though Henri Barbusse's novel, *Under Fire*, was, as it happens, an

---

17 Michael Alexander, *The Poetic Achievement of Ezra Pound* (London, 1979), p.84.
18 Jacques Darras, 'Remembering the Somme', *Listener*, 14 December 1989.

inspiration to Sassoon and Owen. When the war started the French had already read Mallarmé and Rimbaud and witnessed the explosion of aesthetic energy associated with the Paris avant-garde. Darras remarks, 'Thus to the French, the war, when it came in 1914, was, in aesthetic terms at least, an almost supernumerary event breaking out anachronistically after the real upheaval had already taken place. It would certainly uproot lives, but it added no ideas.'

The French saw art and life on different planes, whereas the English, then and now, wanted to bring them together. Darras develops the argument thus:

> The French incline to analyse their artists in the context of the aesthetic movements of which they formed a part; the English, more emotionally, love to link an artist's life to his art (hence the great success of literary biographies in the English-speaking world). And what could be more emotion-laden than a group of talented poets who wrote, and in some cases, died on a foreign field of battle? But what about art?

In his view, the art was insufficient: 'I cannot help detecting in Owen and others a plea to the reader, not only for sympathy for their plight as warriors, but also for pity towards the inevitable inadequacies of the poetry itself.' He adds that to the French even hell could be exciting, as long as it is a modern hell.

If there is an argument against Darras' position it has to be the relativistic one that there are many kinds of art, and some of them, like certain wines, do not travel well. Indeed, much of the interest of the speculations I have tried to raise is that they bring one up against fundamental questions about the nature of literature, and its relations to the cultures that produce and receive it; and, indeed, about the relation of literature to life. We may believe that the militaristic emotions that inspired so many writers in the opening phase of the Great War are now permanently a thing of the past, though remembering their brief but intense recrudescence in the Falklands War, I am now not so sure. In other parts of the world, as recent history has revealed, they remain appallingly alive. In the face of new wars and their horrors, a degree of Hulme's sceptical pessimism about humanity seems in order. But I will end with an assertion that I think we can all agree with. War poetry is the one literary genre that one hopes will never be extended.

Chronology

1914   H.G. Wells: *The War That Will End War*

1915   Rupert Brooke: *1914 and other poems*
      Arthur Machen: *The Bowmen*
      Robert Nichols: *Invocation*
      Deaths of Rupert Brooke, Julian Grenfell, Charles Sorley

1916   Robert Graves: *Over the Brazier*
      F.W. Harvey: *A Gloucestershire Lad*
      Charles Sorley: *Marlborough and other poems*
      H.G. Wells: *Mr Britling Sees It Through*

1917   Henri Barbusse: *Under Fire* (English translation)
      Robert Graves: *Fairies and Fusiliers*
      Ivor Gurney: *Severn and Somme*
      F.W. Harvey: *Gloucestershire Friends*
      Frederic Manning: *Eidola*
      Robert Nichols: *Ardours and Endurances*
      Ezra Pound: *Homage to Sextus Propertius*
      Siegfried Sassoon: *The Old Huntsman*
      Edward Thomas: *Poems*
      Francis Brett Young: *Marching on Tanga*
      Deaths of Edward Thomas, T.E. Hulme and Arthur Graeme
        West

1918   Rupert Brooke: *Collected Poems*
      Ford Madox Ford (Hueffer): *On Heaven*
      Siegfried Sassoon: *Counter-Attack*
      Deaths of Isaac Rosenberg and Wilfred Owen

1919   Richard Aldington: *Images of War*
      Ivor Gurney: *War's Embers*

Herbert Read: *Eclogues, Naked Warriors*
Bernard Shaw: *Heartbreak House*
Charles Sorley: *Letters*
Arthur Graeme West: *The Diary of a Dead Officer*

1920   D.H. Lawrence: *The Lost Girl*
Wilfred Owen: *Poems* (ed. S. Sassoon)
Ezra Pound: *Hugh Selwyn Mauberley*
Edward Thomas: *Collected Poems*

1921   John Dos Passos: *Three Soldiers*

1922   E.E. Cummings: *The Enormous Room*
T.S. Eliot: *The Waste Land*
C.E. Montague: *Disenchantment*
Isaac Rosenberg: *Poems* (ed. G. Bottomley)

1923   D.H. Lawrence: *Kangaroo*
C.E. Montague: *Fiery Particles*

1924   Ford Madox Ford: *Some Do Not*
R.H. Mottram: *The Spanish Farm*

1925   Ford Madox Ford: *No More Parades*
R.H. Mottram: *Sixty-Four, Ninety-Four!*
Herbert Read: *In Retreat*

1926   Ford Madox Ford: *A Man Could Stand Up*
R.H. Mottram, *The Crime at Vanderlynden's*

1927   T.E. Lawrence: *Revolt in the Desert*
R.H. Mottram: *The Spanish Farm Trilogy 1914-18*

1928   Edmund Blunden: *Undertones of War*
Ford Madox Ford: *Last Post*
Siegfried Sassoon: *Memoirs of a Fox-Hunting Man*
R.C. Sherriff: *Journey's End* (first performed)
Death of C.E. Montague

1929   Richard Aldington: *Death of a Hero*
Robert Graves: *Goodbye to All That*
Ernest Hemingway: *A Farewell to Arms*

Ernst Jünger: *The Storm of Steel* (English translation)
E.M. Remarque: *All Quiet on the Western Front* (English translation)

1930 Douglas Jerrold: *The Lie About the War*
Frederic Manning: *Her Privates We*
Siegfried Sassoon: *Memoirs of an Infantry Officer*
H.M. Tomlinson: *All Our Yesterdays*
Henry Williamson: *The Patriot's Progress*

1931 Wilfred Owen: *Poems* (ed. E. Blunden)

1933 Guy Chapman: *A Passionate Prodigality*
Frank Richards: *Old Soldiers Never Die*

1935 T.E. Lawrence: *Seven Pillars of Wisdom*
Deaths of T.E. Lawrence and Frederic Manning

1936 Cecil Lewis: *Sagittarius Rising*
Siegfried Sassoon: *Sherston's Progress*

1937 David Jones: *In Parenthesis*
Wyndham Lewis: *Blasting and Bombardiering*
Collected Works of Isaac Rosenberg (ed. G. Bottomley and
D. Harding)
Siegfried Sassoon: *The Complete Memoirs of George Sherston*
Death of Ivor Gurney

1938 Siegfried Sassoon: *The Old Century*

1939 Death of Ford Madox Ford

1942 Siegfried Sassoon: *Weald of Youth*

1944 Death of Robert Nichols

1945 Siegfried Sassoon: *Siegfried's Journey*

1947 Siegfried Sassoon: *Collected Poems*

1949 Isaac Rosenberg: *Collected Poems* (ed. G. Bottomley and
D. Harding)

1954   Ivor Gurney: *Poems (ed. E. Blunden)*
       Henry Williamson: *How Dear is Life*

1955   Henry Williamson: *A Fox Under My Cloak*

1956   *The Prose of Rupert Brooke* (ed. C. Hassall)
       T.E. Hulme: *Further Speculations* (ed. S. Hynes)

1957   Henry Williamson: *The Golden Virgin*
       Deaths of Wyndham Lewis and F.W. Harvey

1958   Henry Williamson: *Love and the Loveless*
       Death of H.M. Tomlinson

1960   H.D.: *Bid Me to Live*
       Henry Williamson: *A Test to Destruction* (This novel and the
          others by Williamson shown as appearing from 1954 are
          part of his sequence *A Chronicle of Ancient Sunlight*)

1961   Death of Frank Richards

1962   J.B. Priestley: *Margin Released*
       Death of Richard Aldington

1963   *Oh What a Lovely War!* (first performed)
       Wilfred Owen: *Collected Poems* (ed. C. Day Lewis)
       Harold Owen: *Journey From Obscurity: I: Childhood*
       Herbert Read: *The Contrary Experience*

1964   Christopher Hassall: *Rupert Brooke*
       Harold Owen: *Journey From Obscurity: II: Youth*

1965   Harold Owen: *Journey from Obscurity: III: War*

1967   Wilfred Owen: *Collected Letters* (ed. H. Owen and J. Bell)
       Death of Siegfried Sassoon

1968   Rupert Brooke: *Letters* (ed. G. Keynes)
       Death of Herbert Read

1969   Death of Osbert Sitwell

1971   Death of R.H. Mottram

1974 David Jones: *The Sleeping Lord and Other Fragments*
Jon Stallworthy: *Wilfred Owen*
Deaths of Edmund Blunden and David Jones

1975 Paul Fussell: *The Great War and Modern Memory*
Joseph Cohen: *Journey to the Trenches: the Life of Isaac Rosenberg*
Jean Liddiard: *Isaac Rosenberg: a Half-Used Life*
Jean Moorcraft Wilson: *Isaac Rosenberg: Poet and Painter*

1976 Nicholas Mosley: *Julian Grenfell*

1977 Death of Henry Williamson

1978 Michael Hurd: *The Ordeal of Ivor Gurney*
Edward Thomas: *Collected Poems* (ed. R.G. Thomas)

1979 *Collected Works of Isaac Rosenberg* (ed. I. Parsons)

1980 *Dai Greatcoat: A Self-Portrait of David Jones in his Letters* (ed. R. Hague)

1982 *In Broken Images: Selected Letters of Robert Graves* 1914- (ed. P. O'Prey)
Martin Seymour-Smith: *Robert Graves: His Life and Work*
Ivor Gurney: *Collected Poems* (ed. P.J. Kavanagh)
Death of Edgell Rickword

1983 Siegfried Sassoon: *Diaries 1915-1918* (ed. R. Hart-Davis)
Wilfred Owen: *Complete Poems and Fragments* (ed. J. Stallworthy)

1985 *Collected Poems of Charles Hamilton Sorley* (ed. J.M. Wilson)
R. George Thomas: *Edward Thomas: A Portrait*
Death of Robert Graves

1986 R.P. Graves: *Robert Graves: The Assault Heroic 1895-1926*

1987 Ivor Gurney: *Severn and Somme and War's Embers* (ed. R.K.R. Thornton)

1988 Jonathan Marwill: *Frederic Manning: An Unfinished Life*

1989   Charles Doyle: *Richard Aldington*
Charles Hobday: *Edgell Rickword: A Poet at War*

1990   Barry Webb: *Edmund Blunden*

1991   Ivor Gurney: *Collected Letters* (ed. R.K.R. Thornton)
Edgell Rickword: *Collected Poems* (ed. C. Hobday)

Acknowledgements

RICHARD ALDINGTON: For extracts from *Death of a Hero*, to Rosica Collin Ltd., Mme Catherine Guillaume, and Mr Alister Kershaw; for quotations from *Images of War* to George Allen & Unwin Ltd.

HENRI BARBUSSE: For extract from *Under Fire* to J.M. Dent & Sons Ltd.

LAURENCE BINYON: For extract from 'For the Fallen' to the author's estate and Hodder & Stoughton Ltd.

EDMUND BLUNDEN: For extract from *War Poets 1914-1918* to Longmans for the British Council; for extracts from *Undertones of War* and *After the Bombing* to A.D. Peters & Co.

RUPERT BROOKE: For extracts from the *Collected Poems* and *The Prose of Rupert Brooke* to the estate of Rupert Brooke and Sidgwick & Jackson Ltd.

G.K. CHESTERTON: For extract from *The Napoleon of Notting Hill* to A.P. Watt Ltd and Miss D.E. Collins.

CYRIL CONNOLLY: For extract from *Enemies of Promise* to Routledge & Kegan Paul Ltd.

D.J. ENRIGHT: To Penguin Books Ltd, for extracts from 'The Literature of the First World War' included in *The Modern Age*, edited by Boris Ford.

FORD MADOX FORD: For extracts from *Of Heaven* and *Parade's End* to the author's estate and the Bodley Head Ltd.

E.M. FORSTER: For extract from *Howards End* to the estate of E.M. Forster and Edward Arnold Ltd.

ROBERT GRAVES: For extracts from *Goodbye to All That* to A.P. Watt Ltd., International Authors N.V., and Cassell & Co.; for extract from 'The Fight to a Finish in 1914-1918' to A.P. Watt Ltd, International Authors N.V., and *The Sunday Times*. Acknowledgements are also due to the Robert Graves Copyright Trust in respect of quotations from 'It's a Queer Time', 'Big Words', 'Dead Boche', and 'Goliath and David'.

JULIAN GRENFELL: For extracts from poetry and letters, to Lady Salmond.

IVOR GURNEY: For extract from *War's Embers* to the author's estate and Sidgwick & Jackson Ltd., and from *Poems* to the author's estate and Hutchinson & Co.

RENE HAGUE: For extract from 'David Jones: A Reconnaissance' to the author and *Twentieth Century*.

D.W. HARDING: For extracts from *Experience Into Words* to the author and Chatto & Windus Ltd.

THOMAS HARDY: For extract from *The Collected Poems of Thomas Hardy* to Macmillan & Co Ltd.

F.W. HARVEY: For quotations from *A Gloucestershire Lad* to the author's estate and Sidgwick & Jackson Ltd.

JOSEPH HELLER: For extract from *Catch-22* to the author and Jonathan Cape Ltd.

T.E. HULME: For extracts from *Further Speculations* to the University of Minnesota Press.

DOUGLAS JERROLD: For extracts from *The Lie About the War* to the author's estate and Faber & Faber Ltd.

J.H. JOHNSTON: For extract from *English Poetry of the First World War* to the author and Princeton University Press.

DAVID JONES: For extracts from *In Parenthesis* to the author's estate and Faber & Faber Ltd.

ERNST JÜNGER: For extract from *The Storm of Steel* to Chatto & Windus Ltd.

RUDYARD KIPLING: For extracts from 'Tommy', 'The Islanders' and 'All We Have and Are' to A.P. Watt Ltd, Mrs George Bambridge, and Methuen & Co Ltd.

D.H. LAWRENCE: For extracts from *Collected Letters, Kangaroo* and *The Lost Girl* to Laurence Pollinger Ltd, and the Estate of the late Mrs Frieda Lawrence.

CECIL LEWIS: For extract from *Sagittarius Rising* to the author and Peter Davies Ltd.

WYNDHAM LEWIS: For extract from *Blasting and Bombardiering* to the author's estate and Methuen & Co Ltd.

FREDERIC MANNING: For extracts from *Eidola* to John Murray Ltd, for extracts from *Her Privates We to the author's estate and Peter Davies Ltd.*

C.E. MONTAGUE: *For extracts from Disenchantment* to the author's estate and Chatto & Windus Ltd.

R.H. MOTTRAM: For extracts from *The Spanish Farm Trilogy* to the author and Chatto & Windus Ltd.

SIR HENRY NEWBOLT: For extracts from *Later Life and Letters* to A.P. Watt Ltd, the author's executor and Faber & Faber Ltd.

ROBERT NICHOLS: For extract from *Ardours and Endurances* to the author's estate and Chatto & Windus Ltd.

WILFRED OWEN: For extracts from *Collected Poems* to the author's estate and Chatto & Windus Ltd.

PETER PORTER: For extract from *Once Bitten, Twice Bitten* to the author and Scorpion Press.

EZRA POUND: For extracts from *The Cantos* and *Hugh Selwyn Mauberley* to the author and Mr A.V. Moore; acknowledgements are also due to the author in respect of three lines quoted from 'Sestina: Altaforte'; for extracts from *Gaudier-Brzeska: A Memoir* to the Marvell Press.

J.B. PRIESTLEY: For an extract from *Margin Released* to the author and A.D. Peters & Co.

SIR HERBERT READ: For extracts from *The Contrary Experience* and *Collected Poems* to the author and Faber & Faber Ltd.

EDGELL RICKWORD: For extracts from *Collected Poems* to the author's estate and the Bodley Head Ltd.

ISAAC ROSENBERG: For extracts from *Collected Works* and *Collected Poems* to the author's estate and Chatto & Windus Ltd.

SAKI (H.H. MUNRO): For extract from *When William Came* to the author's estate and the Bodley Head Ltd.

SIEGFRIED SASSOON: For extracts from *Collected Poems* and *The Complete Memoirs of George Sherston* to the author's estate and Faber & Faber Ltd.

VERNON SCANNELL: For quotation from 'The Great War' to the author.

BERNARD SHAW: For extract from *Heartbreak House* to the Public Trustee and the Society of Authors.

R.C. SHERRIFF: For extract from *Journey's End* to Curtis Brown Ltd.

SIR OSBERT SITWELL: For extract from *Selected Poems – Old and New* to the author and Gerald Duckworth & Co., Ltd.

GEORGES SOREL: For an extract from *Reflections on Violence* to George Allen & Unwin Ltd.

CHARLES SORLEY: For extracts from *Marlborough and Other Poems* and *The Letters of Charles Sorley* to the author's estate and Cambridge University Press.

EDWARD THOMAS: For extracts from *Collected Poems* to Mrs Helen Thomas and Faber & Faber Ltd.

H.M. TOMLINSON: For extracts from *All Our Yesterdays* to the Society of Authors as the literary representative of the estate of the late H.M. Tomlinson.

H.G. WELLS: For extracts from *Mr Britling Sees It Through* to Cassell & Co., A. P. Watt Ltd, and the executors of H.G. Wells, and from *The World Set Free* to A.P. Watt Ltd and the Executors.

ARTHUR GRAEME WEST: For extracts from *The Diary of a Dead Officer* to George Allen & Unwin Ltd.

HENRY WILLIAMSON: For extracts from *The Golden Virgin* to the author and Macdonald & Co.

W.B. YEATS: For extract from 'An Irish Airman Foresees His Death' to Mrs Yeats and Macmillan & Co Ltd.; for extract from *The Letters of W.B. Yeats* to Mrs Yeats and Rupert Hart-Davis Ltd.

Acknowledgements are also due to those copyright-owners whom it has not been possible to trace.

Index

(Principal accounts are indicated by bold type)

Printed in the United Kingdom
by Lightning Source UK Ltd.
107837UKS00001B/52